Rethinking Historical Time

Rethinking Historical Time

New Approaches to Presentism

Edited by
Marek Tamm and Laurent Olivier

BLOOMSBURY ACADEMIC
LONDON • NEW YORK • OXFORD • NEW DELHI • SYDNEY

BLOOMSBURY ACADEMIC
Bloomsbury Publishing Plc
50 Bedford Square, London, WC1B 3DP, UK
1385 Broadway, New York, NY 10018, USA
29 Earlsfort Terrace, Dublin 2, Ireland

BLOOMSBURY, BLOOMSBURY ACADEMIC and the Diana logo are trademarks of
Bloomsbury Publishing Plc

First published in Great Britain 2019
Paperback edition published 2021

Copyright © Marek Tamm and Laurent Olivier, 2019

Marek Tamm and Laurent Olivier have asserted their right under the Copyright, Designs
and Patents Act, 1988, to be identified as Editors of this work.

For legal purposes the Acknowledgements on pp. xiv, 161, 190 and 203 constitute
an extension of this copyright page.

Cover image: *Celestial news*, 2000 © Peeter Laurits

A catalogue record for this book is available from the British Library.

A catalog record for this book is available from the Library of Congress.

ISBN: HB: 978-1-3500-6508-6
        PB: 978-1-3501-9622-3
        ePDF: 978-1-3500-6509-3
        eBook: 978-1-3500-6510-9

Typeset by RefineCatch Limited, Bungay, Suffolk

To find out more about our authors and books visit www.bloomsbury.com
and sign up for our newsletters.

Contents

List of Figures

List of Contributors

Aleida Assmann is Professor Emerita of English and Literary Studies at the University of Constance. Her visiting professorships include Rice University in Houston (2000), Princeton University (2001), Yale University (2002, 2003, 2005) and the University of Chicago (2007), among others. The subjects of her early works are English literature and the history of literary communication; since the 1990s her specific interests have centred around the history of German memory since 1945, the role of generations in literature and society, and theories of memory. Professor Assmann is a member of the Academies of Science in Brandenburg, Göttingen and Austria, and she received an honorary doctorate from the Faculty of Theology at the University of Oslo in 2008. Her recent book publications include *Der europäische Traum: Vier Lehren aus der Geschichte* (2018), *Menschenrechte und Menschenpflichten: Schlüsselbegriffe für eine humane Gesellschaft* (2018), *Im Dickicht der Zeichen* (2015), *Ist die Zeit aus den Fugen? Aufstieg und Fall des Zeitregimes der Moderne* (2013) and *Das neue Unbehagen an der Erinnerungskultur* (2013).

Torgeir Rinke Bangstad is a postdoctoral researcher at UiT – The Arctic University of Norway. He earned his PhD degree at the Norwegian University of Science and Technology in Trondheim where he wrote his doctoral dissertation on the historic preservation of industrial heritage in three former industrial communities in Northwestern Europe. He is co-editor with Þóra Pétursdóttir of a forthcoming volume for Routledge that seeks to reorient thinking in critical heritage studies in line with the ontological turn and the turn to things. He has contributed to the anthology *Ruin Memories: Materialities, Aesthetics and the Archaeology of the Recent Past* (2014) and is a member of the research project *Object Matters: Archaeology and Heritage in the 21st Century*. He is currently investigating the materiality and memory of a reconstruction house that will be re-erected at Norsk Folkemuseum in 2019. His main research interests lie within the fields of heritage studies, museology, memory studies and theories of history.

Shannon Lee Dawdy is Professor of Anthropology and of Social Sciences at the University of Chicago. She is an anthropologist whose fieldwork combines archaeological, archival and ethnographic methods with a regional focus on the United States, the Caribbean and Mexico. The central thread running through her work concerns how landscapes and material objects mediate human relationships, whether this means an examination of the historical ecologies of capitalism, or the emotional trajectories of those who lost their intimate object worlds to Hurricane Katrina. Her first book, *Building the Devil's Empire* (2008), offers 'rogue colonialism' to explain how French New Orleans, and many colonies like it, functioned outside state controls, developing a political economy loosely moored to metropolitan interests. Her recent book, *Patina: A Profane Archaeology* (2016), investigates nostalgic practices surrounding antiques, heirlooms, historic houses and ruins. It argues that these practices provide a means of critiquing the capitalist present and of bonding people together through a type of kinship. Her current research focuses on rapidly changing death practices in the United States, particularly around disposition and transformation of the body.

Caitlin DeSilvey is Associate Professor of Cultural Geography at the University of Exeter's Penryn Campus, where she has been employed since 2007. Her research explores the cultural significance of material and environmental change, with a particular focus on heritage contexts. She has worked closely with environmental scientists, artists, archaeologists, photographers and heritage practitioners on a range of interdisciplinary projects, supported by funding from UK research councils, the Royal Geographical Society, the Norwegian Research Council and the European Social Fund. She is currently co-investigator on the AHRC-funded Heritage Futures award, a four-year project that works with eighteen non-academic partner organizations to support the development of transformative approaches across a range of heritage-related domains. She co-founded Exeter's Centre for Environmental Arts and Humanities and directs the Creative Exchange art-science programme at the Environment and Sustainability Institute. Recent publications include *Anticipatory History* (2011, with Simon Naylor and Colin Sackett), *Visible Mending* (2013, with Steven Bond and James R. Ryan) and *Curated Decay: Heritage Beyond Saving* (2017).

Victoria Fareld is Associate Professor of Intellectual History at Stockholm University. She earned her PhD in 2007 with a dissertation about the concepts of recognition, vulnerability and exposure in contemporary political philosophy in light of Hegel's philosophy and German Idealism. She was a visiting scholar at The New School for Social Research during 2005–2006, at the Institut für Philosophie, Potsdam Universität and at Sophiapol, Université de Paris-X Nanterre in 2008; fellow researcher at University of Gothenburg during 2009–2012; and co-director of Studies at the Centre for European Studies, University of Gothenburg during 2011–2012. Her current research focuses on the theory of history, historical time, ethics, memory and historical justice. Among her recent publications are 'History, Justice and the Time of the Imprescriptible', in *The Ethos of History* (eds S. Helgesson and J. Svenungsson, 2018); '(In) Between the Living and the Dead: New Perspectives on Time in History', *History Compass* 14:9 (2016); and 'Ressentiment as Moral Imperative: Jean Améry's Nietzschean Revaluation of Victim Morality', in *Re-Thinking Ressentiment* (eds M. Gallagher and J. Riou, 2016).

Anne Fuchs is Director and Professor of the University College Dublin (UCD) Humanities Institute. She studied German and English Literature at the University of Konstanz, Trinity College Dublin and the Freie Universität Berlin. Between 1992 and 2010 she was Lecturer, Senior Lecturer and then Professor of Modern German Literature and Culture at UCD. In 2005/6 she received an IRCHSS Senior Research Fellowship, which enabled her to carry out research for her monograph *Phantoms of War in Contemporary German Literature, Films and Discourse* (2008). The award of a

UCD Senior Fellowship in 2010 helped her to complete her monograph, *After the Dresden Bombing: Pathways of Memory, 1945 to the Present* (2012). Her sixth monograph, *Precarious Times: Temporality and History in Modern German Culture*, is due to be published by Cornell University Press in 2019. In 2011 she accepted the Chair and Professorship of German at the University of St Andrews before moving to the University of Warwick in January 2012, where she was Professor of German Studies until September 2016. She is a Member of the Royal Irish Academy and in 2014 she was elected a Fellow of the British Academy.

Johannes Grave is Professor of Art History and Historical Image Studies at Bielefeld University. He received his PhD at Jena University, was fellow at Basel University (NCCR Iconic Criticism) and deputy director of the Centre allemand d'histoire de l'art in Paris. His research focuses on Early Renaissance painting, art around 1800, theories of the image and the temporality of image perception. His publications include *Der 'ideale Kunstkörper'. Johann Wolfgang Goethe als Sammler von Druckgraphiken und Zeichnungen* (2006), *Caspar David Friedrich* (2012), *Architekturen des Sehens. Bauten in Bildern des Quattrocento* (2015), which was awarded by the Göttingen Academy of Sciences and Humanities, and *Giovanni Bellini. The Art of Contemplation* (2018). Since 2015 he has been one of the editors of the journal *Zeitschrift für Kunstgeschichte*.

Helge Jordheim is Professor of Cultural History at the University of Oslo. He has a PhD in German Literature and has published widely on politics and literature in the eighteenth century. During the academic year 2015–2016 he was Visiting Professor at New York University. He has since moved into the field of conceptual history, exploring concepts like empire, civilization and world. In recent years his main interest has been time and temporality, especially how to think about times in plural, multiple temporalities and layers of time. At present, he is running a research project, funded by the Norwegian Research Council, titled 'Lifetimes: A Natural History of the Present', which seeks to investigate the entanglements of different scales of time through recent global history, in the four lifetime orders of bio-, geo-, cosmo- and quantum-. His recent book publications include two edited volumes, *Universal History and the Making of the Global* (ed. with Hall Bjørnstad and Anne Régent-Susini, 2018) and *Conceptualizing the World: An Exploration across Disciplines* (ed. with Erling Sandmo, 2018).

Liisi Keedus is Professor of Political Philosophy at the School of Humanities in Tallinn University. She has worked on twentieth-century German-Jewish political thinkers, Weimar social, legal and humanist thought, historicism, as well as the making of the 'new political science' in post-Second World War America. Her first monograph, *The Crisis of German Historicism: The Early Political Thought of Hannah Arendt and Leo Strauss*, was published in 2015. Her current research focuses on the interdisciplinary roots, connections and legacies of inter-war political thought, as well as the emergence of shared political concerns and ideas across different national contexts in Europe. She has been a research fellow at the Institute of Politics and Government at Tartu University and a Marie Curie fellow at the Erik Castrén Institute for International Law and Human Rights at the University of Helsinki.

Jean-Pierre Legendre has been General Curator for Cultural Heritage at the French Ministry of Culture since 1985. He has served at the Regional Services of Archaeology of the Alsace region (1985–1989), the Lorraine region (1989–2014) and the Auvergne-Rhône-Alpes region (since 2014). His current research focuses on the epistemology of archaeology (mainly the role of ideology in archaeology) and the archaeology of the recent past (mainly archaeology of the Second World War). His book publications include *L'archéologie nazie en Europe de l'ouest* (co-edited with Laurent Olivier and Bernadette Schnitzler, 2007), *Vestiges de guerre en Lorraine: le patrimoine des conflits mondiaux* (co-edited with Stéphanie Jacquemot, 2011) and *Clashes of Times: The Contemporary Challenge for Archaeology* (co-edited with Jean-Marie Blaising, Jan Driessen and Laurent Olivier, 2017). He was also co-editor for twenty-five years of the scientific journal *Archaeologia Mosellana*.

Chris Lorenz is Professor Emeritus of German Historical Culture at VU University Amsterdam and International Research Fellow at the Institute for Social Movements in Ruhr-University Bochum. He was visiting professor at the universities of Graz, Erfurt, and Michigan at Ann Arbor. His research themes comprise modern historiography, philosophy of history and higher educational policies. His most recent book publications are *Entre filosofia e historia* (2 vols, 2015); *Breaking Up Time. Negotiating the Borders between Present, Past and Future* (co-edited with Berber Bevernage, 2013); *Popularizing National Pasts: 1800 to the Present* (co-edited with Stefan Berger and Billie Melman, 2012); *Wahrheit oder Gewinn? Über die Ökonomisierung von Universität und Wissenschaft* (co-edited with Christian Krijnen and Joachim Umlauf, 2011); *Nationalizing the Past. Historians as Nation Builders in Modern Europe* (co-edited with Stefan Berger, 2010) and *The Contested Nation: Ethnicity, Class, Religion and Gender in National Histories* (co-edited with Stefan Berger, 2008).

Laurent Olivier is archaeologist, curator in chief of the Celtic and Gallic Department at the French National Museum of Archaeology (MAN) in Saint-Germain-en-Laye. He received his Doctorate in Anthropology, Ethnology and Prehistory at the University of Paris I (Panthéon-Sorbonne), his PhD in Archaeology at the University of Cambridge and his Habilitation at the University of Paris I. His main area of research being the archaeology of the European Iron Age, he is leading a multidisciplinary research programme on a complex of sites devoted to the intensive extraction of salt in Lorraine, and its long-term impact both on the natural and social environment. An important part of his work is focused on the history of the archaeological discipline and its place in the building of collective identities. Amongst others, he has published *Le sombre abîme du Temps. Mémoire et archéologie* (2008, English translation in 2011), *Nos ancêtres les Germains. Les archéologues allemands et français au service du nazisme* (2012) and *Le Pays des Celtes. Mémoires de la Gaule* (2018).

Laurence Ollivier has been Research Engineer at the French Ministry of Culture since 1985. She has served at the Regional Services of Archaeology of the Lorraine region (1985–1987), the Languedoc-Roussillon region (1987–1997), the Pays-de-la-Loire region (1997–2003) and the Auvergne-Rhône-Alpes region (since 2003). She was a pioneer in rescue archaeology (especially on motorway projects) and carried out important excavations on several sites, including the Roman baths of Sainte-Ruffine (Moselle). She also led a research programme on the site of the famous Saint-Benoît abbey in Aniane (Hérault). She is currently working in landscape archaeology, including surveys and digital mapping.

Hans Ruin is Professor of Philosophy in Södertörn University in Stockholm, as well as the co-founder and former president of the Nordic Society for Phenomenology. During 2010–2015 he was director of the multidisciplinary research programme 'Time, Memory, and Representation – recent developments in historical consciousness'. His main research interests include phenomenology, hermeneutics (especially Heidegger and Nietzsche), modern French thought (especially Derrida and Foucault), early ancient philosophy (especially Heraclitus), theory of history and memory, philosophy of religion and philosophy of technology. Ruin's main book publications include: *Metaphysics, Facticity, and Interpretation* (ed. with D. Zahavi and S. Heinämaa, 2003); *The Past's Presence: Essays on the Historicity of Philosophical Thought* (ed. with M. Sá Cavalcante, 2006); *Phenomenology and Religion: New Frontiers* (ed. with J. Bornemark, 2010); *Re-Thinking Time: Essays on History, Memory and Representation* (ed. with A. Ers, 2011); and *Ambiguity of the Sacred. Phenomenology, Politics, Aesthetics* (ed. with J. Bornemark, 2012). His most recent monograph, *Being with the Dead: Burial, Ancestral Politics, and the Roots of Historical Consciousness*, was published by Stanford University Press in January 2019.

Zoltán Boldizsár Simon is a research fellow at Bielefeld University and a board member of the Centre for Theories in Historical Research (Zentrum für Theorien in der historischen Forschung). He has written extensively on the theory and philosophy of history and on the challenge posed by technology and the Anthropocene to modern historical thinking in the journals *History and Theory*, *The Anthropocene Review*, *History of the Human Sciences*, *Rethinking History*, *European Review of History*, the *Journal of the Philosophy of History* and the *European Journal of Social Theory*. His recent publications include '(The Impossibility of) Acting upon a Story That We Can Believe', *Rethinking History* 22:1 (2018), 105–25; 'History Begins in the Future: On Historical Sensibility in the Age of Technology', in S. Helgesson and J. Svenungsson (eds), *The Ethos of History: Time and Responsibility* (2018), 192–209; 'The Story of Humanity and the Challenge of Posthumanity', *History of the Human Sciences* (2018). His book, *History in Times of Unprecedented Change: A Theory for the 21st Century*, was published by Bloomsbury in June 2019.

Marek Tamm is Professor of Cultural History at the School of Humanities in Tallinn University and also Head of Tallinn University Centre of Excellence in Intercultural Studies. His primary research fields are cultural history of medieval Europe, theory and history of historiography, and cultural memory studies. He has recently published *Debating New Approaches to History* (ed. with Peter Burke, 2018), a collective handbook on cultural studies, *How to Study Culture? Methodology of Culture Studies* (in Estonian, 2016), an edited volume, *Afterlife of Events: Perspectives on Mnemohistory* (2015), a study of Estonian historical culture, *Monumental History: Essays on the Historical Culture of Estonia* (in Estonian, 2012), and a companion to the *Chronicle* of Henry of Livonia, *Crusading and Chronicle Writing on the Medieval Baltic Frontier* (co-edited with Linda Kaljundi and Carsten Selch Jensen, 2011), as well as numerous articles in various anthologies and journals.

Acknowledgements

This volume is the outcome of an interdisciplinary workshop entitled 'Past Presences: Or, How to Study the Past in the Age of Presentism?' held at the Centre for Advanced Study in Oslo on 9–10 December 2016. The workshop was organized in the framework and with the support of the research project 'After Discourse: Things, Archaeology and Heritage in the 21st Century', led by Professor Bjørnar Olsen. We are truly grateful to Bjørnar for having associated us with his research project and for his unrelenting support and encouragement. We remain indebted also to the kind help of Professor Vigdis Broch-Due, Scientific Director of the Centre for Advanced Study in Oslo (2015–2018).

Almost all the participants of the Oslo workshop were generously able and willing to transform their papers into book chapters. In addition, some other colleagues agreed to endorse the enterprise with their new chapters. We are also particularly grateful to Aleida Assmann who kindly agreed to write a concluding chapter to the volume. Our thanks go as well to Beatriz Lopez and to Dan Hutchins, editorial assistants at Bloomsbury, who have graciously managed the book project. The work of editing this volume was partly supported by Estonian Research Council's project IUT 18–8.

Marek Tamm and Laurent Olivier
Tallinn–Paris, August 2019

Introduction

Rethinking Historical Time

Marek Tamm and Laurent Olivier

Shifting notions of time

'Is time out of joint?', asks the German cultural theorist Aleida Assmann (2013) in the title of her recent book on modern and contemporary time regimes. 'Where has the future gone?', inquires the French anthropologist Marc Augé (2008). We no longer live in historical time, argues the American literary scholar Hans Ulrich Gumbrecht, but within an ever broader present: 'The ways the horizons of the future and the past are experienced and connect with an ever broader present give form to the as yet unnamed chronotope within which globalized life in the early twenty-first century occurs' (Gumbrecht 2014a: 73, see also Gumbrecht 1997: 420; 2013: 199–200). The British historian Michael Bentley seconds Gumbrecht's diagnosis: 'The prevailing chronotype in the West [has] shifted' (2006: 350). A temporal turn has taken place in contemporary art, claims the Canadian art historian Christian Ross (2012: 15), 'it is a shift *away* from time conceptualized as pure continuity, unity, and succession, together with history as progress, acceleration, and teleology; *towards* a post-metaphysical "presentifying" aesthetics of reorientation of modern conventions of historical time'. A new 'regime of historicity' prevails in the contemporary Western world, asserts in turn the French historian François Hartog (2003). While for the past couple of centuries the dominant Western regime of historicity has been future-oriented, the orientation has shifted during the last few decades with the future clearly relinquishing its position as the main tool for interpreting historical experience and giving way to a present-oriented regime that Hartog terms 'presentism'. This presentist regime of historicity, Hartog argues, implies a new way of understanding temporality, an abandoning of the linear, causal and homogeneous conception of time characteristic of the previous, modern regime of historicity.

There is, indeed, an increasing consensus among many scholars in different fields of humanities and social sciences that something has changed in our vision of temporality which we now perceive as more variable, less monolithic – something that affects our way of thinking about the transformation of past phenomena over time. What is the nature of this change? First, according to theories of presentism, the present has ceased to be regarded as a transitional state from what has been to what has not yet been. The past and the future do not exist as separate categories but are always projections of specific presents, they exist as the present's own immanent modes. Second, it is becoming more and more clear today that the material environment of human societies has always been composite, in the sense that it has always been principally composed of elements coming from their past while still continuing to exist in their present (Olivier 2013a: 169). 'The past endures, it accumulates in every corner and crevasse of existence becoming "now", making these presents chronological hybrids by definition and thus objecting to the common conception of time (and history) as the succession of instants' (Olsen 2013: 182). This new situation, described shortly, presents several challenges to the disciplines working on the matters of the past or, in Chris Lorenz's felicitous expression, 'the past is no longer what it used to be, and neither is the academic study of the past' (Lorenz 2010: 67).

Over recent years, various approaches to time and temporality have been offered and discussed in different disciplines, helping to form an emergent new field of 'time studies' (Burges and Elias 2016). For an increasing number of authors, time has become non-linear, complex and constituted in part by the preservation of the past in the present. We can conceptualize this type of time as 'percolating', 'multilayered', 'heterogeneous', 'multitemporal' or 'polychronic'. Michel Serres observed in the early 1990s that 'time doesn't flow; it percolates', and that 'every historical era is likewise multitemporal, simultaneously drawing from the obsolete, the contemporary, and the futuristic' (Serres and Latour 1995: 58 and 60). The philosopher Jacques Rancière (1996) reminds us that every historical study deals with a temporal heterogeneity, with a friction of various temporalities, unchangeable to each other. 'The essential thing is the idea that there are always several presents in the present, several times in the time' (Rancière 2012: 259). In anthropology, the idea of 'multiple temporalities ha[s] become central to recent anthropologies of time' (Born 2015: 367). In the field of history, it has been argued that historians 'must embrace the richness and variability of different forms of time that exist throughout our lives' (Tanaka 2015: 161). From a postcolonial perspective, Dipesh Chakrabarty (2000: 108) has stated in a similar vein: 'The writing of history must implicitly assume a plurality of times existing together, a disjuncture of the present with itself.' He is supported in turn by Berber Bevernage (2015: 351), who argues that 'philosophers of history should break with the idea of the fully contemporaneous present and instead embrace that of radical noncontemporaneity or noncoevalness'. A proper critical history, Ethan Kleinberg and his colleagues recently declared, 'links past to present dynamically, recognizes both the persisting or repeating character of the past in the present and the non-necessary character of pasts present and presents past' (Kleinberg, Scott and Wilder 2018, see also Kleinberg 2017: 133). Also, contemporary archaeology denies the past its radical absence and distance by reminding us that it is still present through its vestiges. 'It follows that, archaeologically, the present is not actually what is happening right now, but rather the accumulation of all past times that have been materially preserved' (Olivier 2013b: 124). Or, in other words, the 'past as it was is at all times the outcome of the gathering of previous pasts' (Olsen et al. 2013: 145). Similar arguments are easy to find across many other disciplines in social sciences and humanities.

In his *Archaeology of Knowledge*, Michel Foucault compared the history of knowledge to a powerful geological process: it happens sometimes that deeply buried plates of commonly acknowledged ideas and concepts, covered over time by a continuous accumulation of sediments – made of successive interpretations – suddenly break down under the huge pressure of events and come to the surface, making the world shake (Foucault 1989: 4). Is that what is happening now? Like seismographs, most of the various fields of human and social sciences – and particularly those dealing with the past – are recording the rising of new objects of enquiry that emerge under the thrust of a new force, previously hidden and unnoticed – that of the present. This volume aims to take a stance in respect to these shifts and changes and to enter into a transdisciplinary dialogue with the contemporary conceptualizations of time. With this aim in mind, it brings together scholars in various disciplines – anthropology, archaeology, geography, history, philosophy, literary and visual studies – and intends to explore what are the main epistemological consequences of the shifts in today's Western time regime of the present made up of multiple temporalities. We consider this to be one of the main issues in contemporary humanities and social sciences, clearly demanding a transdisciplinary discussion.

The volume is divided into three sections. The four chapters of the first part, entitled 'Presentism and New Temporalities', evaluate and discuss critically the nature and impact of 'presentism', as diagnosed by Hartog and other scholars, on the one hand, and, on the other, explore different transformations of temporal experiences in various branches of the humanities. In the second part, 'Multiple Temporalities', genealogical and critical discussions of multiple temporalities in history, philosophy, religious studies and visual arts are offered. The last section, 'Material Temporalities', includes four case studies on the various aspects of conceptualizing the multiplicity of times and presentism in material culture and heritage studies.

The crisis of historicism and alternative temporalities

Although it might seem that contemporary changes in the conceptualization of time are unprecedented, it is important to keep in mind that the roots of the current notion of non-linear and multiple temporalities go back at least to the First World War. Lucian Hölscher (2013) has convincingly shown that the First World War was a turning point in Western temporalities, marking the loss of the modern notion of time as a coherent and future-oriented whole. 'For the generation of World War One, the war was an existential thunderstorm that turned the experience of time upside down,' Hölscher argues, and adds: 'their most notable contribution to the concept of history was to notice that the centre of history had shifted from the past to the present' (2013: 148).

New notions of time developed in the aftermath of the First World War were turned against the historicist understanding of temporality. And yet, even nowadays, the main obstacle to working out new conceptualizations of time is the deeply rooted historicist way of thinking. Jeremy Telman aptly explains our paradoxical situation: 'We cannot abandon historicism . . . it is a part of us and our professional institutions. Historicism was so successful that it has been completely integrated into our culture' (Telman 1996:

305). In trying to capture the essence of the historicist paradigm, we can rely on a recent account by Hans Ulrich Gumbrecht (2014b), who reduces the historicist paradigm or chronotope, as he calls it, following Mikhail Bakhtin, to five main aspects. First, the historicist chronotope always leaves the past behind, causing its orientational value to fade and obliging us to work through the past if we want to have an open future that we can shape. Second, the historicist chronotope counts on the future as an open horizon of possibilities among which we can choose. Third, in the historicist chronotope the present becomes an 'imperceptibly short moment of transition', as Charles Baudelaire wrote in his 'The Painter of Modern Life' (1863). Fourth, for the historicist construction of time, this present is the habitat and the condition of human self-understanding as subject and agency, that is, as being synonymous with the functional potential of consciousness. Finally, in this historicist chronotope, time appears to be an irresistible agent of change, which means no phenomena can escape their own transformation in time and through time, however fast or slow the pace of the specific transformation may be.

Thus, historicism is not merely one of many possible approaches to the past but a comprehensive philosophy and cultural practice which views all social reality as a historical stream or river where no two instances are comparable or reversible (Iggers 1983: 30; Fulda 2010: 142). Frederick Beiser, in his *The German Historicist Tradition*, fittingly captures this position: 'Hence the historicist is the Heraclitean of the human world: everything is in flux; no one steps twice into the river of history' (Beiser 2011: 2). In other words, 'historicism may be regarded as a sustained attempt to transcend the discontinuities that trouble us in the present by making sense of history' (Runia 2010: 237). This historicist paradigm or chronotope, briefly described, came under criticism quite early on, particularly after the First World War. The term 'crisis of historicism' had acquired currency from the early 1920s, thanks largely to the theologian and philosopher Ernst Troeltsch. In 1921, Troeltsch wrote a popular article for the *Deutsche Rundschau* with the captivating title 'Die Krisis des Historismus'. Since Troeltsch's article appeared, the crisis of historicism has become a common trope in debates of the topic. Here, however, is not the place to reopen the discussion of the 'crisis of historicism' widely explored elsewhere by various authors (see, e.g., Bambach 1995; Paul 2008; Keedus 2015; Esposito 2017). We could simply ask – was there a real crisis of historicism at all? As Allan Megill (1997: 114) has observed, 'the relatively late naming of the crisis of historicism' – in 1921 – 'and its lack of any well-defined material or institutional embodiment, give a lot of freedom to the historian in reconstructing – or, perhaps better, in constructing – the thing'. Indeed, what if all these talks about a crisis or decline of historicism merely conceal its actual triumph and success? This is very much the approach adopted by Frederick Beiser in his recent history of German historicism. He argues that 'historicism was not an abject failure but an astonishing success'. This tradition has shaped our intellectual universe to an extraordinary degree, so that today, as Beiser claims, we are all historicists in our ways of thinking (Beiser 2011: 26).

This collective volume argues that the main challenge we face today in our efforts to develop a more complex and nuanced theory of temporality is the overcoming of the historicist or modern notion of time. In this effort, some early critics of historicism are particularly helpful. Perhaps the earliest and most famous example is young Friedrich

Nietzsche in his first 'Untimely Meditation', *On the Use and Abuse of History for Life* (1874), which has not lost its topicality. In this context many other authors could be named, including Wilhelm Dilthey, Henri Bergson and Sigmund Freud; here, however, we would like to focus briefly on two German thinkers of the inter-war period who proposed some of the most important ideas for a non-linear and heterogeneous notion of time, namely Aby Warburg and Walter Benjamin.

Aby Warburg (1866–1929) was an eccentric art historian of the early twentieth century. He preferred to call himself an 'image historian', *Bildhistoriker*, interested primarily in objects and more generally in the discipline of art history (McEwan 2009: 2). The project of his life was a massive atlas of images entitled *Mnemosyne*, a visual account of how and why symbolic images of great pathos persist in Western cultural memory from antiquity to the early twentieth century. Warburg presents his atlas as a way of mapping the 'roaming streets of culture' (*Wanderstraßen der Kultur*), thereby self-consciously reproducing the very errors he finds shaping the spatial and temporal dynamics of cultural history (Johnson 2012: x). He indeed considered culture a dynamic and unpredictable process rather than a one-way street. For Warburg, Renaissance is not the process of a simple repetition of antiquity, but one of appropriation. Recasting Renaissance in this manner, he opens it up to completely new kinds of inquiries; the classical tradition is no longer a monolithic entity whose presence must be either acknowledged or neglected. 'Instead, everything hangs on its transformation through successive acts of remembering, and on what such remembering might consist of and how it might occur' (Rampley 2000: 92, see also Rampley 2001: 305–6).

The key concept in Warburg's thinking is *Nachleben* ('afterlife'), a term that captures his intention to redefine the relations between past and present, to anachronize and disorient history, to show how each period simultaneously comprises elements from the past, the present and the future (see Tamm 2015). For Warburg, *Nachleben* was a concept that helped to make historical time more complex, to recognize specific, non-linear temporalities in the cultural world. Historicist time conceived as a succession of direct relationships ('influences') had no appeal for Warburg. 'Instead he pursued, as a counterpoint or counterrhythm to influence and chronology, a *ghostly and symptomatic time*' (Didi-Huberman 2003: 274). In other words, Warburg's concept of *Nachleben* assumed a temporal model for art history, radically different from any employed at the time. We can see his aspiration to move beyond traditional temporal terms of history writing, for instance, in a study that he published in 1920, titled 'Pagan-Antique Prophecy in Words and Images in the Age of Luther'. As Warburg explains, in rejecting both positivist and historicist approaches to history, he aims to make visible 'hitherto debased epistemological values' and adopt a kind of 'timeless' approach to past matters (Warburg 1999: 599).

In 1965, Warburg's former assistant Gertrud Bing lucidly explained how the concept of *Nachleben* should transform our idea of time and tradition: 'Influences are not a matter of passive acceptance but demand an effort of adjustment, *eine Auseinandersetzung* as Warburg put it, which includes that of the present with the past' (Bing 1965: 310). No longer imaginable as an unbroken stream or river where accumulations are carried from upstream down, tradition should be conceived of as a tense drama that unfolds between the river's flow and its whirling eddies (Didi-Huberman 2003: 276). One of the most interesting interpreters of Warburg nowadays, the French art historian and theorist Georges Didi-Huberman, has very pertinently summarized Warburg's main lessons for contemporary debates on time and temporality: 'By recognising the need to broaden canonical models of history – narrative models, models of temporal continuity, models of objective realisation – by directing himself little by little toward a theory of memory of forms made up of leaps and latencies, Aby Warburg decisively broke with notions of "progress" and historical "development"' (Didi-Huberman 2002b: 69).

Belonging to the next generation of scholars but remaining very close to Warburg's way of thinking, the German philosopher and cultural critic Walter Benjamin (1892–1940) offers a more elaborate and even more radical anti-historicist theory of time and temporality. As it has been pertinently said, Benjamin's work as a whole proceeds from a distinctive notion of an alternative temporality (Pensky 2004: 191). Even in his very earliest writing he explores this alternative conception of historical time. His essay on 'The Life of Students', written in 1914 to 1915, begins by dismissing a predominant conception of progressive, linear historical time and instead advocates 'a particular condition in which history appears to be concentrated in a single focal point, like those that have traditionally been found in the utopian images of the philosophers' (Benjamin 1996: 37). *The Arcades Project* (*Passagenwerk*), the gigantic and unfinished study into nineteenth-century urban life in Paris that Benjamin undertook in the late 1920s, contains many entries contrasting the false continuity postulated by historicism with the reality of discontinuity manifest in the always unpredictable appearance of new phenomena. In one of the notes to *The Arcades Project* explaining the methodological aims of the enterprise, Benjamin makes an important argument, stating that the founding concept of the book 'is not progress but actualization' (Benjamin 1999: 460). In other words, Benjamin presents a vision of history in which nothing is lost forever but each moment of the past can be re-actualized in the future, replayed under other conditions in a new situation.

It is interesting to note that following Warburg, Benjamin re-introduces the concept of *Nachleben* in his *Arcades Project*, defining 'historical understanding' as what is 'to be viewed primarily as an afterlife (*Nachleben*) of that which has been understood: and so what came to be recognized about works through the analysis of their afterlife, their fame, should be considered the foundation of history itself' (Benjamin 1999: 460). But it is in his 'On the Concept of History' (1940), written towards the end of his life, that Benjamin succeeds in summarizing his new vision of history with the greatest clarity. He accuses historicism of imposing on history the model of mechanical causality in which the cause of an effect must immediately precede it (or at least be very close) on the temporal chain. Historicism, claims Benjamin, is happy to establish causal connections between moments in history, threading together sequences of events as if they were the stringed 'beads of a rosary'. For Benjamin, the establishment of a causal link between two successive events does not, in itself, create historical intelligibility. This can stem only from the encounter between a past and a present moment, the one where the historian is located. For Benjamin, history survives only when its pulsations are perceptible in the present. In his view, very similar to Warburg's, this could be done mainly through montage and assemblage, creating dialectical images that are revelatory, evocative and condensed (Benjamin 2007: 263).

To sum up: what both Warburg and Benjamin, as well as many of their contemporaries, had in common was a profound scepticism concerning the triumphalism of historicist thinking and the linear model of time sustaining it (Rampley 2000: 105). They proposed some alternative concepts and approaches, in order to emphasize the percolating and heterogeneous nature of time and the complexity of past, present and future relations. However, due to the widespread popularity of the historicist notion of time, the multilayered time of Warburg, Benjamin and others did not gain a dominant position in humanities and social sciences (as opposed to geology, for instance).

The emergence of presentism and the Anthropocene

Since the second half of the twentieth century, a profound change has slowly been taking place in our perception of time. Indistinct at first, the change became increasingly obvious over the final decades of the century (Esposito 2017). By now, it is so well established as to affect all disciplines in humanities and social sciences. During this period, anthropology and its cognate disciplines underwent what is now referred to as an 'ontological turn' (Holbraad and Pedersen 2017), coinciding with a change in perspective that essentially denied *anthropos* its status as focal point and thus finally doing away with the notion of the 'human exception' (Schaeffer 2007). Human beings have been deposed from their position at the centre of cultures and societies; they are no longer understood to be the only factor forging their history and their fate. As many scholars have noted, the actions and thinking of humans are not alone responsible for the creation of social structures and cultural objects and settings. Other kinds of 'life', in the form of a variety of 'non-human' organisms, are involved, as well. The latter include not only places but also what we generally refer to as 'things': objects, built structures, materials (Olsen 2010) – in fact, all the organic and inorganic components of the world about us.

The most significant of our long-held beliefs that have been undermined in recent decades are those that concern our relation to nature. One needs but reread Jules Michelet to grasp how far we have come from the nineteenth century's triumphant view of history: 'History', said Michelet in his *Introduction à l'histoire universelle*, 'is nothing more than the story of man's never-ending struggle [. . .] against nature, of mind against matter, of freedom against fate.' And, in a purely theoretical proposition affirming man's primacy over nature, now debunked by facts, he emphasized that 'nature remains unchanged while with every passing day man gains advantages over her' (Michelet 1843: 9). The spectacular fashion in which climate conditions in the Holocene have, after remaining more or less unchanged for some 11,700 years, been destabilized has demonstrated that human beings, their societies, and their actions are an integral part of the earth system. As climatologists have noted, anthropogenic factors do not constitute an external force capable of disturbing some intrinsically 'natural' environmental system (Oldfield and Steffen 2004). They are part of that system, and thus dependent upon it. Above all, as Bruno Latour pointed out, we shall need to come to terms with the force the environment can deploy, as well as with the fact that it is not mere background against which human actions play out (Latour 2017: 56). In response to the pressures that human actions bring to bear upon it, the environment changes very quickly and, in doing so, constitutes a historical entity inseparable from the history of humankind. The history of the world, heretofore basically political, economic and socio-cultural, now resembles, in the long-term perspective of geologists, a geo-history (Chakrabarty 2009) or, archaeologically speaking, what some French scholars have called an 'archaeo-geography' (Chouquer 2007, 2008).

The breakdown of the long-standing dichotomy between nature and culture that this ontological shift has led to is not devoid of practical consequences for the very way in which we practise the study of the past. It has effectively stripped humans of their privileged status as the only beings endowed with knowledge and capable of action in an incognizant world subjected to their undertakings. As Bruno Latour (2015: 182) pointed out, the New Climate Regime, known as the Great Acceleration, that we entered with the beginning of the period of Anthropocene now requires us to rethink our own 'ontology', inherited from the modern period, while simultaneously raising the question of history's role in this massive process that has so drastically altered living conditions on Earth.

Having identified a new regime of historicity – which we had supposedly entered at some time around 1989 – and labelled it 'presentism', François Hartog was clearly overwhelmed by the enthusiasm with which his proposition was received. Initially, he had sought to demonstrate that the increasing number of 'sites of memory' (Nora 1984–1992) where the past is commemorated and reinterpreted in the light of the present was indicative of a new attitude to historical time (Hartog 1995). This 'way of entwining past, present and future' makes the present 'the category in which we understand ourselves' (Hartog 2003: 136–40, 157–61), while the pre-eminence granted to the here-and-now which simultaneously comprises both past and future, creates 'a past that does not pass and a future that is closed' (Hartog 2010: 770). Presenting his concept of presentism, Hartog carefully pointed out that he believed this new notion of historical time was closer to a new 'regime of *historicity*' than to one of *temporality* (Hartog 2010: 767–8), meaning that presentism deals above all with the way we apprehend and interpret historical time. Nevertheless, this altered perception of historical time that has distanced itself from the modern regime of historicity does have a beginning point. The latter, according to Hartog, coincides with the social and economic changes that have been taking place since the 1970s and that, notably, led to the fall of the Berlin Wall and the illusion of an 'end to history' (Hartog 2003: 12, 114–18).

In other words, the temporality peculiar to the latter half of the twentieth century triggered the emergence of this regime of historicity that is unique to the Western post-industrial societies of the 'Second Age of Capitalism' and subjected us, as Jérôme Baschet (2018) puts it in his recent book, to the 'tyranny' of a 'perpetual present'. This is why we believe that we need to distinguish presentism as a way of representing history (i.e., as historicity) from the contemporary historical situation of presentism (as temporality). As Chris Lorenz has pointed out in his contribution to the present volume, Hartog's ambiguous use of the term has created a certain confusion. Thus, in our use of the term in this introduction, 'presentism' is to be understood only as a regime of historicity (what Lorenz calls Hartog's 'presentism no. 2').

The pertinence of Hartog's analysis is widely accepted today. Scholars now focus on matters relating to the temporality of presentism, which is effectively the case with several of the articles in the present collection. In this sense, the emergence of the new regime of historicity appears to be more a symptom of the transformations undergone by the contemporary world than a theoretical definition of the current state of our historical situation. But what, one might ask, is Hartog's presentism a symptom of with regard to the way in which we relate to the world? It is not just that the past has dissolved and the future has been enclosed within 'what has already been thought' (Baschet 2018: 215), but also, more profoundly, that the very conditions under which humanity exists have fundamentally changed.

Beginning with the end of the Second World War, human activity has been radically transforming the climate conditions of the period known as the Holocene, which began after the last glacial period that followed the end of the Pleistocene, more than 10,000 years ago (Bonneuil and Fressoz 2016; Lewis and Maslin 2018). We have entered a new climate regime most notable for the rapid rise in temperatures and sea levels and the accelerating disappearance of species. In one or two centuries' time, the latter could affect 75 per cent of living species, leading to a sixth mass extinction comparable in scope to those of geological times (Ceballos, Ehrlich and Dirzo 2017). The change became clearly visible with the onset of the Industrial Revolution in the nineteenth century (Crutzen and Steffen 2003). Since 1945, it has been accelerating at a tremendous pace (Zalasiewicz et al. 2015) and the increasing rate at which carbon emissions are being released into the atmosphere shows no sign of abating, for it is the product of a capitalist economy driven by an extensive exploitation of fossil fuels (Angus 2016; Malm 2017). Climatologists fear that with climate destabilization in the Holocene now reaching the tipping point, the state of the global system will be altered and eventually catapult us into a chaotic period similar to that of the Pleistocene. But the Holocene, it would seem, is the only state in which the planet can sustain contemporary societies (Steffen et al. 2015). We thus now live under the threat of a collapse of human civilization equal in magnitude to the impact the post-industrial world has had upon the Earth system.

Some may question what bearing these external happenings may have on how we apprehend the historical time. The answer lies in the way they affect the future, the way they destroy the 'future-to-which-we-look-forward' so emblematic of the modern period (Baschet 2018: 106) and thrust us into a 'period of latency' (Gumbrecht 2013) that denies us a 'horizon of expectation' (Koselleck 2004: 255–75), leaving us in a sort of 'end-time' (*Endzeit*), as Günther Anders said when mankind entered the nuclear age in the wake of Hiroshima and Nagasaki (Anders 2007). It is because these irreversible transformations redefine the future that they have an impact on the past (Simon 2019). In effect, as Hartog pointed out, the modern regime of historicity was 'dominated by the point of view of the future' from which history was forged (Hartog 2003: 119–20, 2013: 230), with the past being constantly changed by the progress that had brought us to the present (Hartog 2003: 135–6). This was why observers, i.e., historians, considered the past to be an area of study clearly outside the context in which they found themselves and believed that they could examine it in an objective and informed manner. This is no longer the case, and has not been the case for some time, for, as Hartog noted, presentism has absorbed the futurist, that is: open future. It has reduced the future to an immediate continuation of the present and drained the past of its meaning by inscribing it in memorialization (Hartog 1995: 1225–7).

No matter from what angle we approach presentism, we draw much the same conclusion: the modern regime of historicity that emerged in the second half of the eighteenth century definitively lost its domination in the last quarter of the twentieth, while the changes generated by the 'Second Age of Capitalism' (Boltanski and Chiapello 2007) were 'confining us to a hyper-extended present that undid the historical relation to the past and obstructed horizons that might offer a new kind of future' (Baschet 2018: 244). The Anthropocene, Baschet affirms, delivered 'the coup de grace to the modern regime of historicity' (Baschet 2018: 87). Presentism, like the Anthropocene, can thus be considered as a product of the over-exploitation of the world's resources that has accelerated rapidly since 1945, so much so in fact that some scholars have suggested that we replace the term Anthropocene, whose geological appropriateness is contested with 'Capitalocene', to identify clearly the origin of the present environmental crisis (Moore 2015, 2016).

But is this to say that we find ourselves inevitably subjected to an immutable, absolute, totalitarian present? Hartog himself was not convinced. He saw presentism as a temporary state, 'until something else comes along' (Hartog 2010: 770). In effect, presentism understood as historicity is not to be confused with presentism understood as temporality. The rise of the presentist regime of historicity may be a sign, as Baschet suggests, that we are 'moving towards exhausting the conditions under which capitalism can exist' (Baschet 2018: 245). The matter is far from settled, and the collapse of the traditional historicist model has not occurred without resistance and restructuring. It has, though, created a space for the emergence of other still fledgling 'ways of experiencing time' that have long been marginalized and rejected from the thinking of historians (for some possible future scenarios, see Baschet 2018: 237–91).

Multiple temporalities

In his classic study, *We Have Never Been Modern*, Bruno Latour (1993: 75) proposed an alternative, spiral vision of time:

> Let us suppose, for example, that we are going to regroup the contemporary elements along a spiral rather than a line. We do have a future and a past, but the future takes the form of a circle expanding in all directions, and the past is not surpassed but revisited, repeated, surrounded, protected, recombined, reinterpreted and reshuffled. Elements that appear remote if we follow the spiral may turn out to be quite nearby if we compare loops. Conversely, elements that are quite contemporary, if we judge by the line, become quite remote if we traverse a spoke. Such a temporality does not oblige us to use the labels 'archaic' or 'advanced' since every cohort of contemporary elements may bring together elements from all times. In such a framework, our actions are recognized at last as polytemporal.

As this volume argues, a Latourian manner of understanding the polytemporality of human life is gaining ground in contemporary humanities and social sciences. But it is interesting to note that a similar trend is visible also in physics. 'Time has lost its first aspect or layer: its unity,' states the Italian theoretical physicist Carlo Rovelli in his recent bestselling book, *The Order of Time*. 'Times are legion: a different one for every point in space. There is not one single time; there is a vast multitude of them' (Rovelli 2018: 16, 17).

The idea of multiple temporalities is not new in scholarly thinking, but it has long remained in the margins of discussions about time. In the context of historical studies, there have been at least two important attempts after the Second World War to abandon, at least to a certain degree, the idea of the unity of time. In the 1950s, the French historian Fernand Braudel launched his campaign against standard uses of temporality in history by arguing for the importance of multiple times and for the *longue durée* as the methodological ground for a unified historical social science. 'Whether it is a question of the past or the present,' Braudel claims (1958: 727), 'an awareness of the plurality of social time is indispensable for a common methodology shared by human sciences.' Braudel constructs his model of multiple times in terms of three temporalities. First, the *longue durée*, the longest conceivable historical temporality; second, cyclical time or the conjuncture, a structural time of intermediate duration; and third, the event or the (very) short term. Taken together, these three temporalities form a framework that allows for the examination of temporally complex historical phenomena (see Tomich 2011; Sawyer 2015).

In the 1980s, Reinhart Koselleck offered an alternative theory of multiple temporalities. Arguing that time was not linear and progressing from one period to another, he proposed that, instead, there were multiple historical times present within the same moment, layer upon layer pressed together. To capture this phenomenon, Koselleck coined the powerful concept of *Zeitschichten*, 'layers or sediments of time':

'Sediments of time' (*Zeitschichten*), just like their geological prototype, refer to multiple temporal levels of differing duration and varied origin that are nonetheless simultaneously present and effective. Even the non-simultaneity of the simultaneous (*die Gleichzeitigkeit des Ungleichzeitigen*), one of the most informative historical phenomena, is taken up in this concept. Everything that happens at the same time, everything that emerges from heterogeneous life circumstances, both synchronically and diachronically.

Koselleck 2000: 9

Koselleck's aim was, therefore, to circumvent the linear–cyclical dichotomy characteristic of historicist thinking, claiming that 'historical times consist of multiple layers that refer to each other in a reciprocal way, though without being wholly dependent upon each other' (Koselleck 2018: 4). Helge Jordheim (2012: 170) remarks, concerning Koselleck's approach to this issue: 'Thus the fact that historical time is not linear and homogeneous but complex and multilayered accounts for the futility of all efforts to freeze history in order to delimit and define breaks, discontinuities, time spans, beginnings, and endings.'

It is our belief that we have reached the point where the historicist trust for a single overarching coherence of time is vanishing. In this respect, we subscribe to the recent diagnosis of our new temporal condition, delivered by Chris Lorenz:

> The dominant time conception has changed from a linear, irreversible and progressivist time conception to a non-linear, reversible and non-progressivist one. The non-linear time conception allows us to think of a temporal simultaneity and coexistence of past, present and future, because it does not presuppose that the three dimensions of time are separated and 'closed off' from one another – as linear time does – but instead regards them as mutually interpenetrating, meaning that the past can live on in the present just as the future can be present in the present. Non-linear time allows for a pluralisation of times and to conceive of the present, past and future as multidimensional and purely relational categories.
>
> Lorenz 2014: 46, see also Lorenz 2017

However, if we agree that there is no 'homogeneous, empty time' (Benjamin 2007: 261) but only a multiplicity of different times, then the question arises as to how these differential temporalities relate to each other. This is basically a question of understanding historical temporalities as relational and synchronized, in the sense that they articulate material and imaginary ties to one another and among social groups, without returning to the historicist concept of unified time that for many years has been thought to regulate these relations (Lanieri 2014: 613). In other words, the main question is, what are the conceptual and other tools for making sense of the polytemporality?

Helge Jordheim has rightly pointed out that the discussion of multiple temporalities should not be limited to describing pluralities or multitudes of time but also needs to pay attention to the contrasts, oppositions, conflicts and struggles involved in structuring, regulating and synchronizing time. 'The foremost power of time lies in the ability to establish a temporal standard that is the same everywhere and for everyone, to adapt and adjust different times, different temporal regimes, to one another, to merge them into one, or in the terminology I adopt here: to *synchronize* them' (Jordheim 2014: 513, see also Jordheim 2017). The invention of the empty and homogeneous time of historicism is a classic example of how the plurality of historical times is synchronized into the linear, homogeneous, teleological time of progress. For the first time in human history, the practice of temporal synchronization had a global outreach because, as Sebastian Conrad (2018: 841) has demonstrated, this 'linear, empty, and progressive time was imposed upon many societies around the world and triggered the disappearance of indigenous ways of relating to past, present, and future'. This synchronization was achieved by means of different practices and methods, from new ways of history writing to new systems of time-reckoning and map making. However, pride of place in this 'work of synchronization' belongs to novel conceptual tools. Helge Jordheim and Einar Wigen (2018) have recently argued that since the late eighteenth century the key concept for structuring the relationship between past, present and future in Western culture has been *progress*, whereas nowadays the concept of *crisis* is about to replace *progress* as the main tool of temporal synchronization in the Western world and beyond. Their diagnosis of the new 'time of crisis' captures well the nature of our new regime of historicity:

> At present, the myth of the uniform time of progress seems to be losing its grip: On the one hand, globalisation has brought with it more complex and heterogeneous temporal relations, in which the global time of commerce, technology and media comes in conflict with the different rhythms in the variety of cultures and communities; on the other hand, the 'deep times' of climate change, giving rise to the geochronological term *the Anthropocene*, challenges the limited temporal horizons of social relations and political decisions and forces us to renegotiate our views of past and future.
>
> Jordheim and Wigen 2018: 436

Recently, the work of the German historian Achim Landwehr (2014, 2016) has made another landmark contribution to contemporary time studies. Countering the conventional concept of historicist time, he argues for time as a social and historical construct. For Landwehr, past, present and future fundamentally do not exist as separate categories but are always projections of specific presents which, moreover, are mobilized differently and for various purposes by different collectives. In order to analyse the permanently changing relations between 'present' and 'absent' times, he introduces the concept of 'chronoference' (*Chronoferenz*). Chronoference signifies the 'ability of collectives to refer to absent times and to produce a culturally specific web of timings' (Landwehr 2018: 266). By analysing these kinds of chronoferences or temporal relations we become able to understand the ways and conditions of how the respective present time of a culture builds relations with the unpresent times at its disposal, how 'any past contains past futures and past pasts that might play a role in a future, and that this future will in turn deal with future pasts and future futures' (Landwehr 2018: 267).

We can provisionally conclude that the concept of *present*, even more than *crisis*, has become one of the key conceptual tools for synchronizing multiple temporalities in the contemporary Western world. In the footsteps of Saint Augustin we might confirm that 'there are three times, a present of things past, a present of things present, a present of things to come' (*praesens de praeteritis, praesens de praesentibus, praesens de futuris*) (Saint Augustin 1998: 235), or, more precisely, that there are many more times but these are all the present's own various modes of existence. The present time is multitemporal or polychronic in the sense that an event does not merely occur in the present, but also simultaneously actualizes sections of the past within itself. 'Understood this way, the present may be grasped as textured and stretched, latent and current – a mediation of presence and distance in time. The present is both in and out of time and takes time; it is made up of multiple temporalities,' as Joel Burges and Amy J. Elias (2016: 4) felicitously summarize the argument. This also means that historical time can be explained neither by the simple schema of a straight line nor by the absence of any kind of line (Baschet 2018: 234). Our aim should be to grasp historical time in its entanglement or synchronization of multiple temporal lines.

Material temporalities

Yet what if, in interpreting the multiplication of memorial sites as a characteristic mark of presentism, François Hartog had somehow missed the point, namely that sites hold memory? 'Historians have always dealt with memory,' he said, 'but warily, always' (Hartog 1995: 1228). Historians, including Hartog himself, have kept memory apart from the study of history and preferred to see it as an area unrelated to their research. This is how Hartog's view of sites as symptoms degrades them to indications of the presentist state of the 1980s (Hartog 1995: 1233), a period marked by a round of memorializing similar to those of 1830, 1880 and 1914 that had previously influenced the way in which history was recorded. This is the perspective in which Hartog reduces Benjamin to a critic of historicism and the latter's call for remembrance merely to a sign of the crisis that the modern regime of historicity underwent during the early decades of the twentieth century (Hartog 1995: 1222, 1229). Hartog downgrades memory to a matter of commemoration and an obsession with preservation, assimilating it to an anti-historical attitude indicative of the collapsed future that presentism led to. 'It is remarkable,' he says, 'that the dimension of the future has primarily been reintroduced negatively, through our concern for preservation' (Hartog 1995: 1235).

As an historian, a reader, in sum a 'man of the written word', Hartog probably failed to see the potential for transmitting history that sites or places hold, regardless of whether they have been 'memorialized'. Like things, inanimate objects, non-human subjects and places are not simply inert matter fashioned by individuals or (re)interpreted by the collective memory of societies. Places and things are material entities that evolve over time and pass on a 'heritage of form' through transformations that dictate their shape and that of future constructions. Archaeologists speak of 'transformission' (Chouquer 2007) to describe this astonishing phenomenon that proves the existence of a veritable 'material memory' of places and things (combining transformation and transmission). The vestiges of historical pasts gone by subsist as material remains, and are always in the here and now of the futures that follow. They can reappear in different forms or be put to different uses. They do not belong to the unilinear time of conventional history; rather, they transcend it (cf. Fitz-Henry 2017).

In contrast to the sequential time of historicist thinking, this enduring time defies measurement (Bergson 2009: 47). It is the time peculiar to memory and it rolls out heterochronicity (Green 2000). In effect, memory always opens onto the past from the present. More profoundly still, this timeless time of memory is one of returns and reappearances. Sites can be reactivated after periods of latency that may stretch over thousands of years. In the processes through which they are brought back into play, as it were, their presence is often hidden, buried beneath an accumulation of subsequent constructions that make them unrecognizable. The time of memory is built on repetition and reiteration (Olivier 2017), which constantly transforms what exists while generating, in the here and now, a multiplicity of 'revivals' (Hamel 2006) and 'survivals' (Didi-Huberman 2002a). The time of the material memory of places and things is thus in no way that of the 'perpetual present' of presentism, with which Hartog might have confused it. It is rather an indication that there may be 'other times of history', of which the crisis of the modern regime of historicity that was provoked by the advent of presentism has given us a glimpse.

As for the new regime of historicity heralded by our current situation, its identity is far from clear. In truth, we are now at a stage of re-composition, and it would be rash to attempt to predict the outcome. The best we can do is to seek solutions that can take us beyond the impasse the Anthropocene has backed us into by eradicating memory and, on the whole, the possibility for history. From this perspective, presentism appears as a fertile ground whose limits and features need to be explored and whose resources, as yet new to us, we would do well to harness.

Conclusion

We have already noted Michel Foucault's reference to the tectonic upheavals seemingly wrought by subterranean forces that occasionally occur in the history of ideas. '[B]eneath the shifts and changes of political events,' he wrote in *The Archaeology of Knowledge*, lies a vast bedrock of 'great silent, motionless bases', 'sedimentary strata' that 'traditional history' has layered over with the deposits of successive interpretations. It is upon this 'thick layer of events' that the 'sedimentation' from historical sources – that is, the succession of various readings of the world, of various 'ways of approaching things' – settles (Foucault 1989: 4). Then suddenly these seemingly permanent bases are forcefully upended, carrying away with them the intricate web of traditional tales that we had thought to relate reality. With the emergence of presentism, we now seem to find ourselves in one of these times of upheaval whose negative aspects have been the principal focus of commentators.

And yet, these great uncontrollable movements are also capable of generating creative forces. While the old foundations of knowledge crack and become mired in the magma of oblivion, other previously inaccessible substrata that had been buried deep rise to the surface, and the fault lines that now run through the 'layers of interpretation' yield a cross-cut much like what one finds on an archaeological site, making the stratification visible. As they bring to light the manner in which these outmoded 'traditional histories' are interwoven, upheavals like the one that resulted from the impact of presentist temporality also provide new research perspectives, for they prompt us to use new 'interpretative bases' in carrying out our research.

As Bruno Latour (2015: 182) pointed out, the dominance of presentist temporality has brought history back centre-stage, but this is no longer history as we knew it. This is history that operates from within the present, not a history of some past locked inside the past. History has become the discipline that studies the living memory of the past as it exists in the present, along with the dialectical relation between present and future. Rather than seeking moments of origin, we now seek movements of emergence. We now pay more attention to interactions than to actions, more to trajectories than to events. We now look at environments as active contexts that are fully endowed agents, not simply as passive backgrounds that we reduce to objects. We need to find new concepts with which to consider hybridity: the blended, the impure, the discontinuous, the contaminated, or the monstrous. Perhaps we need, as Michel Serres suggested, 'to summon the concept of chaos, which just a while ago was mythical, and which remains so derided by reason that we invoke it only in speaking of madness' (Serres 1982: 161).

History's place, its legitimate place, is thus the present, the here and now of things, beings, and places. As Michel de Certeau (1987: 76) has alerted us, we are being called upon to re-politicize history. In the age of presentism, the study of history effectively demands that we envisage it as a political stance, that we adopt an approach that not only places history in its place – within the present, not adjoining it – but also gives a voice to active entities that the former regime of historicity had reduced to simple objects. It falls to history, as it pronounces testimony in the name of both the human and the non-human, to explore the new ways of knowledge and creation at the time of the Anthropocene.

References

Anders, G. (2007), *Le temps de la fin*, Paris: Les Cahiers de l'Herne.

Angus, I. (2016), *Facing the Anthropocene: Fossil Capitalism and the Crisis of the Earth System*, New York: Monthly Review Press.

Assmann, A. (2013), *Ist die Zeit aus den Fugen? Aufstieg und Fall des Zeitregimes der Moderne*, Munich: Hanser.

Augé, M. (2008), *Où est passé l'avenir?*, Paris: Panama.

Bambach, C. H. (1995), *Heidegger, Dilthey, and the Crisis of Historicism*, Ithaca, NY: Cornell University Press.

Baschet, J. (2018), *Défaire la tyrannie du présent. Temporalités émergentes et futurs inédits*, Paris: La Découverte.

Baudelaire, C. ([1863]2010), *The Painter of Modern Life*, London: Penguin.

Beiser, F. C. (2011), *The German Historicist Tradition*, Oxford: Oxford University Press.

Benjamin, W. (1996), 'The Life of Students', in his *Selected Writings*, vol. 1: 1913–1926, ed. M. Bullock and M. W. Jennings, 37–47, Cambridge, MA and London: The Belknap Press of Harvard University Press.

Benjamin, W. (1999), *The Arcades Project*, transl. H. Eiland and K. McLaughlin, Cambridge, MA and London: The Belknap Press of Harvard University Press.

Benjamin, W. (2007), 'Theses on the Philosophy of History', in W. Benjamin, *Illuminations: Essays and Reflections*, ed. H. Arendt, transl. H. Zohn, 253–64, New York: Schocken Books.

Bentley, M. (2006), 'Past and "Presence": Revisiting Historical Ontology', *History and Theory*, 45: 349–61.

Bergson, H. (2009), *Durée et simultanéité. À propos de la théorie d'Einstein*, Paris: Presses universitaires de France.

Bevernage, B. (2015), 'The Past Is Evil/Evil Is Past: On Retrospective Politics, Philosophy of History, and Temporal Manichaeism', *History and Theory*, 54 (3): 333–52.

Bing, G. (1965), 'A. M. Warburg', *Journal of the Warburg and Courtauld Institutes*, 28: 299–313.

Boltanski, L. and Chiapello, E. (2007), *The New Spirit of Capitalism*, transl. G. Elliott, London and New York: Verso.

Bonneuil, C., and Fressoz, J.-B. (2016), *L'Événement Anthropocène. La Terre, l'histoire et nous*, Paris: Le Seuil.

Born, G. (2015), 'Making Time: Temporality, History, and the Cultural Object', *New Literary History*, 46 (3): 361–86.

Braudel, F. (1958), 'Histoire et sciences sociales: la longue durée', *Annales: Économies, Sociétés, Civilisations*, 13 (4): 725–53.

Burges, J., and Elias, A. J. (2016), 'Introduction: Time Studies Today', in J. Burges and A. J. Elias (eds), *Time: A Vocabulary of the Present*, 1–32, New York: New York University Press.

Ceballos, G., Ehrlich, P., and Dirzo, R. (2017), 'Biological Annihilation via the Ongoing Sixth Mass Extinction Signaled by Vertebrate Population Losses and Declines', *Proceedings of the National Academy of Sciences of the United States of America*, 25 July, available online: www.pnas.org/cgi/doi/10.1073/pnas.1704949114 (accessed 25 November 2018).

Certeau, M. de (1987), *Histoire et psychanalyse. Entre science et fiction*, Paris: Gallimard.

Chakrabarty, D. (2000), *Provincializing Europe: Postcolonial Thought and Historical Difference*, Princeton, NJ: Princeton University Press.

Chakrabarty, D. (2009), 'The Climate of History: Four Theses', *Critical Inquiry*, 35 (2): 197–222.

Chouquer, G. (2007), *Quels scénarios pour l'histoire du paysage? Orientations de recherche pour l'archéogéographie*, Coimbra, Porto: CEAUCP.

Chouquer, G. (2008), *Traité d'archéogéographie. La crise des récits géohistoriques*, Paris: Errance.

Conrad, S. (2018), '"Nothing is the Way It Should Be": Global Transformations of the Time Regime in the Nineteenth Century', *Modern Intellectual History*, 15 (3): 821–48.

Crutzen, P. J. and Steffen, W. (2003), 'How Long Have We Been in the Anthropocene Era?', *Climatic Change*, 61 (3): 251–7.

Didi-Huberman, G. (2002a), *L'image survivante. Histoire de l'art et temps des fantômes selon Aby Warburg*, Paris: Les Éditions de Minuit.

Didi-Huberman, G. (2002b), 'The Surviving Image: Aby Warburg and Tylorian Anthropology', *Oxford Art Journal*, 25 (1): 59–70.

Didi-Huberman, G. (2003), 'Artistic Survival: Panofsky vs. Warburg and the Exorcism of Impure Time', *Common Knowledge*, 9 (2): 273–85.

Esposito, F. (2017), 'Zeitenwandel. Transformationen geschichtlicher Zeitlichkeit nach dem Boom – eine Einführung', in F. Esposito (ed.), *Zeitenwandel. Transformationen geschichtlicher Zeitlichkeit nach dem Boom*, 7–62, Göttingen: Vandenhoeck & Ruprecht.

Fitz-Henry, E. (2017), 'Multiple Temporalities and the Nonhuman Other', *Environmental Humanities*, 9 (1): 1–17.

Foucault, M. (1989), *The Archeology of Knowledge*, transl. A. M. Sheridan, New York: Routledge.

Fulda, D. (2010), 'Historicism as a Cultural Pattern: Practising a Mode of Thought', *Journal of the Philosophy of History*, 4 (2): 138–53.

Green, A. (2000), *Le temps éclaté*, Paris: Les Éditions de Minuit.

Gumbrecht, H. U. (1997), *In 1926. On the Edge of Time*, Cambridge, MA: Harvard University Press.

Gumbrecht, H. U. (2013), *After 1945: Latency as Origin of the Present*, Stanford: Stanford University Press.

Gumbrecht, H. U. (2014a), *Our Broad Present: Time and Contemporary Culture*, New York: Columbia University Press.

Gumbrecht, H. U. (2014b), 'The Future of Reading? Memories and Thoughts Toward a Genealogical Approach', *boundary 2*, 41 (2): 99–111.

Hamel, J.-F. (2006), *Revenances de l'histoire. Répétition, narrativité, modernité*, Paris: Les Éditions de Minuit.

Hartog, F. (1995), 'Temps et histoire. "Comment écrire l'histoire de France?"', *Annales: Économies, Sociétés, Civilisations*, 50 (6): 1219–36.

Hartog, F. (2003), *Régimes d'historicité. Présentisme et expériences du temps*, Paris: Le Seuil.

Hartog, F. (2010), 'Historicité/régimes d'historicité', in C. Delacroix, F. Dosse, P. Garcia, and N. Offenstadt (eds), *Historiographies. Concepts et débats*, vol. 2, 766–71, Paris: Gallimard.

Holbraad, M., and Pedersen, M. A. (2017), *The Ontological Turn: An Anthropological Exposition*, Cambridge: Cambridge University Press.

Hölscher, L. (2013), 'Mysteries of Historical Order: Ruptures, Simultaneity and the Relationship of the Past, the Present and the Future', in C. Lorenz and B. Bevernage (eds), *Breaking up Time: Negotiating the Borders between Present, Past and Future*, 134–51, Göttingen: Vandenhoeck & Ruprecht.

Iggers, G. G. (1983), *The German Conception of History: The National Tradition of Historical Thought from Herder to the Present*, rev. edn., Middletown, CT: Wesleyan University Press.

Johnson, C. D. (2012), *Memory, Metaphor, and Aby Warburg's Atlas of Images*, Ithaca, NY: Cornell University Press and Cornell University Library.

Jordheim, H. (2012), 'Against Periodization: Koselleck's Theory of Multiple Temporalities', *History and Theory*, 51: 151–71.

Jordheim, H. (2014), 'Introduction: Multiple Times and the Work of Synchronization', *History and Theory*, 53: 498–518.

Jordheim, H. (2017), 'Synchronizing the World: Synchronism as Historiographical Practice, Then and Now', *History of the Present*, 7 (1): 59–95.

Jordheim, H., and Wigen, E. (2018), 'Conceptual Synchronisation: From Progress to Crisis', *Millennium: Journal of International Studies*, 46 (3): 421–39.

Keedus, L. (2015), *The Crisis of German Historicism: The Early Political Thought of Hannah Arendt and Leo Strauss*, Cambridge: Cambridge University Press.

Kleinberg, E. (2017), *Haunting History: For a Deconstructive Approach to the Past*, Stanford: Stanford University Press.

Kleinberg, E., Scott, J. W., and Wilder, G. (2018), 'Theses on Theory and History'. Available online: http://theoryrevolt.com/ (accessed 22 October 2018).

Koselleck, R. (2000), *Zeitschichten: Studien zur Historik*, Frankfurt am Main: Suhrkamp.

Koselleck, R. (2004), *Futures Past: On the Semantics of Historical Time*, transl. K. Tribe, New York: Columbia University Press.

Koselleck, R. (2018), *Sediments of Time. On Possible Histories*, transl. and ed. S. Franzel and S.-L. Hoffmann, Stanford: Stanford University Press.

Landwehr, A. (2014), *Geburt der Gegenwart. Eine Geschichte der Zeit im 17. Jahrhundert*, Frankfurt am Main: Fischer.

Landwehr, A. (2016), *Die anwesende Abwesenheit der Vergangenheit. Essay zur Geschichtstheorie*, Frankfurt am Main: Fischer.

Landwehr, A. (2018), 'Nostalgia and the Turbulence of Times', *History and Theory*, 57 (2): 251–68.

Lanieri, A. (2014), 'Resisting Modern Temporalities: Toward a Critical History of Breaks in Time', *History and Theory*, 53: 603–15.

Latour, B. (1993), *We Have Never Been Modern*, transl. C. Porter, Cambridge, MA: Harvard University Press.

Latour, B. (2015), *Face à Gaïa. Huit conférences sur le nouveau régime climatique*, Paris: La Découverte.

Latour, B. (2017), *Où atterrir? Comment s'orienter en politique*, Paris: La Découverte.

Lewis, S. L., and Maslin, M. A. (2018), *The Human Planet: How We Created the Anthropocene*, New Haven and London: Yale University Press.

Lorenz, C. (2010), 'Unstuck in Time. Or: the Sudden Presence of the Past', in K. Tilmans et al. (eds), *Performing the Past. Memory, History and Identity in Modern Europe*, 67–105, Amsterdam: Amsterdam University Press.

Lorenz, C. (2014), 'Blurred Lines: History, Memory and the Experience of Time', *International Journal for History, Culture and Modernity*, 2 (1): 43–62.

Lorenz, C. (2017), '"The Times They Are a-Changin". On Time, Space and Periodization in History', in M. Carretero, S. Berger and M. Grever (eds), *Palgrave Handbook of Research in Historical Culture and Education*, 109–31, London: Palgrave Macmillan.

Malm, A. (2017), *Fossil Capital: The Rise of Steam-Power and the Roots of Global Warming*, London: Verso.

McEwan, D. (2009), 'Aby Warburg's and Fritz Saxl's Assessment of the "Wiener Schule"', *Journal of Art Historiography*, 1. Available online: https://arthistoriography.files.wordpress.com/2011/02/media_139130_en.pdf (accessed 22 October 2018).

Megill, A. (1997), 'Why was There a Crisis of Historicism?', *History and Theory*, 36 (3): 416–29.

Michelet, J. (1843), *Introduction à l'histoire universelle*, Paris: Hachette.

Moore, J. (2015), *Capitalism in the Web of Life: Ecology and the Accumulation of Capital*, London and New York: Verso.

Moore, J. (ed.) (2016), *Anthropocene or Capitalocene? Nature, History, and the Crisis of Capitalism*, Oakland, CA: PM Press.

Nietzsche, F. ([1874]2010), *Untimely Meditations*, Cambridge: Cambridge University Press.

Nora, P. (ed.) (1984–1992), *Les Lieux de mémoire*, 8 vols, Paris: Gallimard.

Oldfield, F., and Steffen, W. (2004), 'The Earth System', in W. Steffen et al., *Global Change and the Earth System: A Planet Under Pressure*, 7, Berlin: Springer.

Olivier, L. (2013a), 'Time', in P. Graves-Brown, R. Harrison, and A. Piccini (eds), *The Oxford Handbook of the Archaeology of the Contemporary World*, 167–77, Oxford: Oxford University Press.

Olivier, L. (2013b), 'The Business of Archaeology is the Present', in A. González-Ruibal (ed.), *Reclaiming Archaeology: Beyonds the Tropes of Modernity*, 117–29, New York: Routledge.

Olivier, L. (2017), 'La répétition dans les processus archéologiques', *Cliniques: Paroles de praticiens en institution*, 14: 172–86.

Olsen, B. (2010), *In Defense of Things: Archaeology and the Ontology of Objects*, Lanham, MD: AltaMira Press.

Olsen, B. (2013), 'Reclaiming Things: An Archaeology of Matter', in P. L. Carlile, D. Nicolini, A. Langley, and H. Tsoukas (eds), *How Matter Matters. Objects, Artifacts and Materiality in Organization Studies*, 171–96, Oxford: Oxford University Press.

Olsen, B., Shanks, M., Webmoor, T., and Witmore, C. (2012), *Archaeology: The Discipline of Things*, Los Angeles, CA: University of California Press.

Paul, H. J. (2008), 'A Collapse of Trust: Reconceptualizing the Crisis of Historicism', *Journal of the Philosophy of History*, 2: 63–82.

Pensky, M. (2004), 'Method and Time: Benjamin's Dialectical Images', in D. S. Ferris (ed.), *The Cambridge Companion to Benjamin*, 177–98, Cambridge: Cambridge University Press.

Rampley, M. (2000), *The Remembrance of Things Past: On Aby M. Warburg and Walter Benjamin*, Wiesbaden: Harrassowitz.

Rampley, M. (2001), 'Iconology of the Interval: Aby Warburg's Legacy', *Word & Image: A Journal of Verbal/Visual Enquiry*, 17 (4): 303–24.

Rancière, J. (1996), 'Le concept d'anachronisme et la vérité de l'historien', *L'inactuel*, 6: 53–68.

Rancière, J. (2012), *La méthode de l'égalité. Entretien avec Laurent Jeanpierre et Dork Zabunyan*, Paris: Bayard.

Ross, C. (2012), *The Past is the Present; It's the Future Too. The Temporal Turn in Contemporary Art*, New York: Continuum.

Rovelli, C. (2018), *The Order of Time*, transl. E. Segre and S. Carnell, New York: Riverhead Books.

Runia, E. (2010), 'Inventing the New From the Old – From White's "Tropics" to Vico's "Topics"', *Rethinking History*, 14 (2): 229–41.

Saint Augustin (1998), *Confessions*, transl. H. Chadwick, Oxford: Oxford University Press.

Sawyer, S. W. (2015), 'Time after Time: Narratives of the Longue Durée in the Anthropocene', *Transatlantica*, 1. Available online: http://transatlantica.revues.org/7344 (accessed 22 October 2018).

Schaeffer, J.-M. (2007), *La fin de l'exception humaine*, Paris: Le Seuil.

Serres, M. (1982), *Genèse*, Paris: Bernard Grasset.

Serres, M. with Latour, B. (1995), *Conversations on Science, Culture, and Time*, Ann Arbor: The University of Michigan Press.

Simon, Z. B. (2019), *History in Times of Unprecedented Change: A Theory for the 21st Century*, London: Bloomsbury Academic.

Steffen, W., Richardson, K., Rockström, J., Cornell, S., Fetzer, I., and Bennet, E. (2015), 'Planetary Boundaries: Guiding Human Development on a Changing Planet', *Science*, 347 (6223): 736–47.

Tamm, M. (2015), 'Introduction: Afterlife of Events: Perspectives on Mnemohistory', in M. Tamm (ed.), *Afterlife of Events: Perspectives on Mnemohistory*, 1–23, Basingstoke: Palgrave Macmillan.

Tanaka, T. (2015), 'History Without Chronology', *Public Culture*, 28 (1): 161–86.

Telman, J. (1996), 'Historismuskritik: Aufarbeitung der Vergangenheit oder Selbstkritik', in O. G. Oexle and J. Rüsen (eds), *Historismus in den Kulturwissenschaften. Geschichtskonzepte, historische Einschätzungen, Grundlagenprobleme*, 289–305, Cologne: Böhlau.

Tomich, D. (2011), 'The Order of Historical Time: The *Longue Durée* and Micro-History', *Almanack*, 2. Available online: http://www.scielo.br/pdf/alm/n2/en_2236-4633-alm-02-00038.pdf (accessed 22 October 2018).

Warburg, A. (1999), 'Pagan-Antique Prophecy in Words and Images in the Age of Luther', in A. Warburg, *The Renewal of Pagan Antiquity: Contributions to the Cultural History of the European Renaissance*, transl. D. Britt, 597–697, Los Angeles: Getty Research Institute for the History of Art and Humanities.

Zalasiewicz, J., Waters, C. W., Barnosky, A. D., Cearreta, A., Crutzen, P., Ellis, E., Ellis, M. A., Fairchild, I. J., Grinevald, J., Haff, P. J., Hajdas, I., Leinfelder, R., McNeill, J., Odada, E. O., Poirier, C., Richter, D., Steffen, W., and Summerhayes, C. (2015), 'When Did the Anthropocene Begin? A Mid Twentieth Century Boundary Level Is Stratigraphically Optimal', *Quaternary International*, 383: 196–203.

Part One

Presentism and New Temporalities

1

Out of Time?

Some Critical Reflections on
François Hartog's Presentism

Chris Lorenz

If it would not sound a bit pathetic, one could say that *anno* 2019 there is a spectre haunting Europe, the spectre of presentism. In my contribution to this volume I will depart from this *Zeitdiagnose* basically in order to question it. I will do so by problematizing the influential analysis of 'presentism' by the French historian François Hartog.[1] Although Hartog did not invent or discover the word 'presentism', as he sometimes suggests, he has certainly played a fundamental role in its spread in history and in historical theory over the last fifteen years.[2]

I take Hartog's analysis of presentism as a point of departure and I argue that his notion of presentism is fundamentally ambiguous. Actually Hartog has presented *two* versions of presentism that cannot be reconciled. The first version I call presentism no. 1 according to which presentism basically means our 'present', 'contemporary' period. This periodizational interpretation of presentism fits in the linear and progressive time conception of modern history, because modern history basically conceives of the past as a progressive succession of periods. Modern History with the capital H is conceived of as the train of time that travels on one (linear) track with an accelerating speed (as Koselleck among others emphasized[3]) from the past to the present and towards the future.[4]

The second version of presentism however, that I call presentism no. 2, conceives of presentism *not* as the contemporary period – *not* as a specific, substantially filled block of time – but as an analytical ideal type of what Hartog calls an 'order of time' or a 'regime of historicity'. This version characterizes a particular view on the relationship between past, present and future, in which one of them is dominant – and presentism represents the regime of historicity in which the present is dominant. Order of time and regime of historicity are Hartog's conceptual instruments to *pluralize* the notion of time by clarifying that the relationship between past, present and future varies over times and cultures. Hartog explicitly presents presentism no. 2 as the interpretation that he intends: presentism is meant to be a heuristic tool for further research concerning experiences of time. Therefore presentism no. 2 is *not* a chronological block of time and does *not* fit in the linear time track of modern history. Hartog's ambiguity in this case exemplifies more general problems of thinking beyond linear time in terms of multi-layeredness and to conceive of 'history without chronology', in Stefan Tanaka's (2016) phrasing.[5]

In order to develop my arguments I proceed in four steps. First, I analyse how Hartog has introduced presentism in the context of the memory wars in France and how his presentism is firmly rooted in what he calls 'a crisis of time'. Second, I argue that his analysis of presentism is basically an inversion of modernism, and that some of the problems of presentism therefore can best be understood as the inverted problems of the modern regime of historicity. Third, I develop my argument that Hartog's presentism actually comes in two varieties and that both versions of presentism are at odds with each other and why. Fourth and last, I draw conclusions from my analysis and put Hartog's presentism in a comparative perspective.

Hartog's presentism, the memory wars and the crisis of time

When analysing texts in the history of ideas and in philosophy it is good practice to start with their contexts. This maxim also holds for the texts that Hartog has published on presentism and there cannot be much doubt that Hartog's ideas on presentism were and are embedded in the crucial context of the so-called memory boom and memory wars in France (Joutard 2013). In this situation many historians were – and still are – extremely worried that professional history was being threatened in its core values by all brands of collective memory (see Van de Mieroop 2016). Hartog is of one mind with Pierre Nora that 'the age of commemoration' began in the 1980s – the bi-centennial of the French Revolution was celebrated in 1989, later followed by many 'round' years connected to events concerning both world wars – and that this age coincides with the rise of 'memory', of 'patrimony' and of 'identity', that simultaneously represent the four master concepts of the age of presentism.[6] The age of memory and the age of presentism thus boil down to the same thing: almost everything, varying from (local, regional, national, European, global) traditions like carnival, songs and recipes to make cheese to all possible built structures and even landscapes, can be transformed into heritage and patrimony and can be taken as an occasion of commemoration and claimed as a basis for some (local, regional, national, European, world) identity.[7]

In Hartog's view Holocaust memory and post-colonial memory are the forerunners of presentism and its four key concepts – at least in France. And each of them is a threat to the autonomy and the authority of history, because each represents an unhistorical if not anti-historical way of dealing with the past. They represent four ways to *erase* the very distance between the past and present because they are striving after an emotional = authentic connection between an identification of the past and the present – the distance that is a precondition for the existence of history as a modernist, truth-seeking practice, as Michel de Certeau had already argued.[8] During the modern period it had been the historian's task to clarify the past to an audience in the present in the light of the future – usually that of the Nation or of another collective identity. Modern histories were characterized by a progressive development because the past in the light of the future was the modern key category of self-understanding. The present was always conceived as a temporary station between the past and the future-in-the-making:

The future illuminating the past and giving it meaning constituted a *telos*, called, by turns, 'the Nation', 'the People', 'the Republic', 'Society', or 'the Proletariat', each time dressed in the garb of science. If history dispensed a lesson, it came from the future, not the past. It resided in a future that was to be realized as a rupture with the past, or at least as a differentiation from it.

Hartog 2015: 102

In presentism this is no longer the case because the present itself has become the key category of self-understanding: the past and the future have become mere extensions of the present. This extended present lacks the senses of both openness and of direction that were so typical of modern history. Now we all inhabit the new – one could say: one-dimensional – territory of memory, in which we all have become contemporaneous according to Hartog (2016: 41, 48).[9]

The new (especially digital immersive and interactive) media technologies have made the 'presentification' of the past possible – including in the form of experiential museums (*Erlebnismuseen* in German) and in the form of virtual reality headsets (Hartog 2005, 2016).[10] While history in principle acknowledges and respects the alterity of the past and its discontinuity with the present, memory is always in search of sameness and continuity according to this Halbwachsian, antagonistic view of the relationship between history and memory. And, as Hartog obviously regrets, somewhere along this road the historians have lost their power over their own agenda because what history is, is increasingly determined by the political agenda of commemorations and not by the historical profession (Hartog 2016: 42–3).

The stellar rise of memory from the 1980s onwards was accompanied by the simultaneous rise of the notions of victim/witness and the notion of trauma (see Goltermann 2017). In Hartog's view the – traumatized – victim in its role as the – emotional – witness has replaced the historian as the authentic authority concerning the past. This replacement began with the Eichmann trial in 1961 to 1962 and continued in the French trials of the 1980s and 1990s against the nazi-'butcher of Lyon' Klaus Barbie, and the French nazi-collaborateurs Maurice Papon and Paul Touvier – trials that were also meant to be 'moments de mémoire' for the future (Hartog 2016: 34, 85).[11] *Contemporary* historians were usually present in these trials – not on their own professional authority but only to answer the questions of the judges in the roles of expert-witnesses.[12]

While memory has advanced as the 'alternative thérapeutique' for history, the task of the judges in presentism has become to treat and cure public and private ailments by means of a 'thérapie judiciaire' (Hartog 2016: 53, 61). This idea was first expressed in the rehabilitation of the most famous victim in recent French history: the Jewish French officer Dreyfus in 1906 – an event that typically called for a commemoration 100 years later (Hartog 2016: 65). Between 1906 and 2006 journalists – and *not* historians – had become the experts in the media in reporting trials and immediately historicizing them in our present 'temps médiatique d'historisation' (Hartog 2016: 61).[13] Since then the present event has actually become identical with its immediate representation in the media, preferably in 'real time' and as 'breaking news'.[14] Also since then the witness and the historian have typically changed places in the public space: while during the

Dreyfus affair witnesses acted like historians, 100 years later historians have to act like witnesses (Hartog 2016: 69). The creation of 'witness-archives' like the Spielberg Archive is just another part of this process.

From the 1980s onwards the witness has been conceived as the victim of past violence and as the carrier of wounds that resist healing. Therefore the witness literally becomes the carrier of the past – including of the truth about the past – into the present. Hartog basically posits that *all* presentist time is trauma-time because 'the past won't go away'.[15] Below we will see that the traumatic character of time in Hartog's view also explains its 'double debt'. And we can observe that unlike modern (Newtonian) time, trauma-time is *not* linear, homogeneous and empty.

According to Freudian theory the only way to deal with trauma-time for the victims – that is: (the descendants of) the victims of the Holocaust, of slavery, of colonialism – is to 'work it through', but Hartog does not elaborate this issue. He only signalizes the new institution of the Truth and Reconciliation Commission that has been invented to fulfil this function in situations of 'transitional justice', starting in post-Apartheid South Africa – without going into its many problems (Hartog 2016: 82–5; cf. Bevernage 2012).

For those in the present who take responsibility for the fate of the victims and who want to 'repair' past injustices, the only way is 'to make whole what has been smashed', that is: to embark on the entirely new road of 'reparation politics' *for specific groups of victims* – and *not* for victorious states after wars, as had been the case before. Therefore the Allied trial of the (surviving) leaders of Nazi-Germany in Nuremberg in 1945 to 1946 was the beginning of an entire new era in Hartog's view – the era of the imprescriptable crimes against humanity and the era of human rights – although it would take another fifty years for this development to become 'fully visible' (Hartog 2016: 31–2).[16] This new era also brought the change from the former view 'let the court of History judge' to 'taking History to court' – in the form of putting perpetrators to trial, irrespective of the temporal distance of their crimes – thus acknowledging the continued suffering of their victims.[17] Since '9/11' victimhood has become even more central because victims for the first time have also acquired heroic attributes (Hartog 2016: 76).

So the omnipresent 'memoralization' of the past – especially signalized by the omnipresence of victims and trauma – is accompanied by the simultaneous *juridification* of the past – observable in the growing presence of human rights and the imprescriptable crimes against them. Human rights make perpetrators *for ever* contemporaneous with their crimes against humanity and thus imply a politico-juridical *a-temporalization of time*:

> If the 'very nature' of crimes against humanity makes statory time limitations fall away, then they ground a *'legal atemporality'* which can be understood as a sort of *past in the present*, a *present past* or rather an *extension of the present*, as from the present of trial. The only place for historians in this temporality is, logically enough, as witnesses, called to express orally what they remember.
>
> Hartog 2015: 201[18]

Therefore the juridification of the past remarkably seems to imply the downgrading of the historical past and of the autonomy of the historical profession in Hartog's view.

The juridification of the past also manifests itself in the form of so-called memory laws. In order to protect some victim groups and their descendants quite a few states since the 1990s have adopted memory laws, which make the denial of specific genocides – especially the Holocaust and the Armenian genocide – punishable by law.[19] In a counter-reaction France under President Nicolas Sarkozy also adopted a memory law in 2005 regulating the 'balanced' contents of history education concerning French colonialism – thus 'snatching' another part of the historical pie away from the historian's table by subjugating it to memory law.[20] Many known historians, like Nora and Rousso, protested in vain against this 'usurpation' of the past by politics for present-day purposes. Hartog is obviously on their side, but he can only draw the conclusion that historians are unmistakably fighting an uphill battle: history seems 'un territoire menacé' and their role as 'régisseur de temps' seems to have come to an at least provisional end since historical time is 'overruled' in the public sphere by memorial and juridical time. 'Memoria magistra vitae' has displaced 'historia magistra vitae' – for an indefinite future (Hartog 2016: 107). As far as Hartog's diagnosis of presentism holds water, for historians presentism definitely means a 'crisis of time'.[21]

Hartog's presentism as the inversion of the modern regime of historicity

So far I have established that Hartog's ideas about presentism and its relationship with history as a discipline are rooted in a critical diagnosis of the present, which assumes that the present is in a general state of crisis – Hartog frequently refers to the present 'crisis of time'. Therefore I think Aleida Assmann is certainly right in identifying a strong nostalgia in Hartog's *Zeitdiagnose* concerning the discipline of history before the memory wars had disrupted it and had plunged it into a crisis (Assmann 2013: 256–63). On similar grounds Kenan Van de Mieroop (2016) has labelled Hartog's *Zeitdiagnose* as a 'pathogen', because Hartog analyses the rise of memory and presentism as a symptom of an illness.

The basic characteristic of the presentist crisis in Hartog's view is that the future is no longer perceived as a promise – as in modern, progressive time – but as a threat and a catastrophe in the making (Hartog 2015: xviii, 197–204). So the presentist 'crisis of time' is actually 'le temps des catastrophes' (Hartog 2016: 100). Characteristic for these (climatic, ecological, nuclear, genetic etc.) catastrophes is that they are already present and are both global and irreversible. Even if drastic precautions are taken immediately in order to further our security – which is the main presentist concern regarding the future – the catastrophic developments can only be slowed down and not reversed (Hartog 2016: 101–2). So in a sense there is a return of time in the present, but with the difference that the train of history is now experienced as definitely heading in the wrong direction – it is no longer making progress, as it used to do in modern times, but is moving towards the abyss (and, as the First World War and Walter Benjamin had taught, the abyss may be deep enough to bury us all).[22] Moreover, the abyss is already present in the form of catastrophic developments, so the future is just an extension of the everlasting present (Hartog 2016: 288). The previsions and precautions in the present therefore only have a very reactive, limited and short-term character, and most certainly not the long-time character of modern projects (including the – unfinished – project of modernity itself). In no way are they a solution for the 'crise du future', that is part and parcel of the crisis of the present (Hartog 2016: 102–3, 287).

What I want to signalize here is that the dystopian and catastrophical view of the present in Hartog's *Croire en l'histoire* basically acquires its contours in a comparison with – and as an *inversion* of – the utopian and progressive view of the present that is characteristic of the modern regime of historicity since the Enlightenment.[23] This already begins with the semantic origins of presentism because Hartog coined presentism after the concept of futurism, meaning 'a more or less "radiant" future, a futurist type of future' – which was the fundamental temporal concept of modern history (Hartog 2015: xvii).[24] 'The West has spent the last two hundred years dancing to the tune of the future – and making others do likewise', Hartog claims, strongly suggesting that presentism is the epochal successor of futurism (Hartog 2015: xvii; 2016: 283).

Simultaneously, however, Hartog also repeatedly emphasizes that at present it may be too early to diagnose the present, and it therefore may not be accidental that in the beginning of *Regimes of Historicity* presentism remains a remarkably elusive notion (Hartog 2015: xviii). There Hartog only tells that 'at present' – he provides no temporal markers[25] – 'the production of historical time seems to be suspended' in a permanent 'acceleration' and that 'perhaps this is what generates today's sense of permanent, elusive, and almost immobile present, which nevertheless attempts to create its own historical time' (Hartog 2015: 17–18).

In the new foreword to *Regimes of Historicity*, Hartog uses the same images and vocabulary. Presentism is 'the sense that only the present exists, a present characterized by the tyranny of the instant and by the treadmill of an unending now' (Hartog 2015: xv). Presentist time points neither to the past, nor to the future, it points only to itself – so we can conclude that it cannot be represented by an arrow, like modern, linear time, but only by a pulsating point. Typical adjectives Hartog uses to characterize the present are omnipresent, omnipotent and omnivorous – adjectives with unambiguous critical normative connotations (Delacroix, Dosse and Garcia 2009: 145–6). Therefore Hartog pictures presentism as a black hole in time: it absorbs both its past *and* its future. As such it is the inversion of the radiant future of futurism, that enlightened both its present and its past.[26]

In line with some postmodern thinkers Hartog argues that the primarily temporal, future-oriented concepts that characterized modern history – especially its master concept of modernization/civilization and progress – have been replaced in presentism by primarily spatial concepts – like modernity, postmodernity, globalization (or multiple c.q. alternative modernities) and crisis – although his suggestion that time can be *reduced* to space is exceptional for a historian (Hartog 2016: 270, 288–9) and is not consistent with the A-theory of time.[27] In his new foreword Hartog uses the spatial metaphor of the 'Generic City' of the Dutch architect Rem Koolhaas to illustrate 'presentist experiences'. Koolhaas coined the concept 'Generic City' for a 'certain city-scape, replicated around the globe'. Hartog comments: 'This is where presentism is really at home, eating up space and reducing or banishing time. The Generic City, freed from its enslavement to the center, is without history, even if it goes at great lengths to advertise its pseudo-historical district' (Hartog 2015: xviii–xix).[28]

Again Hartog embraces a strongly critical, negative stance towards presentism and contrasts it with a notion of authentic history by using the adjective pseudo-historical. It is the same problem that pops up in his characterizations of the presentist obsession with memory, commemoration, patrimony and the present craze for heritage and identity: Hartog is smuggling in normative judgements through the backdoor, without making them explicit and without argument. In Hartog's view 'real' history is apparently completely unrelated to issues of identity and identity politics, although he obviously recognizes the intimate relationship between the rise of academic history and the nation-state.[29] Hartog, however, nowhere explains at which point in his view the normal historical way of dealing with the past ends and the pathological, non-historical obsession with the past and the craze for heritage begin.[30] This omission is noteworthy because he is aware of the problem in case since he explicitly denies that his analysis of presentism is somehow motivated by normative considerations – he denies that he is motivated by 'nostalgia' or by an 'accusatory position' (Hartog 2015: xvii).[31] His only stated aim is purely of a cognitive nature. As a good modern historian, he wants to 'create a distance' to the present by 'viewing from afar', and thus to 'have a finer understanding at the end of the process of what is close by' (Hartog 2015: xv). His only interest is to answer the question of whether 'our way of articulating past, present and future has something specific to it, something which makes today's present, here and now, different from previous presents' (Hartog 2015: xvii–xviii). And as we have seen Hartog presents a sustained argument that 'our way of articulating the past' (and I will come back to the 'our') is fundamentally different from both ancient and modern times – and this leads me to his introduction of the notion of 'indebtedness' and the idea 'indebted time'.

In the last chapter of *Regimes of Historicity* Hartog introduces the notion of debt in order to explain the double craze for memory and heritage. This concerns 'our' contemporary feeling of being indebted to both the past and to the future – and again he does not specify who the implied 'we' are. According to Hartog 'our doubly indebted present' is characterized by the double duty to remember and to preserve:

> The present has [...] extended both into the future and into the past. Into the future, through the notions of precaution and responsibility, through acknowledgement of the irreparable and the irreversible, and through the notions of heritage and debt, the latter being the concept which cements and gives sense to the whole. And into the past, borne by similar concepts such as responsibility and the duty to remember, the drive to make everything into heritage, the lifting of time limitations, and last but not least the notion of debt.
>
> Hartog 2015: 201

So debt for Hartog is what one could call '*the normative glue*' of presentism, because the feeling of debt basically explains *why* the present has *extended* both into the future and into the past. Again, Hartog does not make a distinction between a normal care concerning the past and the future, and a pathological feeling of indebtedness, thus avoiding the implied normative issues in case. Neither does he explain why the notion of debt presently has become so all encompassing that it has become 'ours'.

In *Croire en l'histoire* Hartog tries to fill in this argumentative gap by connecting the notion of debt to the notions of trauma and trauma-time. It is the generalization of trauma into a societal condition outside the therapeutical context that has produced 'un nouveau rapport au temps, à la mémoire, au deuil, à la dette, au malheur et aux malheureux' (Hartog 2016: 81–2, citing Didier Fassin and Richard Rechtman).[32] Instead of hope and trust in progress there is suffering and debt – and the obligation to pay. Therefore the notion of trauma turns out to be the 'missing link' between the state of general indebtedness in presentism and the victims of injustices: the indebtedness concerns the victims of injustices and of catastrophes, past, present and future. No wonder that presentism also implies an inversion of the meaning of the modernist project of the Nation: the dead in the past have no longer died *for* the sake of the Nation, but *because* of the Nation.

So much for Hartog's characterization of presentism as an inversion of the modern regime of historicity. This leads me to the third part of my chapter, which addresses the relationship between presentism as a period and presentism as an analytical category.

Hartog's two versions of presentism: Presentism no. 1 and presentism no. 2

If my analysis of presentism as an inverted form of the modern regime of historicity is correct, and if modern history is basically a period, then there are good grounds also to consider presentism as a period label (presentism no. 1). This line of interpretation suggests a reading of Hartog's analysis as a direct continuation of Koselleck's analysis of modern history – and Hartog makes no secret of Koselleck's huge influence on his own thinking about temporality. Now I am referring to Koselleck's famous explanation of the birth of modern history in terms of a fundamental change during the *Sattelzeit* from the classical exemplary orientation to the past (exemplified in 'historia magistra vitae') to the modern progressive orientation to the future (exemplified in the rise of the -isms, like nationalism, liberalism, socialism etc.).[33] Hartog takes Koselleck's explanation and his dating as a point of departure and baptizes this change in temporal orientation as the transformation from the classical to the modern regime of historicity.[34] Next Hartog introduces a third regime of historicity, which cannot be traced back to Koselleck: the presentist regime of historicity, with which Hartog has made a name for himself as a theoretician of present times. He usually, but not exclusively, dates this transformation of the modern to the presentist regime of historicity between 1980 and 1990. In that decade

the light beaming in from the future was beginning to wane, what was ahead seemed increasingly unpredictable, the category of the present prevailed and the recent past – which to everyone's surprise wouldn't move on or, on the contrary, passed with worrying speed – had to be constantly and compulsively revisited.

[Note the psychoanalytical imagery here. – C.L.] As a result, history could no longer be written from the perspective or in the name of the future (or of any of its various hypostases).

Hartog 2015: 139

Note that by 'adding' the presentist regime of historicity to the classical and modern regimes and by dating it Hartog is identifying presentism as a block of time, that is: as the successor period of the modern regime of historicity (presentism no. 1). Although Hartog does not support this interpretation (to my knowledge) I want to argue that presentism no. 1 is a plausible and well-founded interpretation of a substantial part of his writings. Therefore it is no wonder that this interpretation of Hartog has probably become the most widespread – among others Aleida Assmann has interpreted Hartog in this manner (Assmann 2013: 265–70, 275). Moreover, his *Croire en l'histoire* is chock-full of characterizations of presentism as a period, including various concepts identifying presentism and modernism as periods ('epoque', 'era', 'age') as we saw in the first paragraph.[35]

According to Hartog the transition of the modern to the presentist regime of historicity took place in a gradual manner between 1980 and 1990. Hartog mentions the fall of the Berlin Wall in 1989 occasionally as the key event in case, next to the political and historiographical changes in France during the 1980s, especially the final eclipse of the revolutionary Left and Nora's hugely successful *Les Lieux de mémoire* project between 1984 and 1992. For Hartog Nora's enterprise represents the very embodiment of presentism *in history*: 'As well as being a History of France for today, it is also, quite explicitly, a history of our present. As a result, the historian can no longer be represented as the intermediary between past and future' (Hartog 2015: 144).[36]

Paradigmatic changes in temporality are definitely not a matter of clean breaks or ruptures – for Hartog there is no such thing as a sudden 'coupure épistémologique' (Gaston Bachelard) or a 'scientific revolution' (Thomas Kuhn). Hartog's representation of the modern and presentist regimes of historicity in *Croire en l'histoire* contain many reflections on events and ideas that are widely spread in time – like the Dreyfus affair (1894–1906), the First and the Second World War, the Holocaust, the Nuremberg trial in 1946, the Eichmann trial in 1961 to 1962 and the following nazi-trials in France, '1968', '1990', '9/11' and the financial crisis of 2007 to 2008. Events like these have produced doubts, cracks, fissures and crises in – and finally the fall of – the modern regime of historicity while they gave rise to its presentist successor.[37] Hartog's qualifier that 'the passage from one regime to another involves periods of overlap', however, implies that normally one regime of historicity reigns supreme (Hartog 2015: 107).

In his methodological reflections Hartog does not interpret presentism in terms of a linear periodization.[38] There he argues that presentism and regimes of historicity as a 'methodological instrument' 'belong together'. 'The two are inseparable' because one can't identify presentism without using the regimes of historicity as a conceptual tool (Hartog 2015: xv–xvi). The very notion of regimes of historicity is only an analytical and heuristic tool for research of experiences of time: it is nothing else than a Weberian ideal type.

According to presentism no. 2, 'regimes do not come in a series, one mechanically following another' (Hartog 2015: xvi). In this reading various regimes of historicity can and do coexist. In historical reality it is always a 'matter of *degrees*, of more or less, of mixtures and composites and an always provisional or unstable equilibrium' (Hartog 2015: xv). The regimes only express 'a dominant *order* of time'.

In *Croire en l'histoire* he argues with Koselleck that there is not one stream of time: times are always 'heterogeneous' and 'multi-layered' (Hartog 2016: 233–4, 290). In line with this pluralistic view he signalizes that completely anti-historical, cyclical theories of time, like those of Mircea Eliade and Claude Lévi-Strauss, existed during the heydays of the modern regime of historicity (not to mention the earlier cyclical theories of Spengler and Toynbee) (Hartog 2016: 263–70). He also presents the German 'conservative revolution' during the 1920s and 1930s and the post-colonial approaches of the post-1980s as structurally similar attempts to refuse modern history. According to Hartog all pre-colonial – pre-Hispanic, autochton, 'first' – movements are based on the idea of a return to a pristine origin and to a fictional authentic identity (and again as to identity-claims Hartog only clarifies what he rejects and not what he accepts). They share this characteristic with the new religious fundamentalisms – especially Islamic fundamentalism.[39]

Regimes of historicity therefore do not disappear when they are no longer dominant, as presentism no. 1 suggests. They can be – and are – reactivated, depending on the events and circumstances. Between 'historical situations' and the concept of history there are always 'tensions' (Hartog 2016: 291). Therefore 'the presentist present is by no means uniform or clear-cut, and is experienced very differently, depending on one's position in society' (Hartog 2015: xviii), although Hartog has literally nothing to say about this connection between social positions and temporal experiences. The fact that his analysis is (almost) exclusively based on published books written by famous individual (white, educated, well-to-do, male) intellectuals from Europe and the United States (Sahlins on Captain Cook and Hawaii, Homer on ancient Greece, Chateaubriand on eighteenth-century France and America, Nora on contemporary France …) makes crystal clear that his body of work is one on the history of ideas and not on the anthropology or sociology of time, as Abdelmajid Hannoum (2008) has rightly observed.[40] This fact is rather surprising because Hartog has repeatedly emphasized the importance of his encounter with anthropology (Lévi-Strauss, Sahlins) in the genesis of the notion of regimes of historicity (see Delacroix, Dosse and Garcia 2009). There is, however, *nothing* in Hartog about time in its relation to social, cultural and political 'positionality' other than his authors' positions in specific blocks of time and space (Cook's Hawaii, Homer's Greece, Chateaubriand's France etc.). 'Other voices' within these 'blocks' – not to mention voices from the margins – are simply lacking – as is the discussion concerning history and identity *within* the discipline of history.[41] Just as in his use of the personal pronoun 'our' in 'our experiences of time' and in 'our debt', the subject-position of the speaker/writer remains completely unreflected. The anthropological and/or sociological gaze is not present in Hartog's writings on time.

The only exception to this rule is the distinction Hartog is making in one article between the very different senses of time that the winners and the losers of the First and Second World War have developed simultaneously, but here again his analysis is based on single (male, white etc.) authors (Hartog 2013).[42] Besides, he mentions in an interview that his analysis of time regimes only pertains to Europe and that his analysis does not claim to be exhaustive. Outside Europe other regimes of historicity may be in place – without substantializing his claim about the 'otherness' of non-European experiences of time, however.[43]

All in all, at times Hartog is paying his dues to temporal and spatial complexity *in abstracto* and once he even goes so far as to state that it may be useless to look for a regime of historicity because of a 'lack of unity':

> it might be useless to look for unity, if a certain dispersion or simply a multiplicity of different regimes of temporality happened to characterize (and distinguish) our present. And it might also be simply premature, given how long it takes to bring and delineate a regime of historicity, as we have seen, and given also that a regime of historicity never exists in pure form.
>
> Hartog 2015: 184

Hartog's reference to premature attempts to identify a new regime of historicity, however, presupposes the real existence of regimes and their linear temporality (Hartog 2015: xviii). Regimes of historicity apparently do need enough – linear – time to grow and blossom before they can be identified properly by the historian. This idea is very reminiscent of Marx's view on the succession of modes of production, in which the new mode of production has already developed in the womb of its predecessor but needs enough time to become visible and flower. This idea presupposes the developmental and periodizational view of presentism no. 1, which is at odds with presentism no. 2.

All in all, Hartog's analysis of presentism keeps wavering between two interpretations that contradict each other. Although Hartog explicitly has broken with linear time in presentism no. 2, this is not the case in presentism no. 1, and in his arguments for presentism no. 2 there are presuppositions derived from presentism no. 1. So much for the two versions of Hartog's 'presentism' and their problematic interrelationship.

Conclusion

If my analysis holds water and if Hartog's presentism can best be viewed as an inversion of modernism/futurism, then the conclusion is inevitable that with Hartog we have basically moved from 'the muddle of modernity', to use Chakrabarty's expression, to the muddle of presentism (AHR Roundtable 2008; Chakrabarty 2011). Alluring, erudite, provoking and intriguing as Hartog's analyses may be – and they certainly have these qualities – they remain stuck in the presuppositions of modernity and of modern linear time, as I have argued in my analysis of the two incompatible variants of presentism. Therefore it is probably not accidental that in *Regimes of Historicity* Hartog actually does not tell us how and why modernist time has been supplanted by presentist time – somewhere between 1940 and 1990 – although later in *Croire en l'histoire* he has provided quite some context and historiographical evidence for his theses on modern history. Nor is it accidental that since the publication of his landmark book Hartog has argued in interviews and new prefaces that we cannot even expect him to tell the 'transformation history' because there is no such story to be told due to the multi-layeredness of time and the simultaneous co-presence of regimes of historicity.

Nevertheless the almost absence of an historical account of the transformation of modernism to presentism during the twentieth century remains puzzling to say the least because of its systematic importance to the central argument of *Regimes of Historicity*.[44] This transformation-history is fundamental because 'the birth of the present' as a separate temporal category was the product of seventeenth-century modernity, as Luhmann and Landwehr have argued. The modern future could only open up after the 'punctuation' of the present and the 'Abkopplung' of the present from the past in Luhmann's phrasing. Therefore futurism and presentism have historically been directly connected.[45]

Hartog is not dealing with this connection and the same goes for the spatial location of the present and of presentism, although it is the explicit aim of his regimes of historicity to investigate experiences of time comparatively. Nevertheless, the book does not actually deliver any spatial or temporal comparison – not even within Europe or within the West. The chapters juxtapose a collection of cases in the broad domain of 'historical culture'– while the problem of the representativity of the cases is not addressed.[46] Probably this is the reason why Hartog states that his goal in *Regimes of Historicity* is 'explorative', to 'explore ways of being in time' by focusing on 'the *diversity* of regimes of historicity' and thus to un-familiarize the familiar (Hartog 2015: 9). Probably because of its dispersive set-up Hartog does not consider the book 'a history of time, nor even a treatise on the notion of regime of historicity' (Hartog 2015: 9, 18). Because he is also quite explicit that the book is not a treatise in historical theory or in philosophy of history, a reflexive reader may keep wondering what it is . . .

However this may be, the fundamental problem with Hartog's analysis of experiences of time is that it remains stuck halfway in its questioning of progressive time. Although it is to Hartog's credit to have pointed out systematically that the conception of the relationship between past, present and future is variable and has varied over space and time – and in this sense has undermined the idea that historical time has *one* fixed linear past–present–future structure – his analysis still presupposes the past, present and future as separate ontological entities (as multi-layered and heterogeneous as they may be). It is precisely the situation of the borderlines between past, present and future currently being threatened that Hartog diagnoses as 'threatening' and as 'the crisis of time', as Aleida Assmann (2013: 269) has justifiedly pointed out. However, if one argues – as Hartog does at book length in *Croire en l'histoire* – that the presupposition of history as *one* flow of time is no longer tenable (and thus the very idea of History as 'container-time'), then the past and future can no longer be distinguished in terms of the spatial down-stream and up-stream areas with clear borders of the same river of time.

Finally, we can develop a clearer view of Hartog's halfway position concerning linear time by comparing it with the more radical position that Achim Landwehr has formulated recently.[47] Landwehr points out that the idea of the present, past and future as separate blocks of time is actually pretty modern because it only originated in the seventeenth century (Landwehr 2014: 248–88). Before, it was usual to conceive of the temporal borders between the earlier, the simultaneous and the later as permeable and as relative. Therefore both Landwehr and Aleida Assmann argue that the present postmodern and fundamentally pluralistic experiences of time signalize a partial return to premodern views (Landwehr 2014: 285–6; Assmann 2013: 269–75).[48]

The differentiations between present, past and future therefore appear to be not of an ontological nature, but situational, relational and social/cultural.[49] This means that pasts and futures are always relative to, and constructions of, a present – as Augustinus argued long ago and Luhmann not so long ago.[50] Therefore it is impossible to locate persons, events and processes unambiguously in one 'layer of time', although historians are usually able to unambiguously date them chronologically. Christ, Elvis and Hitler are usually chronologically located in the past, but as long as living people somehow refer to them they simultaneously must be located in the present and the future. The same argument holds for supraindividual processes like 'globalization', 'global warming', 'environmental pollution' and 'debt crisis': they simulataneously refer to connected phenomena in the past, present and future. Landwehr proposes the concept of 'chronoference' (*Chronoferenz*) to capture this multitemporal quality of historical phenomena and suggests the rebaptism of history as a 'discipline of times' (*Zeitenwissenschaft*) – in the plural.

Landwehr's position also implies a break with the presupposition that there is one (dominant) relationship between future, present and past within 'cultures' or 'societies' as presentism no. 1 presupposes. The break with linear time implies the recognition of a non-reducible multiplicity of times, which is being experienced by different groups *simultaneously*.[51] This fundamental multiplicity of times also implies that the past can no longer be conceived as the ontological object that modernist historians reconstruct from a fixed observer position because past–present–future distinctions are made differently in different 'timescapes' – to use another concept proposed by Landwehr. Instead of linear time and other geometrical time conceptions that presuppose an independent observer position, including the stratigraphical – time-layer – conceptions of Braudel and Koselleck (which Hartog adopts), it might be more fruitful to adopt group-specific relational ideas about past–present–future relationships without presupposing that this condition is pathological, as Hartog does.

Therefore Landwehr's radical proposal is simultaneously a plea to abandon the traditional idea that there is a fixed thing called history or the past, and that the object of the discipline of history is knowledge of the past. For Landwehr it is essential for historians to recognize that the past never was present – and neither will the future ever be present. As a consequence it cannot be the goal of history to represent the past as adequate as possible in the form of narrative – and here Landwehr is fully in line with the recent non-representationalism in philosophy of history as argued for by, e.g., Paul Roth and Jouni-Matti Kuukkanen.[52] Landwehr thus proposes dropping the concept of history (*Geschichte* in German) altogether and replacing it with 'the historical' (Landwehr 2014: 298); essential(!) for thinking 'the historical' is abandoning homogeneous, linear time because homogeneous time is the carrier of homogeneous meaning (Landwehr 2014: 313–14). As far as Hartog is still clinging to linear time – and I have argued that this is partially the case in the form of presentism no. 1 – his analysis is also characterized by homogeneous meaning. This could explain the remarkable fact that Hartog also does not address the spatial variety of the meaning and dating of the modern and the present in history writing (as exemplified in the differences between periodizations in Germany, France, the United States, etc.) (see Nipperdey 2015, 2016).

Hartog's tendency to homogenize exhibits itself in a number of remarkable reductions of complexity in his representation of history in substantial parts of *Croire en l'histoire*: all history is contemporary and public history, the real site of contemporary history is in court, the real role of the historian is the expert witness; in short, the time of history has been replaced by the time of law and of present-day jurisdiction. A similar reduction characterizes his conceptualization of the relationship between history and memory: identity, victim, trauma and human rights issues are only located in the domain of memory, heritage and commemoration while real historians apparently are not confronted by them (although Hartog mentions the massive destruction of 'traces' by perpetrators of genocides as an issue for historians). By implication Hartog does not view the post-genocidal condition and the resulting 'historical wounds' (Chakrabarty) and human rights issues as problems for historians and seems to subscribe to the view of Hermann Lübbe and Co according to which the very idea of 'coping with the past' is little else than a category mistake.[53]

Landwehr's semantical swap is also motivated by his insight that since the birth of academic history onwards historians have attributed to History the characteristics that until the nineteenth century were usually attributed to God: meaning and totality. History has thus seized the vacant place of God (after His announced death) and has functioned as His Substitute (*Gottersatz* in German) since. Philosophy of history made it possible to transform religious transcendence and the promise of salvation from a vertical into a horizontal relationship: transcendence and salvation did not disappear, but were projected on the course of History (of the Nation, the Proletariat etc.). History writing transformed into a substitute of religion – and the historians into a caste of priests (Landwehr 2014: 9–31).

In *Croire en l'histoire* Hartog makes very similar observations about modern history and modern historians, without, however, drawing Landwehr's conclusion that we need to revise the very concept of history in order to avoid any further confusion of God/meaning and H/history. In contrast to Landwehr Hartog still seems to have a nostalgia for history before the Age of Memory swept the Age of History away and before the modern belief in the power of both History and history had faded. Although Hartog also knows that there is no way back, his writing at times betrays the spirit of a warrior who calls for a *reconquista* although he does not really believe in a victory.[54] All in all, we can conclude that Hartog does a better job in showing us how and why progressive linear time got historians in trouble than in suggesting them a future way out.

Notes

1   Hartog 2015, with a new foreword (original in French, 2003); Hartog 2016. Although the latter contains the extended arguments and the detailed examples for Hartog's main theses, I will – where possible – stick to the former book for quotes because this one is known best and has been published in English translation.

2   See Delacroix, Dosse and Garcia 2009. The concept of presentism, however, was already in use in American historiography to denote the ideas of 'New Historians' like Charles Beard (1874–1948) and Carl Becker (1873–1945), who both held that the historical past is always framed by the historian in the present. Recently presentism has also been used to denote the tendency of historians to focus on contemporary history at the expense of earlier periods – a tendency that Norbert Elias long ago called 'hodiecentrism'. See, for instance, Hunt 2002 and Walshalm 2017. In philosophy of time the concept of presentism was also already in use to characterize the view that only the present exists, the past exists no longer and the future does not yet exist. Presentism in philosophy of time is opposed by eternalism – which holds that the past and future exist just like the present – and by the growing block theory of time – which holds that the temporal universe is permanently increasing in size. Hartog's presentism appears to combine the three meanings of presentism.

3   This idea of the 'increasing speed' of modern history is known as the 'acceleration thesis' or the 'acceleration theory'. According to Koselleck 'acceleration' explains – among other things – why periods in history have become increasingly shorter. See Koselleck 2003: 150–77.

4   In terms of philosophy of time both presentism and modernism are A-theories of time, that view the distinction between the present, past and future as real and the passage (or 'flow') of time from the future through the present into the past as its fundamental characteristic. B-theories of time, that are in line with relativity theory in physics, contradict these two ideas and posit that all temporal charateristics are analogues of spatial properties. See Sider, Hawthorne and Zimmerman 2008: 209–39, and Markosian 2016.

5   In another article I have argued against the 'standard interpretation' that Reinhart Koselleck is facing similar difficulties. See Lorenz 2017.

6   Hartog uses the expression 'maîtres mots' and 'grands mots d'époque' interchangeably in this context and always in this order: memory, commemoration, patrimony and identity. In line with this characterization is his statement that the 'Trentes Glorieuses' (1945–75) in France have been followed by the 'Trentes Mémorieuses'. See Hartog 2016: 49–51.

7   For a hyper-critical analysis of the 'identity-boom' see Niethammer 2000. Cf. Hall and Du Gay 1996; Assmann and Friese 1998.

8   Hartog 2016: 99, 288. See also 89: 'Authenticité et véracité ne coïncident pas forcément'. Also see Hartog 2005: 16: 'The past attracts more than history. The presence of the past, the evocation and the emotions win out over keeping a distance and mediation.' In an interview Hartog has emphasized the importance of Michel de Certeau's ideas in his development of the notion of 'regimes of historicity'. See Delacroix, Dosse and Garcia 2009: 134. Remarkably, the German historian Martin Broszat had used a very similar argument in the 'Historikerstreit' to distinguish 'distanced' and 'objective' history writing on the Second World War by German historians and 'emotional' and 'mythical' histories of the Holocaust produced by Jewish historians. See Broszat and Friedländer 1988.

9   Hartog is referring to Johannes Fabian's arguments in anthropology that support the 'coavelness' of all cultures and that criticize all – evolutionary – ideas concerning the 'contemporaneity of the uncontemporaneous' (*Gleichzeitigkeit des Unzeitgleichen*).

10 Hartog does not mention the use of virtual reality headsets as a presentist genre, although it fits perfectly in his argument.

11 Hartog posits that the trials were filmed for this reason.

12 Hartog (2016: 42) remarks that in the public sphere the word 'history' is increasingly
   being replaced by 'the past' and 'history' is increasingly identified with 'contemporary
   history'. He also highlights the case of the French historian Henry Rousso, who was
   asked to act as an expert witness in the trial against Maurice Papon in 1997–98 but
   refused to do so because he did not want to participate in the 'mixing' of 'history' and
   'memory'.

13 Hartog lists the journalist next to the judge, the witness, the expert and the victim as
   'les acteurs du présent' (Hartog 2016: 60).

14 This thesis has been argued before by Hayden White for so-called 'modernist events'.
   See White 1996.

15 Hartog uses this phrase coined by the German contemporary historian Ernst Nolte in
   the 'Historikerstreit': 'Mais ce présent avait lui-même cette particularité d'être chargé
   d'un passé qui ne passait pas, selon la formule alors en usage' (Hartog 2016: 50).

16 Although the UN only adopted the declaration of human rights in 1947, the
   Nuremberg trial 'anticipated' this adoption. 'Crimes against humanity' was one of the
   four categories of the specified categories of crimes for this trial.

17 Hartog (2016: 79), citing Yan Thomas on this change: 'La question n'est pas: quels sont
   les effets du temps? Mais: quels effets décidons-nous d'attribuer aux temps?'

18 Hartog (2016: 31–2 and 79), states that the 'opération politico-juridique sur le temps'
   in case produces an 'atemporalité juridique'.

19 Hartog is predominantly referring to memory laws in France, although Eastern
   Europe at present is the region where they are 'booming'. See Koposov 2017.

20 The point was that Sarkozy's government also wanted to emphasize the 'positive'
   aspects of French colonialism (on the model of Monty Python's 'What did the Romans
   ever do for us?').

21 See e.g., Hartog 2015: 144: 'But our contemporary present and its presentism have proved
   almost unsustainable. The demand for memory can be interpreted as an expression of
   this crisis in our relationship with time as well as an attempt at providing a solution.'

22 Hartog 2016: 100–1: 'Le train ou le trend de l'Histoire tend vers la catastrophe', and
   103: 'L'urgence devient permanente'. Hartog also refers to Jean-Pierre Dupuy and his
   'catastrophisme éclairé'.

23 I have elaborated on the role of 'conceptual inversions' in the history of ideas in the
   introduction to my book *Bordercrossings: Explorations between History and Philosophy*
   (published in Polish, Chinese and Spanish). This introduction was republished and
   discussed in English, see Lorenz 2014a.

24 In Hartog 2016: 288, he even calls the 'futurist future' 'le charbon de la locomotive de
   l'Histoire' in modern history.

25 Hartog (2015: 185) states that from the *1960s* onwards 'the present showed signs of
   disquiet in its search for roots and its obsession with memory'. In his introduction
   Hartog's sketch of the fall of modernism begins in *1968* – an event that 'gave
   expression to a loss of faith in time itself as progress' and continues in 'the crisis of the
   1970s (not least the oil crisis)' (Hartog 2015: 5). So although Hartog usually locates the
   rise of 'presentism' *between 1980 and 1990*, sometimes he includes events going back
   to the *1940s* – if we take his inclusion of T. S. Eliot's 'provincialism of time' and the
   Nuremberg Trial seriously.

26 Hartog 2016: 253, on the modern regime of historicity: 'c'est l'avenir qui assigne un
   futur au passé'.

27 The change from modernization to modernity boils down to 'renoncer au temps'
   (Hartog 2016: 270). Although the use of spatial metaphors (long, short, distant, near

etc.) for time is well known given the notorious absence of sensory correlates for time – even time measurement by clocks and calendars is dependent on the spatial representation of time, as Achim Landwehr has recently noticed – the *reduction* of time to space is only argued for by physicists and B-series philosophers of time. Cf. Landwehr 2014: 306–3, for a sustained argument against the reduction of time to space in history.

28 Approvingly Hartog cites T. S. Eliot who already in the 1940s had developed a premonition of presentism when he wrote about a 'new kind of provincialism, not of space but of time' (Hartog 2016: 113).

29 For a more nuanced analysis, see Angehrn 1985. Cf. Assmann 2013; Lorenz 2008.

30 This is remarkable because in *Croire en l'histoire* (2016) Hartog is dealing extensively with the relationship between the historical and the legal ways of handling the past, only to conclude that human rights imply an 'atemporalization of time'.

31 Elsewhere I have argued that also Hayden White, who made a career of criticizing modern history and modern historians, nevertheless kept subscribing to the modern claims concerning the character of the discipline of history. See Lorenz 2014b.

32 For another critical assesment of the generalization of 'trauma', see Kansteiner 2004.

33 Therefore I don't agree with the influential thesis of Helge Jordheim (2012) that Koselleck's theory of time-layers implies that he was 'against periodization' as such. See Lorenz 2017.

34 For the problems of the idea of a *Sattelzeit*, see Osterhammel 2009: 102–16.

35 See also Hartog 2015: 11: 'In "Orders of Time 2" I shall focus on the contemporary period directly, guided by two watchwords: memory and heritage.'

36 Hartog seems to presuppose that teleology is only a problem of futurism and not of presentism but as Chakrabarty and others have pointed out 'teleological directionality was not bound to the future. Ends of history could just as well be located in the present or, in the form of the target envisaged return or merely vague nostalgia, in the past.' See Trüper, Chakrabarty and Subrahmanyam 2015: 12.

37 Hartog 2016: 52, 228–36, already identifies many 'crises' and 'fissures' in the modern regime of historicity during the 'long' nineteenth century around 1820, 1880 and 1914.

38 Hartog is so much at pains to reject the interpretation of 'regimes of historicity' as sequential periods that he must have been aware of its probability: 'les régimes ne sont portés par nulle téléologie, à la façon des stades ou des modes de production et ils ne prétendent pas vous donner le fin mot de l'histoire. [...] Il est un outil, un artefact, dont la finalité est heuristique. Ce n'est pas le point de départ d'une théorie de l'histoire.' See Delacroix, Dosse and Garcia 2009: 140–1.

39 Hartog 2016: 272: 'Le temps des origins qu'on pretend réinstaller, n'a, certes, jamais eu cours sous cette forme-là. On est, du point de vue de temps, du coté des révolutions conservatrices, conjoignant passéisme et futurisme.'

40 Hannoum (2008) also points to the fact that Hartog has completely left out the fundamental controversy in anthropology about Sahlins' interpretation of the encounter of Captain Cook with the Hawaiians. Also the 'other', 'post-colonial' voice of Gananath Obeyesekere is missing.

41 See Hannoum 2008; cf. also Angehrn 1985; Lorenz 1997: ch 14.

42 In this article Hartog is also following the lead of Koselleck.

43 Again following Koselleck Hartog mentions the 'prophetical regime of historicity', that deserves to be studied, see Delacroix, Dosse and Garcia 2009: 147. Cf. Koselleck 2003: 184–95, and Landwehr 2014: 324–29.

44 Hannoum (2008: 467) also notices this 'absence'.

45 Luhmann 1976; Landwehr 2014: 324–51; 2018: 262: 'In the seventeenth-century people found themselves in a temporal maelstrom and were forced to conquer the present as a time-space in which reality could be transformed.' The differentiation of the present from the future and the past was only made possible by the circumstance that modernity is producing *continuous change*, that is: new presents *and* old pasts – first making the 'Abkopplung' of the *historical* past from the present possible.

46 Zoltán Boldizsár Simon has rightly pointed out that the domain of techno-bio-science represents quite different experiences and expectations from those analysed by Hartog. See Chapter 4 by Simon in this volume.

47 Landwehr's arguments are quite similar to the ones of those who have recently pleaded for 'mnemohistory' and for 'history as hauntology', because these approaches also question the fixity of the borderlines between past, present and future.

48 The return is only partial because time in the twenty-first century is viewed as irreversible while in the seventeenth century it was viewed as reversible.

49 Assmann (2013) characterizes this development as a 'Kulturalisierung' of time. Landwehr (2014: 172–3) argues with Luhmann and Elena Esposito in terms of systems theory: 'Danach lässt sich Zeit fassen als die spezifische Unterscheidung zwischen Vergangenheit und Zukunft, die eine Gegenwart jeweils für sich trifft. Diese Unterscheidung ist keineswegs gegeben, vielmehr ist ihr sowohl eine historische wie eine soziale Dimension eigen. Das heisst, Zeit wird im Verlauf der Zeit selbst generiert, regeneriert und transformiert, und dies geschieht durch jeweils unterschiedliche Gruppen auf jeweils unterschiedliche Art und Weise. Diese Umstand lässt eine Mehrzahl differenter Zeiten zu, jede mit eigenen Systembezug.'

50 The basic idea is that we experience time in three modes: as a present present, as a present past, and as a present future. This is so, as Luhmann clarified, because one can only make a distinction between two objects or phenomena if they are *simultaneously* present, just as one can only draw a borderline between two territories that exist simultaneously. And what holds for territories also holds for the temporal modes past, present and future. Therefore the time conception involved can be called relational.

51 Compare Markosian 2016: 5: 'It is also worth asking whether time must be represented by a single line. Perhaps we should take seriously the possibility of time's consisting of multiple time streams, each one of which is isolated from each other, so that every moment of time stands in temporal relations to other moments in its own time stream, but does not bear any temporal relations to any moment from another time stream.'

52 Non-representationalism has broken with the idea that historians are striving to present texts (or other media) that somehow represent a past outside their research-based arguments, and post-narrativism has broken with the idea that historical narratives can somehow represent 'historical reality', *because 'historical reality' is only constructed by historical arguments*. According to Kuukkanen what historians do is present arguments that are evidence-based and that bolster a point of view that claims to be explaining the evidence and to be rationally superior to other points of view concerning a topic and a body of evidence at a particular moment. Therefore historical arguments are always relative to a particular discussion – and in this sense always 'discursive' – and to a particular moment in time. Every historical argument is thus based on and connected to a specific present – and therefore the only way to judge historical arguments is presentist. See Roth 2012; Kuukkanen 2015.

53 For a more nuanced analysis, see Angehrn 1985; Assmann 2013. For a human rights approach to the past, see De Baets 2008, 2015.

54 Hartog 2016: 29: 'Avec la fin du XXe siècle, l'histoire semble être passée de la toute-puissance à l'impuissance', and 292: 'Aujourd'hui, toutefois, *Mnêmosunê* a supplanté *Clio*, du moins dans l'espace public.'

References

'AHR Roundtable: Historians and the Question of Modernity' (2011), *American Historical Review*, 116 (3): 638–751.

Angehrn, E. (1985), *Geschichte und Identität*, Berlin: Walter De Gruyter.

Assmann, A. (2013), *Ist die Zeit aus den Fügen? Aufstieg und Fall des Zeitregimes der Moderne*, Munich: Hanser.

Assmann, A. and Friese, H., eds (1998), *Identitäten*, Frankfurt am Main: Suhrkamp.

Bevernage, B. (2012), *History, Memory and State-Sponsored Violence. Time and Justice*, New York: Routledge.

Broszat, M. and Friedländer, S. (1988), 'Um die Historisierung des Nationalsozialismus. Ein Briefwechsel', *Vierteljahreshefte für Zeitgeschichte*, 36 (2): 339–72.

Chakrabarty, D. (2011), 'The Muddle of Modernity', *The American Historical Review*, 116 (3): 663–75.

De Baets, A. (2008), *Responsible History*, New York and Oxford: Berghahn.

De Baets, A. (2015), *De Universele Verklaring van de Rechten van de Mens en de Historicus*, Amsterdam: Pallas/Amsterdam University Press.

Delacroix, C., Dosse, F. and Garcia, P. (2009), 'Sur la notion de régime d'historicité. Entretien avec François Hartog', in C. Delacroix, F. Dosse and P. Garcia (eds), *Historicités*, 133–51, Paris: La Découverte.

Goltermann, S. (2017), *Opfer. Die Wahrnehmung von Krieg und Gewalt in der Moderne*, Hamburg: Fischer.

Hall, S. and Du Gay, P., eds (1996), *Questions of Cultural Identity*, London: Sage.

Hannoum, A. (2008), 'What is an Order of Time?', *History and Theory*, 47: 458–71.

Hartog, F. (2005), 'Time and Heritage', *Museum International*, 57 (3): 7–18.

Hartog, F. (2013), 'The Modern *Régime* of Historicity in the Face of the Two World Wars', in B. Bevernage and C. Lorenz (eds), *Breaking up Time. Negotiating the Borders between Present, Past and Future*, 124–34, Göttingen: Vandenhoeck & Ruprecht.

Hartog, F. (2015), *Regimes of Historicity. Presentism and the Experiences of Time*, transl. S. Brown, New York: Columbia University Press.

Hartog, F. (2016), *Croire en l'histoire*, Paris: Flammarion.

Hunt, L. (2002), 'Against Presentism', *Perspectives on History*. Available online: https://www.historians.org/publications-and-directories/perspectives-on-history/may-2002/against-presentism (accessed 16 July 2018).

Jordheim, H. (2012), 'Against Periodization: Koselleck's Theory of Multiple Temporalities', *History and Theory*, 51: 151–71.

Joutard, Ph. (2013), *Histoire et mémoires, conflits et alliance*, Paris: La Découverte.

Kansteiner, W. (2004), 'Genealogy of a Category Mistake: A Critical Intellectual History of the Cultural Trauma Metaphor', *Rethinking History*, 8 (2): 193–221.

Koposov, N. (2017), *Memory Laws, Memory Wars. The Politics of the Past in Europe and Russia*, Cambridge: Cambridge University Press.

Koselleck, R. (2003), *Zeitschichten. Studien zur Historik*, Frankfurt am Main: Suhrkamp.

Kuukkanen, J.-M. (2015), *Post-Narrativist Philosophy of Historiography*, Basingstoke: Palgrave Macmillan.

42

Rethinking Historical Time

Landwehr, A. (2014), *Geburt der Gegenwart. Eine Geschichte der Zeit im 17. Jahrhundert*, Frankfurt am Main: Fischer.

Landwehr, A. (2018), 'Nostalgia and the Turbulence of Times', *History and Theory*, 57 (2): 251–68.

Lorenz, C. (1997), *Konstruktion der Vergangenheit. Eine Einführung in die Geschichtstheorie*, Cologne: Böhlau.

Lorenz, C. (2008), 'Drawing the Line: "Scientific" History between Myth-making and Myth-breaking', in S. Berger, L. Eriksonas and A. Mycock (eds), *Narrating the Nation. Representations in History, Media and the Arts*, 35–55, New York and Oxford: Berghahn.

Lorenz, C. (2014a), 'On the Edge of History and Philosophy', *Historein*, 14 (1): 59–70. Available online: https://ejournals.epublishing.ekt.gr/index.php/historein/article/view/2285 (accessed 16 July 2018).

Lorenz, C. (2014b), 'It Takes Three to Tango. History between the "Historical" and the "Practical, Past"', *Storia della Storiografia*, 65 (1): 29–46.

Lorenz, C. (2017), 'Der letzte Fetisch des Stamms der Historiker. Zeit, Raum und Periodisierung in der Geschichtswissenschaft', in F. Esposito (ed.), *Zeitenwandel. Transformationen geschichtlicher Zeitlichkeit nach dem Boom*, 63–92, Göttingen: Vandenhoeck & Ruprecht.

Luhmann, N. (1976), 'The Future Cannot Begin: Temporal Structures in Modern Society', *Social Research*, 43 (1): 130–52.

Markosian, N. (2016), 'Time', *The Stanford Encyclopedia of Philosophy* (Fall 2016 Edition), E. N. Zalta (ed.). Available online: https://plato.stanford.edu/archives/fall2016/entries/time/ (accessed 16 July 2018).

Niethammer, L. (2000), *Kollektive Identität. Heimliche Quellen einer unheimlichen Konjunktur*, Hamburg: Rowolt.

Nipperdey, J. (2015), 'Die Terminologie von Epochen – Überlegungen am Beispiel Frühe Neuzeit/"early modern"', *Berichte zur Wissenschaftsgeschichte*, 38: 170–85.

Nipperdey, J. (2016), 'Abbreviating the Practical Past – the Historiographic Creation of a Short Modern Age', paper delivered at 2nd INTH-conference, Ouro Preto, August.

Osterhammel, J. (2009), *Die Verwandlung der Welt. Eine Geschichte des 19. Jahrhunderts*, Munich: Beck.

Roth, P. A. (2012), 'The Pasts', *History and Theory*, 51 (3): 313–39.

Sider, T., Hawthorne, J. and Zimmerman, D., eds (2008), *Contemporary Debates in Metaphysics*, Oxford: Blackwell.

Tanaka, S. (2016), 'History without Chronology', *Public Culture*, 28 (1): 181–86.

Trüper, H., Chakrabarty, D. and Subrahmanyam, S., eds (2015), *Historical Teleologies in the Modern World*, London: Bloomsbury.

Van de Mieroop, K. (2016), 'The "Age of Commemoration" as a Narrative Construct. A Critique of the Discourse on the Contemporary Crisis of Memory in France', *Rethinking History*, 20 (2): 172–91.

Walshalm, A. (2017), 'Introduction: Past and. . . Presentism', *Past and Present*, 234 (1): 213–17.

White, H. (1996), 'The Modernist Event', in V. Sobchack (ed.), *The Persistence of History: Cinema, Television, and the Modern Event*, 17–38, New York: Routledge.

2

Return to Chronology

Helge Jordheim

In 'World Scientist's Warning to Humanity: A Second Notice', published in the journal *BioScience* in December 2017, 15,364 scientists from 184 countries joined forces to issue a warning that mankind has unleashed what they refer to as a 'sixth mass extinction event', wherein many current life forms could be annihilated by the end of this century (Ripple et al. 2017). The first 'notice' came in 1992. Due to mankind's presence on the planet, causing pollution, resource depletion and global warming, large populations of vertebrates, invertebrates and plants are dying out, and since 1992 this 'mass extinction' has been speeding up. Both textually and graphically the article tracks the time that has passed between 1992 and 2017, around a third of an average human life span and a period of time that can easily be included in the term 'present'. In his famous book on 'presentism', François Hartog dates the beginning of the 'present' at 1989, when the 'modern regime of historicity' collapsed together with the Berlin Wall (Hartog 2003: 11–29). To reconceptualize the present as the 'sixth mass extinction event' caused by human presence on the Earth opens it up to a very different scale of time – initially in a purely numerical way: That mankind is the sixth event means there have been five others before us. Together these events span 540 million years. The fifth mass extinction event took place 66 million years ago and was caused by the impact of an asteroid; the third and biggest – a volcanic eruption – happened 251 million years ago and killed 96 per cent of life on Earth. The sixth mass extinction event is happening now and is caused by human overpopulation and overconsumption (Ceballos, Ehrlich and Dirzo 2017) – in other words, it is our present. Clearly, this is a claim about biological, geological, even cosmological change; but it is also a claim about history – about the past, present and future of human societies.

In this chapter I will attempt to make sense of the 'World Scientist's Warning to Humanity' as a way of thinking about history and historical time, which at the same time fundamentally questions the modern regime of historicity and demands a reconceptualization of the entire past–present–future nexus (Hartog 2003: 28). A key to understanding this shift, I argue, is by returning to a discipline and a knowledge practice that for almost 300 years has been gone from historiography – *chronology*.

Chronology and the temporal turn

In the ongoing revaluation of the role of time and temporality in the social and human sciences, chronology is systematically accorded the role of the negative, against which multiplicities of temporal experiences, practices and narratives are allowed to stand out. Chronology means time-reckoning or the metrics of time – or, in the *OED* definition, 'the science of computing and adjusting time or periods of time, and of recording and arranging events in the order of time'. In the context of 'the temporal turn' (Hassan 2010), chronology has become the symbol for linear, homogenous, singular and quantifiable time, deployed in order to control and discipline the physical, biological and the human world – and not least, to discipline history.

Attacks on chronology have taken their cue from a wide range of thinkers and theorists, from Bergson, Benjamin and Certeau to Ricoeur and Agamben, who all appear to agree that chronology is nothing but 'a way of making use of time without reflecting on it', as Michel de Certeau puts it (1986: 216; see also Bergson 2001; Benjamin 1973; Ricoeur 2004; Agamben 1993). Many of these attacks are summed up in a recent contribution by the historian Stefan Tanaka, entitled simply 'History without Chronology', in which he argues that 'when chronology is used, history becomes a field of study that organizes pasts in relation to a metric that highlights, guides, and perpetuates a system of the recent several hundred years of the thousands of years of happenings on the earth and that has little room for the temporalities at the human or global levels' (Tanaka 2015: 170). As much as I share many, even most of Tanaka's ambitions to break with modernist temporal homogeneity, my point in this chapter is to make the opposite claim about chronology: that at present some of the most decisive influences and inspirations for revaluating our understanding of time and temporality, beyond the time-discipline of capitalism, famously described by E. P. Thompson (1967), come from chronology. Contrary to Tanaka's view that chronology closes history down, and closes it off from most of what is happening on Earth, I argue that chronology represents a force for opening history up to other scales of time and other scales of life, different from the ones contained in the concept of 'historical time' deployed in modernist historiography and experience of history.

In the work to historicize mankind as 'the sixth extinction event', that is to document the pasts, presents and futures mobilized by this concept, the timescales of modernist historiography come up short. On the one hand, the concept prompts us to look back into an all but endless past, made up by other extinction events and the time that has passed between them, encompassing millions of years; on the other hand, it envisions a future, in which the openness, endlessness and teleology of the modernist dogma of progress is efficiently revoked by the idea of extinction, dying-out, the end of many forms of life as we know them. In between deep past and imminent end, we inhabit a present no less 'monstrous' than the one theorized by Hartog (2003: 217), but belonging to a regime of historicity in which chronological concepts and conceptualizations – of duration, periodization, beginnings and endings – are radically different.

Another striking example of how chronology, or rather, different and conflicting chronologies intervene in the political and social fabric of the present, comes to the fore in the revision of the geological timescale, which has caught the cultural imagination of people across the globe (Zalasiewicz et al. 2011). In his recent essay, Dipesh Chakrabarty maps the many uses and effects of the concept of 'the Anthropocene' on different fields of knowledge, especially on historiography (Chakrabarty 2018; see also Quenet 2017). Even though both Chakrabarty and Quenet recognize the role of chronology in the attempts to arrive at a different label for the present period in Earth's history, neither of them pays much attention to what the Anthropocene debate does to the reckoning, or the metric of time in general – how quantifiable time, periodization, beginnings and endings emerge as an all-dominating point of contention. Chakrabarty comes closest to drawing a similar conclusion when he latches on to a remark by the earth system scientist Jan Zalasiewicz, who chairs the International Commission on Stratigraphy's Working Group, that geological time and the geological timescale, of which the Anthropocene is part, is '*simply time* – albeit in very large amounts' (quoted in Chakrabarty 2018: 6). Later on in the article Chakrabarty engages with the ideas of the German historian Lucian Hölscher, who insists that what he calls 'empty time' is both a 'potential bond of life' and 'a common ground for historical narratives, for keeping history as universal reality together' (Hölscher 2014: 591). Still, these reflections about the emergence of 'empty time' and 'simply time' do not spur any general argument about the return of chronology to historiography in the face of climate change and global warming. This is the argument I will present in this chapter.

Chronology as a challenge to history

In modernist historiography, 'historical time' is taken to encompass around 6,000 years at the most, often no more than 2,500 (Smail and Shyrock 2011); it is organized around periodizations like the 'Middle Ages', 'modernity' or 'post-war' (Jordheim 2012) and temporal concepts like 'growth', 'recession' or 'crisis'. None of these timescales or concepts, however, can account for what it means to be an agent or a force on a planetary scale. The idea of humanity as 'the sixth mass extinction event' evokes a timescale that radically disrupts 'history' as we know it, placing mankind – us as humans – at the sixth spot in a series of events that go back 540 million years and aligning us temporally with asteroids and volcanic eruptions. In light of this radical challenge to history in general and to what François Hartog and Aleida Assmann refer to as 'the modern regime of historicity' in particular (Hartog 2003; Assmann 2013), the belief that chronology is nothing but a stable, pre-defined system according to which time can be measured and controlled, can no longer be upheld. On the contrary, today, I argue, the most radical challenges to history as we know it come not from the perception of events and processes, from what we are used to calling 'social or historical time', but from chronology, in our attempts to establish durations, rhythms, speeds and periods in the history of Earth.

If this is true, the kind of transformation I am referring to in this chapter can better be grasped as a return *of* chronology, than a return *to* chronology. Humanity as a 'sixth mass extinction event' puts chronology back on our historians' plates whether we like it or not. This approach, however, makes us forget that chronology is not just, not even primarily, a fact of history, but a specific form of knowledge and scholarship, which for almost 1,000 years dominated Western historiography, before it got first devalued

46 Rethinking Historical Time

and then banished 250 years ago. Until chronology was turned into a homogenous, stable, disciplined and disciplining system at the end of the eighteenth century, it served as a name for a multivocal, multidisciplinary, and not least multitemporal practice, which gave rise to some of the most productive tensions and conflicts in the early modern *res publica literaria* (Colliot-Thélène 2003; Wilcox 1987).

Chronologies existed in plural, and the struggles to align them or to establish a standard made up highly vibrant intellectual projects. Neither Chakrabarty nor Hölscher and Zalasiewicz take into account that the last time 'simple' or 'empty' time came to dominate the practice of historians, theories and methods were framed by the discipline of chronology, also referred to as 'computus', practised by people like Joseph Justus Scaliger and Johann Albrecht Bengel – only that this quantifiable and quantified time was really neither simple nor empty, but invested with contentious claims about Christian faith and political allegiance. As I will discuss below, this potent mix of chronology and ideology led to the separation between chronological time and historical time at the end of the eighteenth century. But today this separation can no longer be upheld, nor can the belief in time as simple, empty, uniform and singular, in accordance with modernist dogma (Benjamin 1973). Chronology is splitting up again, in a way that allows for conflicting durations, periodizations, speeds and rhythms, thus making it a force for multiplying, not unifying our ways of thinking about pasts, presents and futures. This shift of time-reckoning from the periphery to the centre of historiography demands a rethinking of chronology as a knowledge practice.

Turns and returns in the history of chronology: Grafton's Scaliger

Among the most widespread temporal practices in the human and social sciences are the proclamations of 'turns' and 'returns'. Since Richard Rorty announced the 'linguistic turn' in 1967, in reference mainly to language philosophy in the tradition from Wittgenstein and Carnap (Rorty 1967), one turn has been superseded by the next: the cultural turn, the material turn, the iconic turn, the practical turn, the affective turn, etc. There has even been something as all-encompassing, and explicitly Kantian like a 'spatial turn'. According to Robert Hassan, this 'spatial turn' is currently succeeded by a 'temporal turn', which puts time back into the analysis of social phenomena, even foregrounds it (Hassan 2010). Anthropologists, sociologists and human geographers insist in different ways that time is part of the social, indeed that time is social and material, 'enfolded' into everything, as Bruno Latour puts it (2002; Bastian 2013). Of course, this 'temporal turn' in the social sciences has implications for historical understanding as well (for example in Rosa 2005 and Latour 1993) and found an echo in Ethan Kleinberg's proclamation that we are witnessing the emergence of 'a new metaphysics of time' (Kleinberg 2012: 1–2).

As a temporal practice, 'turn' fits well with a general idea of scientific progress. Although it clearly evokes the idea of a change of direction and a shift of gaze, and thus seems to contradict any Popperian idea of linear progress, 'turn', in terms of a somewhat attenuated version of Kuhn's 'revolution', still warrants newness and innovation in scholarship. A 'return', on the other hand, breaks with illusions of progressivist linearity and pushes a more circular view of scholarship, in which it is possible, even recommendable, to return to earlier positions and paradigms, to solve or at least throw new light on current issues.

Turns and returns to chronology as a knowledge practice can usefully be discussed in the context of Anthony Grafton's impressive study of the life and work of Joseph Justus Scaliger, the French philologist and chronologist, one of the most prominent academics in early modern Europe. Grafton begins his study of Scaliger's chronological work by describing the status of the discipline of chronology in Europe in the period between the Renaissance and the Enlightenment: '[I]t won the interest of many of the most innovative European thinkers and gave rise to sophisticated debates. It probably enjoyed more esteem than disciplines now much better known like textual criticism [. . .] and epigraphy' (Grafton 1993: 4). In his two-volume study, Grafton dedicates the first volume to philology, the second to chronology, although he is also well aware that they remain entangled (Grafton 1983 and 1993). Much of Scaliger's work in chronology is based on his philological reconstruction of Eusebius's *Chronicon*, especially its Egyptian and Babylonian sources. But chronology permeated early modern intellectual and material culture in a variety of ways: 'Europeans plastered their walls and filled their travelling-packs with calendars and charts of world history. They produced and consumed majestic books, tiny monographs, and even "machines chronologiques" that laid out the structures and details of historic time' (Grafton 1993: 4). Even beyond the remits of the *res publica litteraria*, he concludes, the study of chronology 'formed part of the fabric of common life' until the eighteenth century (Grafton 1993: 7).

Proclaiming a 'Turn to Chronology' in the first chapter of the book, Grafton does not only refer to Scaliger's life and career, but also to his own contemporary moment. Indeed, some of the Renaissance solutions to chronological problems, he argues, have 'paradoxically become novel and relevant once again' (Grafton 1993: 18). In reading Grafton's incredibly detailed, truly congenial exploration of Scaliger's chronology, it is hard to recognize this relevance and novelty, except as an exceptionally learned contribution to the study of ancient and Renaissance chronology. Today, however, we are in a position to re-evaluate Grafton's claim. As illustrated by the warning that humanity is the 'sixth mass extinction event', the question of co-ordination of human life with various natural phenomena as well as the dating and periodization of events and processes in natural history have again moved to the forefront of history. The natural phenomena in question are not so much the movements of the sun and the moon, but resource depletion, global warming, and extinction of large populations of vertebrates, invertebrates and plants.

Why chronology ended: Koselleck's Kant

Between Scaliger's *turn* to chronology and the present *return* to the same, chronology as a knowledge practice in its own right has been more or less gone from historiography. In the second half of the eighteenth century when philology – Scaliger's other favoured discipline – came into its own as an academic discipline, chronology faded away and was replaced by other ways of organizing and relating to historical time. Or, rather, chronology became the more or less stable unquestioned temporal framework into which philologists and other historians could place their written sources and texts. As Grafton points out, the interest in chronological texts and dating practices, especially pertaining to Antiquity, persisted throughout the nineteenth century, but only as a highly specialized field, with little impact on historical scholarship as a whole (Grafton 1993: 16–17).

Alongside philology, and in the same period, another discipline was on the rise, especially in the German area, namely 'history', *Geschichtswissenschaft*, the theoretically and methodologically elaborated study of past events, peoples, nations and cultures (Muhlack 1991). History in the modern sense was premised on the rupture with the chronological tradition. In historiography and theories of history, this shift has come to be symbolized by a quote from Immanuel Kant, later picked up by Reinhart Koselleck and others. Originally, the way Kant put it to paper in his 1789 *Anthropologie in pragmatischer Hinsicht* [Anthropology From a Pragmatic Point of View], the sentence has a somewhat convoluted structure, and is put in the form of a German *irrealis*: *als ob sich nicht die Chronologie nach der Geschichte, sondern, umgekehrt, die Geschichte nach der Chronologie richten müßte* – 'as if it wasn't chronology that had to conform to history, but the other way around, that history had to conform to chronology' (Kant 1907: 195). Koselleck rewrites Kant in a way that emphasizes and amplifies even more the break with chronology: 'As Kant said at the time: Until now history has adapted to chronology. From now on, however, chronology will have to adapt to history.' And Koselleck adds: 'This was the program of the Enlightenment: to organize historical time according to criteria that were derived from history itself' (Koselleck 1979: 321–2). And in another essay he goes on to list these criteria, or rather these concepts, according to which historical time can be organized: *der Fortschritt, die Dekadenz, Beschleunigung oder Verzögerung, das Noch-nicht und das Nicht-mehr, das Früher- oder Später-als, das Zufrüh oder Zuspät, die Situation und die Dauer* – or, in English, although some of these time-labelling words are almost untranslatable,'progress, decadence, acceleration or deceleration, not yet and not anymore, before or after, too early and too late, situation and duration' (Koselleck 1979: 133).

Returning to Kant, what prompts his confrontation with practices of chronology is a footnote in another text written and published at the same time, *Die Streit der Fakultäten* [The Conflict of the Faculties], in which he takes up a work by the theologian Johann Albrecht Bengel, a well-known scholar of Greek and the editor of a critical commented edition of the Greek New Testament. In his *Ordo Temporum* from 1741, Bengel develops a chronology, in terms of a mathematical system of years and centuries, based solely on biblical sources and especially on the Apocalypse of St. John (Kant 1907: 62). According to Bengel's chronological calculations, Christ was born in 3939 Anno Mundi, after the Creation of the Earth. But in order to account for the *numerus septenarius* Bengel finds a way to make 3939 divisible by the holy number seven, by using so-called 'apocalyptic periods' and by deducting the 'years of rest [*Ruhejahre*]' etc. (Kant 1907: 62). After going through all of Bengel's calculations, Kant sighs: 'What can we say? Did the holy numbers decide the way of the world?' (Kant 1907: 62). In other words, can the world be synchronized to Christian dogma, as expressed in the chronologies of the Bible? And is this really the task of a universal historiographer?

Of course, Kant's rejection of this possibility has been the rejection of every other historiographer and theorist of history since the late eighteenth century. Indeed, it is possible to claim, as Donald J. Wilcox does in his path-breaking book on pre-Newtonian chronologies, that the emergence of modern historiography rests on this shift: when Newton's absolute time, singular, mathematical and independent of 'anything external' – including Christian dogma and holy numbers – found its way into history writing and became the precondition for historicism (Wilcox 1987: 16–50). In other words: Kant's claim that the principles for organizing history must be found in history itself is premised on the existence of a stable, uniform and homogenous chronology, in which the struggles to find the right time to celebrate Easter or establish the age of Metusalech are solved once and for all and have given way to an absolute metrics.

Signs of the times: Wonders and progress

On closer inspection, however, the separation of history from chronology is hardly as clear-cut as that, even in Kant. His remark about chronology and history and who should conform to whom is taken from the first book of part I of *Anthropologie in pragmatischer Hinsicht*, on the *Erkenntnisvermögen*, 'the cognitive faculty', more specifically, from paragraph 37, in which he discusses what he calls *Bezeichnungsvermögen*, 'the faculty of using signs' – he even gives it a Latin heading: 'Facultas signatrix'. Signs can according to Kant be put in three groups: 'arbitrary (artificial), natural, and prodigious' (Kant 1907: 192). Among arbitrary signs, Kant mostly discusses language. But what is important here are the two others. Kant's exploration of natural signs is namely an exploration of time, since what interests him about natural signs is the way their relationship to reality is either 'demonstrative or rememorative or prognostic', referring the present, the past or the future (Kant 1907: 193). 'Demonstrative signs', according to Kant, include a patient's pulse, or smoke from a fire, 'rememorative signs' involve tombs, mausoleums and ruins. The natural signs that he finds most interesting, however, are the signs pointing towards the future, the 'prognostic signs', which he organizes in two groups: astronomic signs, which are pure superstition, and medical signs, which are based on knowledge and experience. And finally, this last category of natural, future-directed signs brings him to the 'prodigious signs', *Wunderzeichen*, which are no longer 'natural' but appear when 'the nature of things is turned upside down', like comets, solar and lunar eclipses, and northern lights, taken by superstitious people to predict the ending of the world (Kant 1907: 194). At this point the main text of §37 on the faculty of using signs ends, and Kant starts an appendix, in which the reference to chronology can be found. Already in Kant, however, what stands out is how the need to discuss chronology is linked to certain rare, dramatic and ominous events in nature, which to a certain extent prefigures the discussions about the Anthropocene and humanity as the 'sixth mass extinction event'.

In the appendix, Kant draws on what he has said about prodigious signs and superstition, and begins in the following way: 'We should, furthermore, take note here of a strange way in which man's imagination plays with him by confusing signs with things, or putting an intrinsic reality into signs, as if things must conform to them' (Kant 1907: 194). Here it is again, the word from the quote, 'conform', *sich richten* – and the signs; actually the only signs Kant is interested in here are numbers. What Kant means by chronology, then, is a knowledge practice, in which numbers are confused with reality and used to foresee the future. And the number most likely to bring about this kind of confusion in time-reckoning is, of course, the number seven. Kant goes on to list examples from different systems of knowledge and beliefs, in which the number seven 'has acquired a mystical importance', and he adds: 'even the creation of the world had to conform to it' (Kant 1907: 194). And finally, he concludes, in Judeo-Christian chronology, it has gone so far that the various computations of number seven not only 'comprise in fact the period of the most important changes (from God's call to Abraham to the birth of Christ), but even determine *a priori*, as it were, the precise limits of that period' (Kant 1907: 194–5). For this reason we can say that history is made to conform to chronology, and not the other way around. In other words, Kant's criticism of chronology is based on a theory of numbers as something between natural signs that are granted purchase not only on future but, indeed, and more interestingly, also on past reality, and *Wunderzeichen*, signs of wonder, that are understood as warnings about the end of the world. Looking back at this moment in the history of the relationship between history and chronology, we might recognize something like an uncanny symmetry between Bengel's belief in the *numerus septuarius* and Koselleck's claim that in the *Sattelzeit* the 'criteria' of historical time emerges from history as such. Isn't progress also a sign, in Kant's sense, much like a number, no more or less intrinsical to history than the 7+7 *Stufenjahre*, or the 70 *Jahrwochen* that governs Christian chronology, according to Kant? As Bengel was searching history for patterns of seven, modern historians search history for signs of progress – when one culture, one people or one field of knowledge and practice advance to the front of history and others are struggling to catch up.

Chronology as a knowledge practice

My point here is not to deny the difference between pre-modern and modern ideas and practices of history, aligning myself with Latour's famous claim that 'we have never been modern' (Latour 1993); rather, my interest is in exploring what might be the conditions for a 'return to chronology' in the present. In my argument, the gesture of return responds to a specific moment in the history of historical experience, often identified as the collapse of 'the modern regime of historicity' (Hartog 2003; Assmann 2013). The past–present–future nexus is put under pressure by two sets of changes: by processes of 'social acceleration', which, according to Hartmut Rosa, have brought about their dialectical opposite, an experience of standstill (Rosa 2003: 18; Rosa 2005: 402–7), of being stuck in a 'monstrous present' (Hartog 2003: 119); and, more importantly, I argue, by events and processes that can no longer be understood, explained and periodized by the timescales of modernist historiography, but demand a radical revision of what we understand by 'history'.

Examples can be found in different sets of lifetimes, geological, cosmological and technoscientific: At present, humans are being recast as 'geological agents', and thus placed on a timescale that *outlasts* 'history' in the modernist sense by millions of years (Zalasiewicz et al. 2011; Ceballos, Ehrlich and Dirzo 2017). At the same time, populations across the globe are currently *outliving* the cultural and social structures put in place to care for a much younger population. In Europe the proportion of people older than 65 is approaching 25 per cent (Oeppen and Vaupel 2002), and in Japan the average life expectancy of women is now 86.5 years, the highest in the world (Christensen et al. 2009). Not least, 'history' is challenged by the projection of radically different, technoscientific futures, both infinitely long and infinitely short, multiplied, and entangled, emerging both in science and fiction. Genetic engineering, quantum physics and Artificial Intelligence (AI) all envision multiple possible future worlds that are absolutely discontinuous, *out of sync* with 'history' (Harari 2016). These processes unfold in different fields of knowledge and indeed on different scales of life; what they have in common, however, is that they do not really register in the standard timescales of modernist history, dealing mainly with written sources, technology and state-building, and hardly looking beyond the last 6,000 years of human history (Smail and Shyrock 2011). After the rise of historicism, chronology has been reduced to a tacit presumption, hardly to be questioned unless someone comes up with a new theory of modernity or reinvigorates earlier speculations about an 'axial age' (Eisenstadt 1986). To return to chronology means to return to a historiographical practice that is able to think about timescales and periodizations in the plural, to try out different durations, periodic structures and rhythms, compare them and map out their similarities and their differences, or, if you like, their synchronicities and their non-synchronicities.

Bengel's struggles to establish the correct age of the world as well as the correct year of the birth of Christ by mathematical procedures are interwoven with Christian dogmatics; hence, alternative chronologies were disqualified as dogmatically wrong or even heretical. His *Ordo Temporum* is a prime example of this kind of chrono-dogmatics, which is also what Kant rejects in his discussion. It serves as a reminder that the metrics of time is not just a neutral, technical and mathematical practice, but also a tool for controlling the people in a society, by convincing them that time moves according to a specific rhythm – and so should their lives and bodies. By contrast, in the works of less dogmatic, more inventive chronologists, such as Scaliger, the inherent multiplicity of chronology and the many possible pasts and futures, going back not only to Greek Antiquity, but also to the Egyptians and the Babylonians, become a source for creativity, experimentation and innovation.

As illustrated by the juxtaposition of Scaliger and Bengel, and as argued by Wilcox (1987: 221–51), returning to chronology means returning to a paradigm of multiple temporalities, which has since been expelled from discussions of history. In Tanaka's essay, chronology functions as a placeholder for uniform, unquestioned time to be disposed of in order to make room for the temporal multiplicities of history: 'One way to use time, but not chronology in history,' Tanaka writes, 'is to recognize multiple timescales.' And he goes on: 'Here time is still linear, but it recognizes the multiple scales that are connected to natural – physical and biological – and social phenomena' (Tanaka 2015: 169). Agreeing with Tanaka's ambition to recognize and reclaim multiple timescales, my argument here is that 'chronology' might be a better tool for achieving this goal than 'history', which is still very much confined to a modern temporal regime.

What I propose is to see chronology not as an absolute, homogenous, metric system, into which events in the past, present and future can be placed, but as a knowledge practice in its own right – not something that is there, but as something we as historians and social scientists are involved in and produce. Around the same time as Kant wrote his dismissal of chronology, Edward Gibbon showed far more interest in this particular element of historiography, at least if we are to believe his posthumously compiled memoirs, published in 1796. None of his 'vague and multifarious reading', he recounts, could teach him 'to think, to write, or to act'; instead he opts for a 'rational application to the order of time and place':

> [F]rom Stranchius I imbibed the elements of chronology: the Tables of Helvicus and Anderson, the Annals of Usher and Prideaux, distinguished the connection of events, and engraved the multitude of names and dates in a clear and indelible series. But in the discussion of the first ages I overleaped the bounds of modesty and use. In my childish balance I presumed to weigh the systems of Scaliger and Petavius, of Marsham and Newton, which I could seldom study in the originals; and my sleep has been disturbed by the difficulty of reconciling the Septuagint with the Hebrew computation.
>
> Gibbon 1966: 43

In the eyes of the young Gibbon, chronology represents a field of theories and methods that any historian worth his salt needs to engage with. Among the most useful works he counts *Annales Veteris Testamenti*, published by bishop James Ussher in 1650, in which Creation is dated to the first part of the night that preceded 23 October in the year of the Julian Period 710, as well as Christoph Hellwig's *Theatrum Historicum*, in which the entire world history was represented in tables designed to prove the headstart of sacred rather than pagan history (Jordheim 2017). As soon as he tries to measure his own ambitions as a historian-chronologist with the works of Scaliger and others, however, Gibbon must admit that he not just overstepped, but indeed 'overleaped' the boundaries for what was useful and even modest, possibly in a religious sense.

In *The Measure of Times Past*, Wilcox welcomes the return of the 'rhetoric of relative time' in works by twentieth-century thinkers and artists in fields as diverse as physics, painting, poetry, psychology and philosophy (Wilcox 1987: 3). In these works he recognized the demise of the 'absolute time line', which was introduced by Isaac Newton and then migrated into history in the eighteenth century (Wilcox 1987: 16). During the twentieth century, however, this 'fall of absolute time' remained a purely theoretical shift, whereas history continued to be written, as if time were an absolute, homogenous and stable system. My claim then is that it took the recognition of global warming and mass extinction as historical events and experiences for the rhetoric of relative time that had dominated pre-Newtonian chronologies to find its way back into historiography.

Deep history and the dating of the Anthropocene

In the works of Scaliger, Bengel, and even Newton, questions of time and time-measurement kept oscillating back and forth between fields of knowledge that we today consider to be separate disciplines. In a similar fashion, ongoing debates about dating and periodization transgress borders between disciplines and raise questions about the beginning and ending of mankind as well as our role on Earth – not, however, in the framework of Christian dogma, but in the context of a form of natural history, in which man is put back into the long history of life on the planet.

In historiography, 'deep history' and 'deep time' have become names for timescales, which have in common that they go far beyond the periodizations that traditionally guide historical inquiries. Since 'the time revolution of the 1860s', when geology took human history into a limitless time before Eden, Andrew Shyrock and Daniel Lord Smail argue, the history of humankind has been haunted by a 'fragmentation of historical time' (Smail and Shyrock 2011: 3). Historians are still largely in 'the grip of sacred history', in which mankind emerged from Eden around 6,000 years ago, ignoring completely close to two million years of human history, or rather, leaving it to archaeologists, anthropologists and evolutionary biologists (Smail and Shyrock 2011: 3). In a methodological perspective, this temporal 'straightjacket' (Smail and Shyrock 2011: 5) – which also serves to exclude an entire continent, Africa, from historiographical interest – was supported by the choice of a specific kind of source as well as a specific set of scholarly procedures: the analysis of written documents, accompanied by serious and sustained *Quellenkritik*. The part of the history of mankind that had no documents, in other words, everything older than 6,000 years, disappears from sight. In much present historiography this extremely short, quasi-Biblical chronology is made even shorter by the relentless interest of historians in progress, modernization and political and economic development, hence, in the last 300 years of human history.

On the contrary, to write 'deep history', in Smail's terms, means 'bundling together the Paleolithic and the Neolithic' – that is the Old Stone Age, which began approximately 2.5 million years ago, and the New Stone Age, 'the period between the shift to agriculture roughly 10,000 years ago and the invention of bronze tools' – 'with the Postlithic', meaning 'everything that has happened since the emergence of metal technology, writing, and cities some 5,500 years ago' (Smail 2008: 1–3). And he adds, in a wishful, rather than analytic mode, evoking the dreams of early modern chronology: 'The result is a seamless narrative that acknowledges the full chronology of the human past' (Smail 2008: 3). The return to chronology taking place in Smail's work is accompanied by an early modern dream about the homogeneity and continuity of history, about the 'seamlessness' and 'fullness' of time, which was handed down from Eusebius to Scaliger and to Engel and which resurfaces in some of the dreams of the 'deep time' of history.

Among scholars who agree that we are currently in the Anthropocene and that humanity has become a geological 'force' or 'agent', which has taken the earth into another period of its history, the question of dating remains highly contested. Alternatives range from the invention of agriculture, expansion and colonization by Europe, the Industrial Revolution, the Great Acceleration, to the first testing of the atomic bomb. In an article from 2014, Zalasiewicz, together with a large group of authors, including Paul Crutzen, who first coined the term, ask 'When did the Anthropocene begin?' They sum up their arguments in the following way:

We evaluate the boundary of the Anthropocene geological time interval as an epoch, since it is useful to have a consistent temporal definition for this increasingly used unit, whether the presently informal term is eventually formalized or not. Of the three main levels suggested – an 'early Anthropocene' level some thousands of years ago; the beginning of the Industrial Revolution at ~1800 CE (Common Era); and the 'Great Acceleration' of the mid-twentieth century – current evidence suggests that the last of these has the most pronounced and globally synchronous signal. A boundary at this time need not have a Global Boundary Stratotype Section and Point (GSSP or 'golden spike') but can be defined by a Global Standard Stratigraphic Age (GSSA), i.e. a point in time of the human calendar. We propose an appropriate boundary level here to be the time of the world's first nuclear bomb explosion, on July 16th 1945 at Alamogordo, New Mexico; additional bombs were detonated at the average rate of one every 9.6 days until 1988 with attendant worldwide fallout easily identifiable in the chemostratigraphic record. Hence, Anthropocene deposits would be those that may include the globally distributed primary artificial radionuclide signal, while also being recognized using a wide range of other stratigraphic criteria.

Zalasiewicz et al. 2015: 196

Not yet a reversal of Kant's statement about chronology and history, the paragraph illustrates how chronological procedures are reinstalled at the core of historiography, raising questions about the quality of time ('geological'), periodization ('the Anthropocene time interval as an epoch'), beginnings and origins ('July 16th 1945'), computation ('the average rate of one every 9.6 days') and claims for universality ('the most pronounced and globally synchronous signal'). In spite of the almost mythological search for the 'golden spike', however, the evidence and arguments for different chronological options are not found in mystical numbers like the *numerus septuarius*, or in Christian dogma, but in the 'chemostratigraphic record', that is 'Anthropocene deposits' containing a 'radionuclide signal'. In other words, the spiritual truth of Christian providence has been replaced by the material truth of the stratigraphical composition of the Earth, and, thus, theology by earth systems science. The point of this analogy is not primarily to bring out the metaphysics of science, but rather to emphasize how both of these disciplines – theology and earth system science – impact human history, and that their impact takes the form of questions of dating, periodization and time-measurement, in other words of chronology.

In conclusion, returning to chronology should not be understood as a return to an early modern knowledge practice, nor should it be taken as a full-fledged historical analogy. Rather, the point of this chapter has been to discuss how new forms of presentism – evoking the present as the scene of a mass extinction event, or of the emergence of humanity as a geological agent – destabilize the modernist principles of time-reckoning and open historiography up to a plurality of competing chronological practices. In the next step, these practices will transform completely the conceptions of subjectivity, agency, and even events in history, as past, present and future humans are inscribed into time frames and timescales that differ radically from the 6,000 years of modernist historiography. In this way the return to chronology will lead to new turns, decentring both the present, the human subject and Western civilization, and giving rise to different narratives of life on the planet.

References

Agamben, G. (1993), *Infancy and History. On the Destruction of Experience*, London and New York: Verso.

Assmann, A. (2013), *Ist die Zeit aus den Fugen? Aufstieg und Fall des Zeitregimes der Moderne*, Munich: Hanser.

Bastian, M. (2013), 'Political Apologies and the Question of a "Shared Time" in the Australian Context', *Theory, Culture & Society*, 30 (5): 94–121.

Benjamin, W. (1973), 'Theses on the Philosophy of History', in *Illuminations*, ed. H. Arendt, transl. H. Zohn, Glasgow: Fontana.

Bergson, H. (2001), *Time and Free Will: An Essay on the Immediate Data of Consciousness*, transl. F. L. Pogson, Mineola, NY: Dover.

Ceballos, G., Ehrlich, P. R. and Dirzo, R. (2017), 'Biological Annihilation via the Ongoing Sixth Mass Extinction Signaled by Vertebrate Population Losses and Declines', *PNAS*, 114 (30), published ahead of print 10 July 2017, https://doi.org/10.1073/pnas.1704949114 (accessed 3 March 2018).

Certeau, M. de (1986), *Heterologies: Discourse on the Other*, Manchester: Manchester University Press.

Chakrabarty, D. (2018), 'Anthropocene Time', *History and Theory*, 57 (1): 5–32.

Christensen, K., Doblhammer, G., Rau, R. and Vaupel, J. W. (2009), 'Aging Populations: The Challenges Ahead', *Lancet*, 374: 1196–208.

Colliot-Thélène, C. (2003), 'Chronologie und Universalgeschichte', in J. Robeck and H. Nagl-Docekal (eds), *Geschichtsphilosophie und Kulturkritik. Historische und systematische Studien*, 21–49, Darmstadt: Wissenschaftliche Buchgesellschaft.

Eisenstadt, S. N. (1986), *The Origins and Diversity of Axial Age Civilizations*, New York: SUNY Press.

Gibbon, E. (1966), *Memoirs of My Life*, ed. G. A. Bonnard, London: Nelson.

Grafton, A. (1983), *Joseph Scaliger. A Study in the History of Classical Scholarship. Vol. I: Textual Criticism and Exegesis*, Oxford: Oxford University Press.

Grafton, A. (1993), *Joseph Scaliger. A Study in the History of Classical Scholarship. Vol. II: Historical Chronology*, Oxford: Clarendon Press.

Grafton, A. (2003), 'Dating History: The Renaissance and the Reformation of Chronology', *Daedalus*, 132 (2): 74–85.

Harari, Y. N. (2016), *Homo Deus: A Brief History of Tomorrow*, London: Harvill Secker.

Hartog, F. (2003), *Régimes d'historicité. Présentisme et expériences du temps*, Paris: Le Seuil.

Hassan, R. (2010), 'Globalization and the "Temporal Turn". Recent Trends and Issues in Time Studies', *The Korean Journal of Policy Studies*, 25 (2): 83–102.

Hölscher, L. (2014), 'Time Gardens: Historical Concepts in Modern Historiography', *History and Theory*, 53 (4): 577–91.

Jordheim, H. (2012), 'Against Periodization: Koselleck's Theory of Multiple Temporalities', *History and Theory*, 51: 151–71.

Jordheim, H. (2017), 'Synchronizing the World: Synchronism as Historiographical Practice, Then and Now', *History of the Present*, 7 (1): 59–95.

Kant, I. (1907), *Gesammelte Schiften. Akademieausgabe, Bd. VII: Der Streit der Fakultäten. Anthropologie in pragmatischer Hinsicht*, Berlin: Meiner.

Kleinberg, E. (2012), 'Introduction: New Metaphysics of Time', *History and Theory*. Virtual Issue 1. Available online: http://tinyurl.com/q5gr5cf (accessed 10 April 2018).

Koselleck, R. (1979), *Vergangene Zukunft. Zur Semantik geschichtlicher Zeiten*, Frankfurt am Main: Suhrkamp.

Latour, B. (1993), *We Have Never Been Modern*, Cambridge, MA: Harvard University Press.

Latour, B. (2002), 'Morality and Technology', *Theory, Culture & Society*, 19 (5/6): 247–60.

Muhlack, U. (1991), *Geschichtswissenschaft im Humanismus und in der Aufklärung. Die Vorgeschichte des Historismus*, Munich: Beck.

Oeppen, J. and Vaupel, J. W. (2002), 'Broken Limits of Life Expectancy', *Science Compass*, 296: 1029–31.

Quenet, G. (2017), 'L'Anthropocène et le temps des historiens', *Annales HSS*, 72 (2): 267–99.

Ricoeur, P. (2004), *Memory, History, Forgetting*, transl. K. Blamey and D. Pellauer, Chicago: University of Chicago Press.

Ripple, W. J. et al. (2017), 'World Scientists' Warning to Humanity: A Second Notice', *BioScience*, 67 (12): 1026–28.

Rorty, R., ed. (1967), *The Linguistic Turn. Essays in Philosophical Method*, Chicago: University of Chicago Press.

Rosa, H. (2003), 'Social Acceleration: Ethical and Political Consequences of a Desynchronized High-Speed Society', *Constellations*, 10 (1): 3–33.

Rosa, H. (2005), *Beschleunigung. Die Veränderung der Zeitstrukturen der Moderne*, Frankfurt am Main: Suhrkamp.

Smail, D. L. (2008), *On Deep History and the Brain*, Berkeley: University of California Press.

Smail, D. L. and Shyrock, A. (2011), 'Introduction', in A. Shryock and D. L. Smail (eds), *Deep History: The Architecture of Past and Present*, 3–20, Berkeley: The University of California Press.

Tanaka, S. (2015), 'History without Chronology', *Public Culture*, 28 (1): 161–86.

Thompson, E. P. (1967), 'Time, Work-Discipline, and Industrial Capitalism', *Past and Present*, 38: 56–97.

Wilcox, D. J. (1987), *The Measure of Times Past. Pre-Newtonian Chronologies and the Rhetoric of Relative Time*, Chicago: University of Chicago Press.

Zalasiewicz, J., Williams, M., Haywood, A. and Ellis, M. (2011), 'The Anthropocene: A New Epoch of Geological Time?', *Philosophical Transactions of the Royal Society*, 369: 835–41.

Zalasiewicz, J. et al. (2015), 'When did the Anthropocene Begin? A Mid-Twentieth Century Boundary Level is Stratigraphically Optimal', *Quaternary International*, 383: 196–203.

3

Coming to Terms with the Present

Exploring the Chrononormativity of Historical Time

Victoria Fareld

To relate to the past today has often to do with coming to terms with it. Whether described in terms of memory, guilt, wound or trauma the past has to a growing extent become a problem in the hands of the present. Thus, for many historians today, their task is not primarily to reconstruct or represent an absent past, but to deal with a past that persists as an immanent dimension of the present.[1]

Put in temporal terms: the boundaries between past and present, so essential to the writing of history, seem to be changing. The idea of a fundamental temporal rupture constitutive of modern historiography – expressed with the words of Gabrielle Spiegel, as 'the disappearance of the past from the present' – is today undergoing a profound transformation (Spiegel 2009: 4). This is, to an extent, some historians argue, that past and future tend to collapse into an ever expanding present; an 'omnipresent present', famously described by François Hartog, a present that only has itself as the horizon and ultimately threatens historical understanding (Hartog 2003: 18).

The turn of phrase in the title of this chapter: coming to terms (not with the past – as the standing expression has it – but) with the present, alludes to this contemporary critique of an expanding presentism. The title also signals, however, an effort to explore our current state of presentism beyond discussions of it connected to threats and crises. It expresses an attempt to call attention to its historiographical potentials.

In this chapter, I will argue that our current situation of presentism can generate a critical time consciousness that can help us see historians' performing of past and present as constitutive temporal figures in historical thinking. Through a chrononormative analysis of a recent debate about the role of monuments in public spaces commemorating today highly debatable historical persons, I will try to show that conflicting ideas about how past and present should be related in a contemporary memorial landscape offer us possibilities to self-reflexively address the temporal norms governing historical thinking.

This attempt to come to terms with the (historical) present is, I will argue, not the same as sacrificing historical understanding in favour of an all encompassing and ever expanding present, but rather a way to continue and intensify the work of historicizing historical time, in the tradition of Reinhart Koselleck, François Hartog and others (Koselleck 2004; Hartog 2003).

Presentism as a denial of otherness

Today, we can see an intense preoccupation with the 'now' in Europe and the Western world, to an extent that it makes many historians worried. In an important text, 'Against Presentism', Lynn Hunt writes:

> There is a certain irony in the presentism of our current historical understanding: it threatens to put us out of business as historians [...] It becomes the short-term history of various kinds of identity politics defined by present concerns and might therefore be better approached via sociology, political science, or ethnic studies [...]. But history should not just be the study of sameness, based on the search for our individual or collective roots of identity. It should also be about difference.
>
> Hunt 2002

According to Hunt history has to a large extent become an instrument to deal with and come to terms with the present, an arena to play out and work through a society's ongoing conflicts, or a mirror in which we can recognize our present selves more clearly. Hunt describes a situation in which the view of the past as something radically different and foreign, in which we, living today, cannot and should not recognize ourselves and our own issues, is fundamentally threatened. Presentism is thus a symptom of a denial of otherness. In our growing difficulty to see the past as something other than the present we are about to lose our ability to historicize the past.

Although Hunt's concern as a historian is presentism, it fits well with attempts in other fields to describe a contemporary situation. It overlaps with media theorist Douglas Rushkoff's claim that digital culture is about to profoundly transform our experience of time. Living in a culture in which 'everything is live, real time, and always-on', makes us suffer from a 'present shock', he asserts (Rushkoff 2013: 8). His diagnosis shares key features with literary theorist Hans Ulrich Gumbrecht's thesis of a 'broad present' (Gumbrecht 2014). In an expanding now, which assimilates the past and the future in an incessant generation of presence, Gumbrecht argues, we gradually come to lose our historical consciousness. This loss is not, however, a result of a disappearing past. On the contrary, in our digital age the past is accessible to us in ways that it has never been before. This always-present-past, Gumbrecht claims, generates an experience of simultaneity which blurs our traditional temporal borders. Or otherwise put: the past is all over the place but we don't relate to it historically any more. It has become yet another dimension of the present. And also the future has lost its otherness. No longer a horizon of possibilities or a place of unfulfilled promises it has primarily become a problem for the present to solve. In this situation, between a past that overwhelms us and a future that is blocked to us as a place for something different,

Gumbrecht states, 'the present has turned into a dimension of expanding simultaneities' (Gumbrecht 2014: xiii).

One further aspect of the idea of a growing present is the juridification of history that has been going on in recent decades, reflecting a growing interest in the fate of the victim of past injuries, trauma and historical wounds. When sociologist and historian John Torpey argues that 'in recent years, the distance that normally separates us from the past has been strongly challenged in favour of an insistence that the past [...] is constantly, urgently present as part of our everyday experience', the past referred to is purely a painful one full of injustices and crimes, measured from present legal and ethical standards (Torpey 2004: 240–1).

Some historians have expressed concerns about this growing intermingling of history and justice. Historian and Vichy specialist Henry Rousso emphasizes that the legal notion of imprescriptibility has led to a new temporal figure not only within the domain of the law but also within the field of history. This change, he claims, 'signifies concretely that the time of justice and the time of history no longer are separated' (Rousso 2001: 265). Against a concept of time in which the past is seen as irreversibly and definitely gone, and which has been constitutive of conventional historical time, the idea of the imprescriptible has introduced a temporality in which the events of the past can be revoked as possible to act upon as if they were part of the present. This revoking of the past is something else than looking back at what has happened. It is an act that reverses time by transforming the past into a present upon which one can act morally and legally (Fareld 2018).

Different as these attempts to describe a present-day situation are, they all seem to point to a state of crisis of successional time, in which both past and future tend to become dimensions of the present rather than horizons of otherness – sameness rather than difference – that, in various ways, is experienced as a threat to historical understanding.

In the following analysis, the idea of a differentiation between past and present as well as the question of otherness – so essential to the idea of historical understanding – will be centre-stage.

Rhodes must fall

One of numerous manifestations of the problematic presence of the past in today's memorial landscape is the student actions that took place in 2015 at university campuses in various parts of the world. Although locally situated and different in size and methods the actions shared the same demand: that statues and names of today's controversial historical persons at campus should be removed.

What soon would become the international student movement 'Rhodes Must Fall' started as a protest action in March 2015 by students at Cape Town University in South Africa (Figure 3.1). The students required that a statue commemorating Cecil John Rhodes, the British imperialist, mining magnate and university patron, should be removed from campus, with the argument that it is not only a symbol of historical colonialism but of the institutional racism that still pervades higher education in South Africa (Chaudhuri 2016). In the 'Mission Statement' of the movement we can read:

The statue has great symbolic power; it glorifies a mass-murderer who exploited black labour and stole land from indigenous people. Its presence erases black history and is an act of violence against black students, workers and staff . . . The statue was therefore the natural starting point of this movement. Its removal will not mark the end but the beginning of the long overdue process of decolonising this university.

'UCT Rhodes Must Fall Mission Statement' 2015: 6

After a month of campaigning, the statue was removed and the protests spread to other parts of the nation as well as to other countries. A couple of months later it had reached Oxford University in the UK. Students demonstrated for the removal of a statue of Cecil Rhodes at Oriel College in Oxford. Although the symbolic significance of the two statues differed – one placed in the former colony and the other in the former colonial metropole – the key message of the movement was the same: it is time to decolonize the universities, in South Africa as well as in the UK.

Figure 3.1 The 'Rhodes Must Fall' protest action in March 2015 at Cape Town University in South Africa. Source: Wikimedia Commons.

The actions in Oxford caused an affected debate in British media. Journalists complained about a generation of egocentric students: 'The little emperors have grown up. The babies of the late 1990s – mollycoddled by their parents, spoon-fed by their teachers, indulged by society – have now reached university' (Mount 2015). Activists, engaged in the movement – some of them studying on Rhodes Scholarships themselves – stressed the importance of a profound transformation of the British system of education (Elgot 2016). Eurocentric curricula as well as questions of representations of students and staff were at the centre of the activists' debate. As was of course the question of iconography in a postcolonial memorial landscape, of who should be commemorated in public space (Chigudu 2015). One of the campaign's organizers, the doctoral student in history, Brian Kwoba, stated: 'The significance of taking down the statue is simple: Cecil Rhodes is the Hitler of southern Africa. Would anyone countenance a statue of Hitler? The fact that Rhodes is still memorialised with statues, plaques and buildings demonstrates the size and strength of Britain's imperial blind spot' (Brian Kwoba quoted in Rawlinson 2016).

A similar high and polemic tone was also adopted by the critics. Historian Niall Ferguson compared the students' iconoclastic demands to Taliban and ISIS destruction of historical sites and monuments (Ferguson 2016). In January 2016, after some months of discussions, the Governing Body of Oriel College published an official statement saying that the statue would remain but that it would 'seek to provide a clear historical context to explain why it is there'. And it continued: 'By adding context, we can help draw attention to this history, do justice to the complexity of the debate, and be true to our educational mission' ('Statement from Oriel College on 28th January 2016' 2016).

Related protests also took place at Princeton University in the United States, where students required the removal of the former president Woodrow Wilson's name (he was also a former student at and Head of the university) from university buildings and centres because of his racist and separatist views. Similar actions were launched against statues of Thomas Jefferson on campuses in the United States, which led to a public discussion about growing presentism and lack of historical understanding (Stack and Fisher 2015; Newman 2015; Jaschik 2015; Svrluga 2016).

My aim here is not to take a stance for or against the actions. Nor is it to judge the legitimacy of the following reactions. The student actions and the following debates could be analysed from different perspectives. My intention is not to discuss the debate as a whole with all its complexities. My focus is to pinpoint the way history and historicization became the battleground for the debate. However, rather than focusing on a past that was, legitimately or not, kidnapped by present concerns, the following chrononormative analysis aims to expose the temporal conflicts at the heart of the debate.[2]

Presentism and erasure of history

A common criticism of the student actions in the UK and the United States was their presentism. Although sympathetic to the campaign against institutional racism, many commentators stressed the dangers in judging the past out of present concerns (Beard

2015; Hutton 2015; Jenne 2015; Garner 2015). The judging of actors and deeds of the past from today's ethical and legal stance was taken as exposing a self-congratulatory attitude of a generation believing itself to be morally superior: none of the commemorated historical figures, not even progressives like Wilson and Jefferson, measure up to our present-day standards. Instead of rushing to judge complex historical figures and turning them into unwanted criminals to be prosecuted and expunged from history, the campaigners should, it was argued, devote more energy in trying to understand the historical context and the complexity of historical legacies (Hutton 2015).

In a similar vein, critics argued that the activists in Oxford were 'treating history as moral therapy' (Lemon 2016: 218). British historian Cheryl Hudson emphasized: 'Flattening out historical meaning for the purpose of producing a therapeutic salve for the slights and injustices of today is a mistake.' Historical understanding, she continued, was sacrificed 'for the sake of present-day emotional well-being' (Hudson 2016).

The various critiques of presentism and identity politics that were articulated during the debates echoed both Hartog's assumption of a self-mirroring present so enclosed in itself that it tends to produce both past and future according to its own image, and Hunt's critique of a present that self-servingly uses the past to come to terms with itself and its own problems.

Closely related to the critique of presentism was the question of falsification of history. Activists and critics accused each other of erasing history. The activists saw their protests as reactions against an already established and ongoing erasure of black history (Chigudu 2015; 'UCT Rhodes Must Fall Mission Statement' 2015). Critics understood the students' demand as attempts to 'whitewash Rhodes out of history', as one historian put it (Beard 2015). Some described 'the dangers of re-writing history' (Lemon 2016) or the mistake of 'expung[ing] Rhodes from history' (Hutton 2015). When the Chancellor at Oxford University, Chris Patten, publicly criticized the movement by stating that '[o]ur history is not a blank page on which we can write our own version of what it should have been according to our contemporary views and prejudices', history itself seemed to be at stake (Chris Patten quoted in Adams 2016).

Chrononormativity and temporal conflicts

In her work *Time Binds* queer theorist Elizabeth Freeman develops the concept of chrononormativity to analyse how we normatively relate to time. Chrononormativity, she explains, is 'a technique by which institutional forces come to seem like somatic facts. Schedules, calendars, time zones, and even wristwatches inculcate ... forms of temporal experience that seem natural to those whom they privilege' (Freeman 2010: 3).

Chrononormativity is thus, according to Freeman, what structures and forms our experience of time. Freeman is interested in the temporalization of the human body, how time is used to socially organize individual bodies. If we self-servingly adapt her notion to the domain of historiography, we can more clearly see historical thinking as forms of temporal regulation, and historicization as a particular epistemic regulation and normative orchestration of time. An analysis of the debates surrounding the Rhodes Must Fall movement from a chrononormative perspective thus aims at exposing the conflicting ideas at the centre of the debates about how past and present should be related, and how we should ethically and epistemically regulate time.

Critics and commentators in the Rhodes Must Fall debate, who referred to the importance of a historical perspective, had as a silent point of departure a view of the present as something qualitatively different from the past. Although many of them saw the actions as expressions of a legitimate struggle against historically conditioned racism, they argued that Rhodes, Wilson and Jefferson should be regarded as men of *their* times – implicitly a time gone by in contrast to the present time, which is *ours*. The statues of these figures from another time should be considered as *historical* objects, and we, living today, should be able to chronologically place them in this 'other' time and recognize the difference (Hutton 2015; Jenne 2015; Garner 2015; Beard 2015).

This idea of historical understanding can be interpreted in light of Michel de Certeau's famous claim that history articulates the conceptual border between the living and the dead. His statement '[historical] writing makes the dead so that the living can exist elsewhere … A society furnishes itself with a present time by virtue of historical writing', captures concisely the performative function of history (Certeau 1988: 101). Critics and commentators in the Rhodes Must Fall debate defended a historical understanding by explicitly stressing the importance of distancing between past and present, and by implicitly organizing and regulating this temporal distance. In classicist Mary Beard's argument against the removal of the statue at Oxford, we read:

> But the battle isn't won by taking the statue away and pretending those people didn't exist. It's won by empowering those students to look up at Rhodes and friends with a cheery and self confident sense of *unbatterability* – much as I find myself looking up at the statues of all those hundreds of men in history who would vehemently have objected to women having the vote, let alone the kind of job I have [. . .]. Wouldn't it be better to celebrate what we have managed to achieve with Rhodes's money, whatever his views. If he was bad, then we have certainly turned his cash to the better [. . .] and maybe, to give him for a moment the benefit of the doubt, if he had been born a hundred years later even he would have thought differently.
>
> Beard 2015

Beard places the statue in a progressive narrative in which the present – to which we living today all belong – has won the battle over its past. Rhodes should be judged by the standards of his time; we should look at the statue as a reminder of a past very different from the present and be strengthened by the fact that we belong to another, better, time.

In contrast to Beard's argument concerning Oxford, the philosopher Achille Mbembe comes to another conclusion about the Rhodes statues in South Africa. Instead of looking up at those statues cheerily and self-confidently, Mbembe emphasizes quite different feelings that the statues provoke, by articulating a narrative which brings past and present together as temporal dimensions that experientially intermingle:

> There is something not only wrong, but profoundly demeaning, when we are asked to bow in deference before the statues of those who did not consider us as human and who deployed every single mean in their power to remind us of our supposed worthlessness. There is something perverse to engage in this ritual of self-humiliation and self-debasement every time we happen to find ourselves in such an environment.
>
>   Mbembe 2016: 32

In this narrative, there is no distance between the historical figures of the statues and ourselves living today ('*those* who did not consider *us* as human'). We all seem to share the same temporal space. In a similar vein, the activists in Oxford presented the past as an ongoing present. The statue commemorating Rhodes was not seen as a remnant of a different and remote time but rather as a reminder of a past that persists in the present; indeed a past that many students experience as a present part of their everyday life (Sims 2015; Ali 2015). As one of the founding activists put it: 'A lot of the time when people talk about colonialism they think of it as a past event that happened. They don't think about it as something that manifests itself in everyday life at institutions like Oxford' (Ntokozo Qwabe quoted in Ali 2015).

The students' actions manifested an experience of temporal coexistence. They drew attention to the question of temporal demarcations: For those who have to deal with a legacy of historical violence, which persists as a formative force in the present, the boundaries between past and present are not neutral or objective categories but indeed cultural and political phenomena, exposing a particular chrononormativity, or, again, 'forms of temporal experience that seem natural to those whom they privilege' (Freeman 2010: 3).

Mbembe's sharp assertion that 'Rhodes' statue has nothing to do on a public university campus', can at first sight be read as an inversion of Beard's argument, presuming the same conception of linear progressive temporality: the statues do not belong to *our* present (Mbembe 2016: 29). They are the true anachronisms, not the demands of the students. Mbembe surely reserves the word 'anachronistic' for Eurocentric curricula and old statues of colonial figures, pointing at something that is chronologically, and ethically, out of place (Mbembe 2016: 32). By letting 'those' living in the past act upon 'us' living today, he also, however, emphasizes the non-successional character of time. In anticipating his critics he moreover touches upon the temporal normativity of historical time by pointing at several ongoing pasts in the present: '[W]e are told that he [Rhodes] donated his land and his money to build the university. How did he get the land in the first instance? How did he get the money? Who ultimately paid for the land and the money?' (Mbembe 2016: 29).

Mbembe's rhetorical questions open a space for other pasts to appear, pasts that are still to be turned into historical narratives in the ongoing realization of the nation's history as a common site of recognition, being and belonging. His criticism thus also exposes the silent primacy of historical time and its complicity with a time politics, which in the end favours the perpetrators rather than the victims of historical violence, or the ones still benefitting from this violence.

If we look at the Rhodes Must Fall debate chrononormatively, we can discern opposing ideas about the very transition between past and present. The activists forced us to rethink our tacit temporal normativity by articulating some basic questions concerning the process of historicization: in what sense is a statue of Rhodes part of the 'past'? When did it become 'past'? In what sense is it part of the 'present'? The campaign gave us an opportunity to self-reflectively interrogate into how the past is produced as an historical object; how the transition between past and present is performed, epistemically and ethically. To critically interrogate the performance of this transition – which is not given to us beyond the realm of theory – is not, I would say, to surrender to the pressure of an expanding presence, but an effort to use the potential in this presence to historicize historical time. Such a rethinking of temporal interrelations is, differently put, a way to historicize the performative temporal categories of past and present constitutive of historical understanding; essentially an effort to historicize the act of historicization itself in order to expose what it silently presupposes.

The materiality of time

Shortly after the Rhodes Must Fall movement had launched its first actions, in Spring 2015, the decommunization process started in Ukraine, where during a six-month period more than 1,300 Lenin statues were removed from public spaces, and 50,000 streets and 1,000 cities and villages were given new names ('Decommunization Reform' 2016). In the international media debate about the Rhodes statues, few commentators referred to the simultaneous removal of Lenin statues, although the question of the role of the past in the present – of how time should be ethically and politically regulated – couldn't be more urgent (Ash 2016; Hatherley 2016). It sharpened the question at stake: do we see an effort to come to terms with a violent past or a dangerous erasure of history, or maybe both?

The many chronoschisms and memory conflicts that have been evoked around statues and monuments in recent years expose their particularity as historical documents. Their very materiality seems to provoke debates about the role of the past in the present revolved around the concept of contemporaneity. Statues and monuments are some of all the things from the past that make up our present. Their material presence, however, is also what makes our present never fully *of* the present but rather always already 'multitemporal' or 'polychronic', saturated with the accumulated, multiple times of their existence. All these material things of the past thus turn the present into 'nothing more than the sum total of all the past times which physically coexist in the present moment', as Laurent Olivier succinctly puts it (Olivier 2004: 205). Statues seem to manifest, more than many other historical objects, the temporal fusion constitutive of the present, indeed its polychronic character. Is the Rhodes statue at Oriel College today out of its 'proper' time? But if so, when was its 'proper' time? Past, present and future seem deeply interconnected through its material manifestations.

In recent years, scholars from different perspectives have tried to rethink the concepts of past and present dominant in historiography and archaeology in favour of conceptual frameworks that can account for several ongoing pasts in the present

(Tanaka 2016; Tamm 2015; Assmann 2013; Bevernage 2012; Olivier 2004). In light of these attempts, the controversy over the statue of Rhodes draws attention to the need to rethink the meaning of temporality as a structural feature of historical understanding. Such a rethinking can help us to move beyond the question of presentism as the opposite to historical understanding. By conceptualizing the present differently, we can become open for a discussion that aims to make visible the many temporal experiences that the present harbours. Framing the present as temporally multidirectional not only helps us to understand how time is produced socially and materially; it gives us conceptual tools that enable us to account for multi-layered temporal experiences, and to recognize the emerging presences of the past, some of which are still to be fully accounted for and narrated in contemporary history.

Presentism as emerging presences of the past

Let us return finally to the question of the otherness of the past. We have seen that critics in the debate about Rhodes Must Fall tended to interpret the students' actions as an unhistorical way of dealing with the past, because of their usage of the past for their own present purposes. In defending a historical understanding the critics stressed the importance of restoring the collapsed temporal boundaries, reinstituting the difference between past and present – from the tacit assumption that it is in this very difference that an historical understanding operates.

From such a silent presupposition of historical time, the campaigns launched against the statues of Rhodes, Wilson and Jefferson can easily appear as flagrant expressions of a temporal superiority, coming from the activists' presentist stance and their failure to treat the past historically, that is, as qualitatively different from the present. What is hidden here, however, is that this otherness of the past – which, indeed, is the historian's task to defend – is not something that belongs to the past as such; it is something that is produced as an effect of a certain chrononormativity.

A defence of a historical understanding against presentism, with the argument that history should be the study of difference (remember Lynn Hunt: we should see something other than ourselves when we engage with the past historically, and we have to learn how to do that), hides the fact that the past that is referred to as different is not there to begin with, it is produced as an historical object. It is an effect of a historiographical operation, which makes the past appear to us as a category of its own neatly separated from the present.

What at first sight might have appeared as yet another manifestation of presentism in the sense of a failure to recognize the otherness of the past, the Rhodes Must Fall movement can in light of the above analysis, be interpreted as manifesting another conception of presentism which, by exposing the temporal norms that govern historical thinking rendered visible the many presences of the past. Against this background, presentism loses its univocality and appears as a more complex and double-edged phenomenon. At worst it can surely make us short-sighted and deceived by illusions of temporal superiority and of the urgency of our own present concerns. At best, however, it has the potential to sharpen our critical time consciousness and make us clear-sighted about the temporal normativity that frames our historical thinking. So interpreted, the Rhodes Must Fall debate gave us an opportunity to critically come to terms with some aspects of our present by inquiring into the temporal categories that underpin what we call a historical understanding.

Note

1   This chapter is a revised and extended version of an article originally published in Swedish, Fareld 2017.
2   This means that I will leave all themes aside that were raised in debates that don't directly relate to the questions considered in this chapter, for instance the issues of freedom of thought, free speech and safe spaces. See Gayle and Khomami 2016; Svrluga 2015, 2016.

References

Adams, R. (2016), 'Oxford's Leaders Present Competing Visions of Future', *Guardian*, 12 January. Available online: https://www.theguardian.com/education/2016/jan/12/oxford-university-vice-chancellor-louise-richardson-tradition (accessed 12 April 2018).

Ali, A. (2015), 'Oxford University Students Call for Greater "Racial Sensitivity" at the Institution and Say it Must Be "Decolonised"', *Independent*, 19 June. Available online: https://www.independent.co.uk/student/news/oxford-university-students-call-for-greater-racial-sensitivity-at-the-institution-and-say-it-must-be-10332118.html (accessed 24 April 2018).

Ash, T. G. (2016), 'Rhodes Hasn't Fallen, But the Protesters Are Making Me Rethink Britain's Past', *Guardian*, 4 March. Available online: https://www.theguardian.com/commentisfree/2016/mar/04/rhodes-oxford-students-rethink-british-empire-past-pain (accessed 24 April 2018).

Assmann, A. (2013), *Ist die Zeit aus den Fugen? Aufstieg und Fall des Zeitregimes der Moderne*, Munich: Hanser.

Beard, M. (2015), 'Cecil Rhodes and Oriel College, Oxford', *Times Literary Supplement*, 20 December. Available online: https://www.the-tls.co.uk/cecil-rhodes-and-oriel-college-oxford/ (accessed 12 April 2018).

Bevernage, B. (2012), *History, Memory, and State-Sponsored Violence. Time and Justice*, New York: Routledge.

Certeau, M. de (1988), *The Writing of History*, transl. T. Conley, New York: Columbia University Press.

Chaudhuri, A. (2016), 'The Real Meaning of Rhodes Must Fall', *Guardian*, 16 March. Available online: https://www.theguardian.com/uk-news/2016/mar/16/the-real-meaning-of-rhodes-must-fall (accessed 24 April 2018).

Chigudu, S. (2015), 'In Defence of Rhodes Must Fall and the Struggle for Recognition at Oxford', Department of International Development Studies, Oxford University. Available online: http://www.qeh.ox.ac.uk/content/defence-rhodes-must-fall-and-struggle-recognition-oxford (accessed 12 April 2018).

'Decommunization Reform: 25 Districts and 987 Populated Areas in Ukraine Renamed in 2016', *Ukrinform.net*, 27 December. Available online: https://www.ukrinform.net/rubric-society/2147127-decommunization-reform-25-districts-and-987-populated-areas-in-ukraine-renamed-in-2016.html (accessed 24 April 2018).

Elgot, J. (2016), '"Take it Down!": Rhodes Must Fall Campaign Marches Through Oxford', *Guardian*, 9 March. Available online: https://www.theguardian.com/education/2016/mar/09/take-it-down-rhodes-must-fall-campaign-marches-through-oxford (accessed 24 April 2018).

Fareld, V. (2017). 'Tiden är nu: Presentism, tidskris och historiska sår', in A. Burman and L. Lennerhed (eds), *Samtider: Perspektiv på 2000-talets idéhistoria*, 19–36, Göteborg: Daidalos.

Fareld, V. (2018), 'History, Justice and the Time of the Imprescriptible', in S. Helgesson and J. Svenungsson (eds), *The Ethos of History: Time and Responsibility*, 54–69, New York: Berghahn Books.

Ferguson, N. (2016), 'Come and Have a Go at Cecil's Statue if You Think You're Hard Enough', *Sunday Times*, 17 January. Available online: https://www.thetimes.co.uk/article/come-and-have-a-go-at-cecils-statue-if-you-think-youre-hard-enough-lb302xv9927 (accessed 30 March 2018).

Freeman, E. (2010), *Time Binds: Queer Temporalities, Queer Histories, Perverse Modernities*, Durham: Duke University Press.

Garner, R. (2015), 'Oxford University Risks "Damaging its Standing" if it Pulls Down Cecil Rhodes Statue, Warns Tony Abbott', *Independent*, 23 December. Available online: https://www.independent.co.uk/news/education/education-news/oxford-university-risks-damaging-its-standing-if-is-pulls-down-cecil-rhodes-statue-warns-tony-abbott-a6784536.html (accessed 24 April 2018).

Gayle, D., and Khomami, N. (2016), 'Cecil Rhodes Statue Row: Chris Patten Tells Students to Embrace Freedom of Thought', *Guardian*, 13 January. Available online: https://www.theguardian.com/education/2016/jan/13/cecil-rhodes-statue-row-chris-patten-tells-students-to-embrace-freedom-of-thought (accessed 23 April 2018).

Gumbrecht, H. U. (2014), *Our Broad Present: Time and Contemporary Culture*, New York: Columbia University Press.

Hartog, F. (2003), *Régimes d'historicité: présentisme et expériences du temps*, Paris: Le Seuil.

Hatherley, O. (2016), 'Rewriting the Past: Must Rhodes Fall?', *Apollo: The International Art Magazine*, 29 January. Available online: https://www.apollo-magazine.com/rewriting-the-past-must-rhodes-fall/ (accessed 12 April 2018).

Hudson, C. (2016), 'History is Not a Morality Play: Both Sides on #RhodesMustFall Debate Should Remember That', *Conversation*, 30 January. Available online: https://theconversation.com/history-is-not-a-morality-play-both-sides-on-rhodesmustfall-debate-should-remember-that-53912 (accessed 12 April 2018).

Hunt, L. (2002), 'Against Presentism', *Perspectives on History: The Newsmagazine of the American Historical Association*, May. Available online: www.historians.org/publications-and-directories/perspectives-on-history/may-2002/against-presentism (accessed 24 April 2018).

Hutton, W. (2015), 'Cecil Rhodes Was a Racist, But You Can't Readily Expunge Him from History', *Guardian*, 20 December. Available online: https://www.theguardian.com/commentisfree/2015/dec/20/atonement-for-the-past-not-censorship-of-history (accessed 24 April 2018).

Jaschik, S. (2015), 'Jefferson is Next Target', *Inside Higher Ed*, 23 November. Available online: https://www.insidehighered.com/news/2015/11/23/thomas-jefferson-next-target-students-who-question-honors-figures-who-were-racists (accessed 24 April 2018).

Jenne, A. (2015), 'Mary Beard Says Drive to Remove Cecil Rhodes Statue from Oxford University is a "Dangerous Attempt to Erase the Past"', *Independent*, 22 December. Available online: https://www.independent.co.uk/news/education/education-news/mary-beard-says-drive-to-remove-cecil-rhodes-statue-from-oxford-university-is-a-dangerous-attempt-to-a6783306.html (accessed 12 April 2018).

Koselleck, R. (2004), *Futures Past: On the Semantics of Historical Time*, transl. K. Tribe, New York: Columbia University Press.

Lemon, A. (2016), '"Rhodes Must Fall": The Dangers of Re-Writing History', *The Round Table*, 105 (2): 217–19.

Mbembe, A. (2016), 'Decolonizing the University: New Directions', *Arts and Humanities in Higher Education*, 15 (1): 29–45.

Mount, H. (2015), 'It's Time to Say No to Our Pampered Student Emperor', *Daily Telegraph*, 29 December. Available online: https://www.telegraph.co.uk/education/educationopinion/12073349/Its-time-to-say-No-to-our-pampered-student-emperors.html (accessed 24 April 2018).

Newman, A. (2015), 'At Princeton, Woodrow Wilson, a Heralded Alum, is Recast as an Intolerant One', *New York Times*, 22 November. Available online: https://www.nytimes.com/2015/11/23/nyregion/at-princeton-addressing-a-racist-legacy-and-seeking-to-remove-woodrow-wilsons-name.html (accessed 24 April 2018).

Olivier, L. (2004), 'The Past of the Present: Archaeological Memory and Time', *Archaeological Dialogues*, 10 (2): 204–13.

Rawlinson, K. (2016), 'Cecil Rhodes Statue to Remain at Oxford After "Overwhelming Support"', *Guardian*, 28 January. Available online: https://www.theguardian.com/education/2016/jan/28/cecil-rhodes-statue-will-not-be-removed--oxford-university (accessed 24 April 2018).

Rousso, H. (2001), 'Juger le passé? Justice et histoire en France', in F. Brayard (ed.), *Le génocide des Juifs: entre procès et histoire, 1943–2000*, 261–87, Paris: Editions Complexes.

Rushkoff, D. (2013), *Present Shock: When Everything Happens Now*, New York: Current.

Sims, A. (2015), 'Oxford Students Call for "Racist" Statue of Cecil Rhodes to Be Pulled Down', *Independent*, 13 July. Available online: https://www.independent.co.uk/student/news/oxford-students-call-for-racist-statue-of-cecil-rhodes-to-be-pulled-down-10385293.html (accessed 24 April 2018).

Spiegel, G. (2009), 'The Task of the Historian', *American Historical Review*, 114 (1): 1–15.

Stack, L., and Fisher, G. (2015), 'Princeton Agrees to Consider Removing President's Name', *New York Times*, 19 November. Available online: https://www.nytimes.com/2015/11/20/nyregion/princeton-agrees-to-consider-removing-a-presidents-name.html?mtrref (accessed 24 April 2018).

'Statement from Oriel College on 28th January 2016 Regarding the College's Decision Concerning the Rhodes Statue' (2016). Available online: http://www.oriel.ox.ac.uk/sites/default/files/statement_from_oriel_college_on_28th_january_2016_regarding_the_college.pdf (accessed 16 April 2018).

Svrluga, S. (2015), 'Princeton Protesters: Why We Need Safe Spaces, and Why Honoring Woodrow Wilson is Spitting in Our Faces', *Washington Post*, 4 December. Available online: https://www.washingtonpost.com/news/grade-point/wp/2015/12/04/princeton-protesters-why-we-need-safe-spaces-and-why-honoring-woodrow-wilson-is-spitting-in-our-faces/ (accessed 24 April 2018).

Svrluga, S. (2016), 'Founding Father or Racist? Free Speech or Hate Speech? Students Debate Thomas Jefferson and Other Icons', *Washington Post*, 12 January. Available online: https://www.washingtonpost.com/news/grade-point/wp/2016/01/12/founding-father-or-racist-free-speech-or-hate-speech-students-debate-thomas-jefferson-and-other-icons/ (accessed 24 April 2018).
Tamm, M., ed. (2015), *Afterlife of Events: Perspectives on Mnemohistory*, Basingstoke: Palgrave Macmillan.
Tanaka, S. (2016), 'History Without Chronology', *Public Culture*, 28 (1): 161–86.
Torpey, J. (2004), 'The Pursuit of the Past: A Polemical Perspective', in P. Seixas (ed.), *Theorizing Historical Consciousness*, 240–55, Toronto: University of Toronto Press.
'UCT Rhodes Must Fall Mission Statement' (2015). Available online: http://jwtc.org.za/resources/docs/salon-volume-9/RMF_Combined.pdf (accessed 13 April 2018).

4

The Transformation of Historical Time

Processual and Evental Temporalities

Zoltán Boldizsár Simon

The question of historical time today

Philosophy of history is dead, so we are told. It died multiple deaths in the early postwar period, at the hands of both philosophers and historians. In a certain sense, it is hardly surprising that proclaiming the end, the death, the unfeasibility, the illegitimacy, the impossibility and even the practical perils of the enterprise had simply been one of the intellectual priorities of the era. After the horrors of the first half of the last century, being sceptical about the idea of a historical process leading to a better future seemed the most honest and reasonable thing to do.

This of course does not mean that philosophy of history ruled the intellectual landscape without any criticism up until postwar times. Since its late Enlightenment invention, the practice of philosophizing about the course of human affairs gathered quite a few adversaries from Friedrich Nietzsche to nineteenth-century historians seeking to professionalize and institutionalize their discipline against the backdrop of the way philosophers approached the question of history. Yet, postwar criticism of the entire enterprise is not just one wave in the long history of voicing concerns, but a moment of spectacular change. Whereas in the nineteenth century there were only a few scattered voices raising serious objections against a common standard of philosophizing about history, the postwar years have turned the tides and criticism of the former standard has become the new standard.

But what exactly is this entire enterprise that postwar intellectuals so eagerly proclaimed dead? And why do I refer to history as a modern invention? Intellectual historians could point out that there was something like a philosophy of history already during Classical Antiquity and the medieval period, not to mention Chinese philosophy of history, or the work of Ibn Khaldun. But the target of postwar criticism was not Christian eschatology, Ibn Khaldun, Orosius, or any ancient concept of 'history'. Its target was the specifically modern idea of a historical process in which human and societal betterment plays out, and the newly emerging intellectual practice responsible for the invention of such an idea: philosophy of history.

Referring to (philosophy of) history as a modern Western phenomenon aligns with the scholarship of Koselleck (2004) about the birth of the temporalized notion of history in the period between 1750 and 1850, but goes against the secularization thesis of Löwith (1949). By claiming that philosophy of history is nothing other than secularized eschatology (a newer version of something old, essentially), Löwith underemphasizes the significance of the modern notion of history. For even if future-orientation or the expected fulfilment of the ultimate purpose of human affairs is a common pattern present in modern philosophy of history and eschatology, the latter does not postulate anything like a *course* of human affairs. In eschatology there is nothing like a *process* that leads to such fulfilment. Change is granted by the Final Judgement, meaning an entry to another world. Contrary to this, the great invention of philosophy of history is precisely a processual notion of 'history', a conceptualization of the possibility of change *within* the mundane world of human affairs as running a *course*.

In this chapter, I argue that contrary to all rumours, the enterprise of philosophy of history is very much alive today, even indispensable. This is of course not to say that postwar criticism can be completely disregarded. The question is not that of how to return to a discredited philosophy of history that invented a processual concept of history with attributes of directionality, teleology, inherent meaning and substance in the course of human affairs. The question is whether the possibility of change over time in human affairs can be conceptualized as 'history' without invoking the aforementioned attributes. This is no easy question. In fact, it even consists of two distinct but heavily interrelated questions: first, whether it is possible to conceive of historical time in other than processual-developmental terms; and second, whether such other-than-processual temporality can still be 'historical' in the sense of retaining the possibility of change over time in human affairs.

The challenge, I believe, lies in answering both questions affirmatively. Consider today's conceptual alternatives to the processual temporality of the modern notion of history. They are able to provide answers to the first question only at the cost of leaving the second unanswered. Theorizing how the past survives, haunts and has a 'presence' in the present most certainly advocates novel ways to think about the relationship between the past and the present (Runia 2006; Lorenz 2010; Beverage 2012; Tamm 2015: 1–23; Kleinberg 2017). In that, such theories offer alternative temporalities to the modern idea of the historical process. Yet, inasmuch as they leave the question of the future out of the equation, inasmuch as they focus only a relation to the past in which the past either permeates or suddenly erupts into the present, these alternative temporalities cannot be conceptual alternatives to modern historical time as an overall configuration of past, present *and* future.

Cultural diagnoses of presentism seem to have an adequately broad scope to tackle the issue of historical time. François Hartog (2015), Aleida Assmann (2013) and Hans Ulrich Gumbrecht (2014) try to understand a new disposition of past, present and future in Western societies, emerging in the last decades and replacing the modern time regime. As to the question of what to call the successor, Gumbrecht (2014: xii, 55, 73) repeatedly invokes a yet nameless chronotope, which he nevertheless consistently refers to as the 'broad present'. What Gumbrecht means by this is very close to what Hartog (2015) calls the reign of presentism and a presentist 'regime of historicity' that has already replaced the future-oriented modern one, while Assmann (2013: 245–80) prefers to talk about a time out of joint.

Naming and different vocabularies aside, the diagnoses accord in their basic understanding of the new situation. They are even congruent with theories of the present past when they concur on mapping current societal relations to the past by investigating the ways in which the past pervades the present and how the past doesn't go away. But for cultural diagnoses this is only one side of the coin, the other being the relationship to the future. For Hartog, the shift from a future-oriented regime to a presentist one – in which the sole viewpoint is that of the present's – did not make the future disappear, only made it seem 'opaque and threatening' (Hartog 2015: 196). The future came to be seen in terms of risks, precaution and responsibility at the same time as when the past came to be seen 'through notions of heritage and debts'. In the view of Hartog (2015: 201), this means nothing other than that the present has 'extended both into the future and into the past'. Gumbrecht (2014: 20) echoes these sentiments by saying that 'today we increasingly feel that our present has broadened, as it is now surrounded by a future we can no longer see, access, or choose and a past that we are not able to leave behind'. Finally, Assmann (2013: 322) interprets the extension of the present as a new concept of the future that revolves around the idea of sustainability as the prolonged existence of the already known and familiarized.

Altogether, there is something deeply bewildering in all the above approaches to historical time. Both theories of the present past and cultural diagnoses seem to imply that historical time today is, in one way or another, anything but historical. For inasmuch as the past does not go away and takes hold of the present, and inasmuch as the future is only the extension of the present, these conceptualizations convey a sense of changelessness. But without the possibility of further change, without a future different from the past and the present, there is no *historical* time; there is only an end to historical time in the present. What the above theories indicate is that the current condition of Western societies, which is no longer supposed to change over time is, actually, *ahistorical*.

Now, I do not wish to claim that this is what cultural diagnoses explicitly and wilfully assert. But this is what I think they entail, and I have three objections to such entailed ahistoricity as changelessness. The first objection concerns the *lack of an actual engagement with future prospects in their own rights*; not in terms of how such prospects are received, but in terms of being mere prospects. Although diagnoses even note that the catastrophism of postwar visions of the future has to do with recent ecological and technological prospects, their discussion is limited to occasional mentions of biotechnology and global warming. They are interested in the future inasmuch as it appears threatening, but they do not examine the question of why and how the future appears as catastrophic and what is the novelty in that. Had they asked such questions, they might have found that artificial intelligence research, biotechnology and climate change are perceived today as *anthropogenic existential risks* (Bostrom 2013), that is, risks arising out of human activity carrying the threat of premature human extinction.

In discussing *responses* to anthropogenic threats without exploring the threats themselves, cultural diagnoses remain inattentive to a handful of critical elements: that the prolongation of existence concerns the prolongation of *human existence* as such;

that the *prospects* themselves are prospects of *changes*; and that the changes envisioned lately in the ecological and technological domains are of a completely other character than changes promised by the modern time regime. Later I will come back to the novel characteristics of prospective changes. What I wish to point out here is only that Western societies are most certainly not presentist concerning *expectations* of the future. Quite the contrary: the societal expectation of the future involves today previously unimaginable changes and transformations in the human condition.

My second objection is closely related to the first: *existential risk prevention concerning worst-case scenarios of human extinction does not mean that nothing changes.* Calling for preventive measures to avoid the most dystopian visions does not exclude the possibility of other kinds of changes that do not threaten to eradicate human life, even as associated with the very same prospects. This leads straight to my third point: *even utopian changes are, in fact, very prominently envisioned today* – especially in the technological domain. For instance, transhumanism and technologies of human enhancement are often understood today as updated versions of familiar Enlightenment ideals of processual human betterment (Alleby and Sarewitz 2011: 1–13; Hauskeller 2014; Cabrera 2015; Jasanoff 2016). Whether rightly or not, is another question.

In any event, catastrophism is not the only vision of the future there is. Many of today's technological prospects are anything but cataclysmic and dystopian in their self-perception. They can be optimistic and utopian not only when they evoke the modern time regime in connection with a retained hope of human betterment, but also when they claim to escape its confines. Sometimes even transhumanists are not aware of the difference between improving on already existing human capacities and aiming at better-than-human capacities (Simon 2018c). They tend to claim compatibility with Enlightenment ideals of progress *in* the human condition and simultaneously announce much stronger programmes 'to overcome limits imposed by our biological and genetic heritage' (More 2013: 4). Either way, for advocates all this is highly desirable, while a large variety of bioconservative criticism (reviewed by Giubilini and Sanyal 2016) finds the very same prospects deeply disturbing and dystopian because of the inherent possibility of leaving behind a condition that can still reasonably be called human.

Again, all this poses the question of the new perception of change over time in human affairs as entailed by technological and ecological prospects, and, more importantly, the question of how they configure the relationship between past, present and future. To answer this question, what needs to be understood first is not that technological-scientific and ecological future prospects are catastrophic and dystopian. Nor it is that most prospects of technology and science are bright in their *self-perception*, promising to continue the betterment of the human condition over a historical process. What needs to be understood is the simultaneity of highly optimistic and extremely pessimistic perceptions, oftentimes even concerning the very same future prospects. What needs to be understood is the inherent dystopianism even of the shiniest prospects of postwar times and the type of perceived change such prospects harbour.

On the coming pages, I will argue that nothing is better suited for providing a conceptual understanding of the current transformation of historical time and an emerging sense of historicity of Western societies than a rebranded philosophy of history. The first step makes the case for the necessity of a reinterpreted intellectual endeavour. The second step returns to and elaborates on the question of the novel type of perceived change in recent ecological and technological prospects. Finally, the third step brings the two previous ones together by conceptualizing the transformation of historical time as an increasing societal invocation of an evental temporality of change against the backdrop of a decreasing belief in a processual one.

On the necessity of the philosophy of history

The necessity of the philosophy of history is best indicated by two antithetical movements in the broadly understood post-Second World War period (stretching until today). On the one hand, there is a growing scepticism about philosophy of history, mostly due to a disbelief about the future as the promise of human and social betterment; on the other, there is the survival of philosophy of history in disguise.

To begin with the former: inasmuch as the modern concept of history is the promise of a better future seen together with the present and the past (history as the way leading to the promised future), and inasmuch as this future collapses, it simply follows that the concept of history itself, together with philosophy of history as the exercise that invents and elaborates that concept, must collapse as well. Pointing at the postwar collapse of a promise, however, is not to say that Enlightenment thinkers and consecutive philosophies of history were naïve believers. Consider the following remark of Kant (1991: 42) from his essay on universal history: 'despite the apparent wisdom of individual actions here and there, everything as a whole is made up of folly and childish vanity, and often of childish malice and destructiveness'. Like Kant, Enlightenment thinkers and subsequent philosophers of history were perfectly aware of the horrors of human affairs. They invented the possibility of a better future and the idea of history precisely to eliminate these horrors by conceptualizing the possibility of change over time in human affairs as history.

What postwar Western societies renounced was then not a naïve belief, but *the will to conceptualize change* for the better in human affairs *in spite of* the primary experience of horrors. It happened in multiple ways. The first thing to point out is to remember that the criticism of philosophy of history is not exclusively postwar. Although it became the standard attitude only after the Second World War, Raymond Aron, as early as 1938 (the date of the first French edition) introduces his book on philosophy of history with a warning that he does not mean 'the great systems of the beginning of the nineteenth century, so discredited today' (Aron 1961: 9). The postwar period, however, discredited not merely the 'great systems of the nineteenth century', but a large set of interrelated general ideas. Horkheimer and Adorno's *Dialectic of Enlightenment* (2002) is a wonderfully instructive example of how to understand what this means. Their story about the way Enlightenment ideals have led to the most gruesome consequences instead of delivering their promise might appear as a critique of philosophy of history. But, in fact, it simply reverses the assumed directionality of human affairs. If Hannah Arendt (1973: vii) is right in claiming that 'Progress and Doom are two sides of the same medal', then a comprehensive critique of the entire enterprise of philosophy of history is that which aims at abandoning the medal itself, instead of holding up one of its sides against the other. In other words, such a comprehensive critique wishes to abandon the general idea of directionality, regardless of the specific directions assumed by particular approaches.

Postwar scepticism about the entire enterprise of philosophy of history meant scepticism about these most general ideas. Without the intention to provide a full overview, I would like to mention a few more, such as the idea of a supposed knowledge of the future (regardless of the particular imaginings of how the future may look); the idea of the self-identical substance of the postulated historical process (regardless of the particular shape this substance may take); the idea that this historical process follows a discernable pattern inevitably governed by an impersonal 'force' of history (whatever that force may be); or the idea that history has an ultimate and inherent purpose or meaning (whatever that meaning may be). To bring these down to concrete examples, sharing with Lyotard (1979: xxiv) the postmodern condition as 'an incredulity towards metanarratives' amounts to sharing a general suspicion about metanarratives of any kind, including Horkheimer and Adorno's. Agreeing with Popper (2002) on the impossibility of predicting the future of human affairs based on the past, or agreeing with Danto (1985) that configuring a course of history based on an illegitimate knowledge of the future results in the illegitimacy of knowledge-claims on the past, is a general agreement on the illegitimacy of knowledge-claims about the future. In a similar vein, being convinced by the criticism of historical inevitability of Berlin (2002: 94–165) entails a distrust in the general idea of a determined historical process on the move.

Postmodern 'end of history' theories, announcing the end of the modern idea of history in the sense of movement and directionality (Vattimo 1987; Baudrillard 2000: 31–57; Jenkins 1997; many of them analysed by Butler 1993), are of a special kind. On the one hand, they attest to the tendency of outright scepticism towards philosophy of history; on the other, they testify its survival by tacitly exercising it. For announcing the 'end of history' necessarily invokes an epochal change as a basic tenet of historical thinking, even if the announced new era is that which is supposed to be void of history. Postmodern 'end of history' theories may nevertheless be very well aware of the ambivalence of their position. Vattimo (1987) is at least reflexive enough not only to associate postmodernity with the idea of the 'end of history', but also to point out that an 'incredulity towards metanarratives' itself tells a metanarrative.

Abandoning the philosophy of history and the idea of a historical process is so hard that even attempts of abandonment are caught *in flagranti* of exercising philosophy of history. No wonder that survival stories are just as manifold as stories of death. According to Louis Mink, the idea of a Universal History survives in historical writing as the presupposition of a past actuality as an untold story. There is even a lack of self-awareness about the survival itself in the practice of historical studies, inasmuch as the transformed idea of Universal History as an untold past actuality 'is implicitly presupposed as widely as it would be explicitly rejected' (Mink 1987: 188). This psychological edge is also present in Hayden White's view on the necessary presence of a philosophy of history in each piece of historical writing. As part of the conclusion of his seminal *Metahistory*, White (1973: 428) claims that 'every philosophy of history contains within it the elements of a proper history, just as every proper history contains within it the elements of a full-blown philosophy of history'. What this means is that regardless of whether knowing it or not, no one can write history without relying on a philosophy of history (understood as the course of human affairs). It simply lurks in the background and tacitly informs the work of historians.

What is implied by every piece of written history is not an altered version of a once celebrated idea, as in Mink's story, but a tacit and necessary appeal to the enterprise of the philosophy of history. This arguably is a strong claim. I nevertheless think that White is right, and not only about the survival of the philosophy of history in professional historical studies, but also in various other disciplines. In fact, such implied philosophy of history seems the most apparent in theories of sociology and political science, that intend to make sense of the constitution of the world over a longer timescale. Theories of modernization, globalization, democratization or secularization – and, for that matter, all '-ization' theories – rely on a processual temporality and sketch a historical development over time. Such '-ization' theories of course appear as authored by historians as well, although they are usually called long-term interpretations instead of being labelled as theories.

This brings me to the last version of survival stories I would like to introduce: the sheer continuation of the enterprise of philosophy of history. Popular scientists and public intellectuals – who otherwise are experts in fields of cognitive science, physiology or geography – have retained the idea of the developmental historical process with humankind as its central subject all along (Diamond 1997; Pinker 2011). Lately even popular historians have given in to the urge to tell universal histories of humanity (Harari 2015), while the big history project – launched by historian David Christian (1991) – aims at telling a history of practically everything since the Big Bang in a single unfolding story. A more detailed enumeration could include deep history, world history, the rise of global history, or the recent fascination with telling large-scale Anthropocene stories. But all this, I believe, already indicates clearly enough that the Western world has serious difficulties with effectively abandoning both the idea of change over time in human affairs as history and philosophy of history as the enterprise conceptualizing such 'history'.

The challenge posed by this situation is just as tough as the situation itself. For what needs to be explained and accounted for is both the scepticism towards the enterprise of the philosophy of history *and* the actual unwillingness to abandon history. Failing to take seriously the scepticism part and merely noting the unwillingness to abandon history very likely ends up in promoting a return to classical philosophies of history, as if nothing had happened in the last seventy years or so. Failing to take seriously the apparent unwillingness to actually abandon history disregards the possibility of identifying a socio-cultural endeavour that craves satisfaction, and very likely ends up in advocating the demolition of an enterprise that is designed to satisfy that very endeavour.

Unlike these options, taking seriously both sides of the equation would simultaneously recognize the indispensability of the philosophy of history and the implausibility of the way it has been exercised throughout Western modernity. What this means is that the indispensability of the philosophy of history is not unconditional or naturally given. It is most certainly a *conditional indispensability* that concerns a context-bound and purpose-dependent human endeavour. Philosophy of history may vanish and the idea of history could be reckoned with one day. But this day comes only when the very purposes and socio-cultural needs satisfied by the philosophy of history vanish. For now, this does not seem the case. Instead, the enterprise of the philosophy of history is still *indispensable as the best effort of Western societies to conceptualize, thereby understand, account for, and enable change in human affairs; and, consequently, it is indispensable inasmuch as Western societies are concerned about change over time.*

In this conditional indispensability, the defining general ideas of modern philosophy of history can indeed be abandoned. Conceptualizing historical change and historical time does not necessarily have to take the shape of conceiving of history as a force or master plan being out there. Instead of postulating a historical process with inherent meaning and purpose concerning humankind, a rebranded philosophy of history can be fully aware of the fact that 'history' is its own conceptual invention. But this awareness should not simply mean the postulation of the same old historical process, this time without determinism and inherent purpose in the course of human affairs. It rather has to mean the conceptualization of a novel notion of history, arising out of present-day concerns about change and perceptions of time as 'historical'. Thus the central question of such a rebranded philosophy of history is: *how to understand historical time when even what seem to be utopian remainders of human and societal betterment in technological and ecological prospects come out as inherently dystopian?*

A novel sense of historicity

In my previous research (Simon 2015; 2018a; 2018b), I have already ventured into answering some aspects of this question. Here I would like to briefly recapitulate two of my earlier points and to elaborate on a more general third point, which will lead, in the concluding section, to a brief sketch about the transformation of historical time.

The first point is that *the type of the perception of change underlying today's prospects is what I came to call unprecedented change.* Both optimistic and pessimistic expectations of the future in the technological-scientific domain typically concern changes which are not merely conceived of as unfolding from past conditions. What makes utopian visions of technology inherently dystopian is precisely that they are not about the prospective development of already known and familiar potentials and yet-underdeveloped capacities. Instead, as indicated in the earlier discussion, technological prospects of artificial intelligence, bioengineering, transhumanism, genome editing and human enhancement entail the possibility of the creation of other-than-human beings with greater-than-human capacities. In the case of ecological prospects, there is of course nothing like an intentional act to bring about anything like this. Nevertheless, the type of change implicit in the prospect and the potentiality of humanity engineering its own demise is *categorically* the same in the technological and ecological domains. The challenge of the ultimate vision of an inhabitable planet and human extinction as the result of anthropogenic climate change is that it defies the continuity of human experience (Chakrabarty 2009: 197–8). Defying this continuity, defying the possibility of having recourse to a familiar configuration of change, defying the possibility of making sense of the future by connecting it to past experiences (on a human timescale) or past occurrences (on a larger-than-human timescale) along a deep processual temporality, is what I call unprecedented.

The second point follows from the first: *conceiving of change over time as unprecedented means conceiving of it as an evental transformation*. That which is conceived of as unprecedented is expected to be brought about in the shape of a sudden game-changer event, instead of being the result of a cumulative historical process. This of course does not mean that prior to the expected event nothing can happen and nothing can change in any way whatsoever. This means only that the expected momentous transformation is supposed to be brought into effect by such an occurrence identified as a disruptive event. My favourite example is that of a technological singularity (Vinge 2013), referring to the anticipated creation of greater-than-human intelligence, with consequences inaccessible to human cognition (which is the primary source of unease and dystopianism in prospects of evental transformations).

These two points tend towards a third one I would like draw attention to: *the scope of a rebranded philosophy of history is not limited to human affairs, meaning that it is not limited to affairs which are exclusively human*. This may be surprising and unsurprising at the same time. It is surprising as measured against the focus of classical philosophies of history on the human and humanity, while unsurprising as measured against the current cacophony of discourses questioning the human in one way or another. Without the intention to introduce all the oftentimes radically conflicting views, I would like to mention only a few.

The manifold discourses on posthumanity/posthumanism are, I believe, the best indicators that Western societies envision unforeseen changes today instead of being presentist. The most trenchant of all is a technological-scientific prospect of posthumanity. It marks a potential new era by the already mentioned prospect of the creation of beings that may be posthuman in the most literal sense. The creation of greater-than-human intelligence (Vinge 2013; Bostrom 2014) and the aforementioned radical enhancement scenarios advocated by transhumanism are the most prominent versions of this technological posthumanity. Then, there is a critical posthumanism focused on dismantling humanism as a long-standing pattern of thought, questioning its anthropocentrism and human exceptionalism, fighting the liberal subject at its centre, and trying to renegotiate the human–animal divide (Braidotti 2013a; Wolfe 2010; Haraway 2008). Ewa Domanska (2010, 2017) has already tried to raise awareness of the importance of such posthumanism for historical theory. Then, often oscillating between critical and technological-scientific versions, there is also the most sophisticated posthumanism of Hayles (1999), which nevertheless has more sympathy for the former in arguing that the posthuman does not necessarily entail biological alteration.

None of this is to say that the human is no longer important or that the human is no longer a central concern. Despite all claims of anti-anthropocentrism in critical posthumanism, it must be clear that the sheer existence of most of these discourses is due to the extent to which human beings became a threat to themselves in the shape of the anthropogenic risks discussed earlier. Critical posthumanists would not call for humility and would not challenge what they call human exceptionalism if the human was not appearing more powerful – both in creation and destruction – than ever before. Nowhere is this clearer than in debates about the Anthropocene, regarding which even Chakrabarty (2017) gives in to the otherwise much criticized tendency to talk about the 'age of humans'. At the same time, Chakrabarty (2015) argues that the *anthropos* of the Anthropocene debate is not a mere reiteration of old conceptions of humanity, but a redefinition of the human within a *zoecentric* worldview focused on life. Similarly, Domanska (2014) situates the Anthropocene with concerns for the wider category of Terrans instead of the narrower category Humans, while Latour (2010) has his own wider category called Earthlings.

Again, the list could be continued with far more examples. But the tendency is hopefully already displayed: with or without much conceptual innovation, both within a narrowly defined historical studies (Chaplin 2017) and an emerging transdisciplinary setting (Braidotti 2013b; Domanska 2015; Robin 2018), the scope of today's historicity extends over a world of entangled human/nonhuman affairs.

The transformation of historical time: Processual and evental temporalities

To avoid any misunderstandings, I am not advocating any of the above views. My intention is rather to provide a conceptual understanding of their shared thematizations, concerns and most profound assumptions as our emerging historical sensibility. I think that the redefinition of the human/nonhuman world as an object of knowledge, the perception of change over time as unprecedented, and the expectation of a singular disruptive event to bring about such unprecedented change, are integral features of an ongoing transformation of historical time.

Running the (not really existential) risk of schematization, it seems useful to distinguish between a processual and an evental understanding of historical time. Changes conceived of along a processual temporality concern changes in the condition of a subject in the human world, unfolding against the backdrop of a deep temporal continuity. This is historical time as we know it in Western modernity. Changes conceived of along an evental temporality concern changes in the entangled human/nonhuman world which bring about a previously inexistent subject in a non-continuous manner, through unprecedented changes. This is historical time as it is emerging in the post-Second World War societies. The transformation of historical time is best understood as the increasing perception of change over time in Western societies along an evental temporality, accompanied by the simultaneous decrease of expecting change to take place in a processual scenario.

However useful such schematic contrast may be in gaining a conceptual understanding of what is at stake in the transformation of historical time, it must be clear that actual views are typically less comprehensive and coherent. Just as it is not necessary for a processual historical sensibility to exhibit in its particular instances all the attributes of an interrelated conceptual toolkit (directionality, self-identical substance, telos and so forth), the above individual examples of an evental conception of historical time do not necessarily hold or imply all the aforementioned three features associated with evental temporality on the conceptual level. Not to mention that the two temporalities are often conflated in certain discourses. For instance, critical posthumanism implies a processual temporality in extending emancipatory concerns of the human world to the entangled world of human/nonhuman affairs, although the tectonic rearrangement of knowledge it advocates qualifies as unprecedented change that does not merely unfold from past conditions as an accumulation of knowledge.

Given such blending of concerns and temporalities in current discourses and views, the main question is that of how processual and evental dispositions of historical time relate to each other today. To begin to answer this question from a distance, the first thing to note is that both processual and evental temporalities can be labelled as 'historical' inasmuch as they configure large-scale change over time in the world without the assumption of otherworldly intervention, either divine or supernatural. It is nevertheless equally tempting to consider evental temporality as the one that brings about other-than-historical change. It would also be possible to propose a new, and at first perhaps odd-sounding, concept for that which is other-than-history, and then to contrast it to history and its processual time. But there is a way in which the result would be the same: insofar as the evental temporality harboured by postwar prospects is not conceived of *exclusively* as a new version of the old historical time, insofar as the occurrence of a novel type of perceived change is conceived of as that which threatens to shatter whatever we have previously thought about historical change, it makes no difference if we stick with the *word* history. The sheer fact of referring to 'historical' time in the case of both a processual and an evental temporality can nevertheless be confusing. But we know, to a large extent due to the work of Reinhart Koselleck, that concepts tend to shift meanings, even to an extent that meanings associated with certain words and concepts completely dissipate with the emergence of new meanings associated with the very same words and concepts.

At the moment, this is not (although perhaps only not yet) the case with 'history'. It rather seems to me that, since sometime around the end of the Second World War, we have been living in a period like the one between 1750 and 1850, to which Koselleck (2004) referred to as *Sattelzeit*. By this, Koselleck meant a saddle period in which a cluster of interrelated concepts (from the concept of history itself to those of revolution or utopia) gained a temporal dimension and thereby new meanings, resulting in the overall conceptual design of the processual historicity of Western modernity. If, as I think, we are in another saddle period of substantial changes, it means that old and new understandings of history and conceptions of historical time exist alongside each other, and sometimes even mingle in particular instances, such as in the case of critical posthumanism. This is also why it is better, for now, to consider both processual and evental temporalities as being 'historical'.

Until we recognize or affirm the transformation as finished and one that irrevocably took place, we cannot even determine its character and settle the question of whether the transformation of historical time itself is processual or evental. Accordingly, the claim I wish to advance asserts only that a processual and an evental historical time can be analytically distinguished in the post-Second World War Western world. A stronger version of this claim, that I also wish to hold, asserts that the evental conception of historical time is gaining prominence at the expense of the former ubiquity of the processual conception of historical time. If there is an ongoing *transformation* of historical time, nothing more about its character can be said with any certainty precisely because what an *ongoing* transformation of *historical time* transforms is the very way in which we can talk about transformations in time.

References

Alleby, B. and Sarewitz, D. (2011), *The Techno-Human Condition*, Cambridge, MA: MIT Press.

Arendt, H. (1973), *The Origins of Totalitarianism*, New York: Harcourt Brace and Company.

Aron, R. (1961), *Introduction to the Philosophy of History: An Essay on the Limits of Historical Objectivity*, transl. George J. Irwin, Boston: Beacon Press.

Assmann, A. (2013), *Ist die Zeit aus den Fugen? Aufstieg und Fall des Zeitregimes der Moderne*, Munich: Hanser.

Baudrillard, J. (2000), *The Vital Illusion*, ed. J. Witwer, New York: Columbia University Press.

Berlin, I. (2002), *Liberty: Incorporating Four Essays on Liberty*, ed. H. Hardy, Oxford: Oxford University Press.

Bevernage, B. (2012), *History, Memory, and State-Sponsored Violence: Time and Justice*, London and New York: Routledge.

Bostrom, N. (2013), 'Existential Risk Prevention as Global Priority', *Global Policy*, 4 (1): 15–31.

Bostrom, N. (2014), *Superintelligence: Paths, Dangers, Strategies*, Oxford: Oxford University Press.

Braidotti, R. (2013a), *The Posthuman*, Cambridge: Polity Press.

Braidotti, R. (2013b), 'Yes, There is No Crisis: Working Towards the Posthumanities', *International Journal for History, Culture and Modernity*, 1 (2): 187–99.

Butler, J. (1993), 'Poststructuralism and Postmarxism', *Diacritics*, 23 (4): 2–11.

Cabrera, L. Y. (2015), *Rethinking Human Enhancement: Social Enhancement and Emergent Technologies*, Basingstoke: Palgrave.

Chakrabarty, D. (2009), 'The Climate of History: Four Theses', *Critical Inquiry*, 35 (2): 197–222.

Chakrabarty, D. (2015), 'The Human Condition in the Anthropocene', *The Tanner Lectures in Human Values*. Delivered at Yale University, 18–19 February. Available online: https://tannerlectures.utah.edu/Chakrabarty%20manuscript.pdf (accessed 25 March 2018).

Chakrabarty, D. (2017), 'The Future of the Human Sciences in the Age of Humans: A Note', *European Journal of Social Theory*, 20 (1): 39–43.

Chaplin, J. E. (2017), 'Can the Nonhuman Speak? Breaking the Chain of Being in the Anthropocene', *Journal of the History of Ideas*, 78 (4): 509–29.

Christian, D. (1991), 'The Case for "Big History"', *Journal of World History*, 2 (2): 223–38.

Danto, A. C. (1985), *Narration and Knowledge: Including the Integral Text of Analytical Philosophy of History*, New York: Columbia University Press.

Diamond, J. (1997), *Guns, Germs, and Steel: The Fates of Human Societies*, New York: W. W. Norton & Company.

Domanska, E. (2010), 'Beyond Anthropocentrism in Historical Studies', *Historein*, 10: 118–30.

Domanska, E. (2014), 'The *New Age* of the Anthropocene', *Journal of Contemporary Archaeology*, 1 (1): 96–101.

Domanska, E. (2015), 'Ecological Humanities', *Teksty Drugie*, Special Issue – English Edition, 186–210.

Domanska, E. (2017), 'Animal History', *History and Theory*, 56 (2): 267–87.

Giubilini, A. and Sanyal, S. (2016), 'Challenging Human Enhancement', in S. Clarke, J. Savulescu, C. A. J. Coady, A. Giubilini and S. Sanyal (eds), *The Ethics of Human Enhancement: Understanding the Debate*, 1–24, Oxford: Oxford University Press.

Gumbrecht, H. U. (2014), *Our Broad Present: Time and Contemporary Culture*, New York: Columbia University Press.

Harari, Y. N. (2015), *Sapiens: A Brief History of Humankind*, New York: Harper.

Haraway, D. (2008), *When Species Meet*, Minneapolis: University of Minnesota Press.

Hartog, F. (2015), *Regimes of Historicity: Presentism and Experiences of Time*, transl. S. Brown, New York: Columbia University Press.

Hauskeller, M. (2014), *Better Humans? Understanding the Enhancement Project*, London and New York: Routledge.

Hayles, K. N. (1999), *How We Became Posthuman: Virtual Bodies in Cybernetics, Literature, and Informatics*, Chicago: University of Chicago Press.

Horkheimer, M. and Adorno, T. W. (2002), *Dialectic of Enlightenment: Philosophical Fragments*, transl. E. Jephcott, Stanford: Stanford University Press.

Jasanoff, S. (2016), 'Perfecting the Human: Posthuman Imaginaries and Technologies of Reason', in J. B. Hurlbut and H. Tirosh-Samuelson (eds), *Perfecting Human Futures: Transhuman Visions and Technological Imaginations*, 73–95, Wiesbaden: Springer.

Jenkins, K. (1997), 'Why Bother with the Past? Engaging with Some Issues Raised by the Possible "End of History as We Have Known It"', *Rethinking History*, 1 (1): 56–66.

Kant, I. (1991), 'Idea for a Universal History with a Cosmopolitan Purpose', in H. S. Reiss (ed.), *Kant: Political Writings*, 41–53, Cambridge: Cambridge University Press.

Kleinberg, E. (2017), *Haunting History: For a Deconstructive Approach to the Past*, Stanford: Stanford University Press.

Koselleck, R. (2004), *Futures Past: On the Semantics of Historical Time*, transl. K. Tribe, New York: Columbia University Press.

Latour, B. (2010), 'A Plea for Earthly Sciences', in J. Burnett, S. Lefferes and G. Thomas (eds), *New Social Connections: Sociology's Subjects and Objects*, 72–84, Basingstoke: Palgrave.

Lorenz, C. (2010), 'Unstuck in Time. Or: The Sudden Presence of the Past', in K. Tilmans, F. van Vree and J. Winter (eds), *Performing the Past: Memory, History, and Identity in Modern Europe*, 67–102, Amsterdam: Amsterdam University Press.

Löwith, K. (1949), *Meaning in History: The Theological Implications of the Philosophy of History*, Chicago: University of Chicago Press.

Lyotard, J.-F. (1979), *The Postmodern Condition: A Report on Knowledge*, transl. G. Bennington and B. Massumi, Manchester: Manchester University Press.

Mink, L. O. (1987), *Historical Understanding*, ed. B. Fay, E. O. Golob and R. T. Vann, Ithaca: Cornell University Press.

More, M. (2013), 'The Philosophy of Transhumanism', in M. More and N. Vita-More (eds), *The Transhumanist Reader: Classical and Contemporary Essays on the Science, Technology, and Philosophy of the Human Future*, 1–17, Malden: Wiley-Blackwell.

Pinker, S. (2011), *The Better Angels of Our Nature: Why Violence Has Declined*, New York: Viking.

Popper, K. (2002), *The Poverty of Historicism*, London and New York: Routledge.

Robin, L. (2018), 'Environmental Humanities and Climate Change: Understanding Humans Geologically and Other Life Forms Ethically', *WIREs Climate Change*, 9:e499.

Runia, E. (2006), 'Presence', *History and Theory*, 45 (1): 1–29.

Simon, Z. B. (2015), 'History Manifested: Making Sense of Unprecedented Change', *European Review of History*, 22 (5): 819–34.

Simon, Z. B. (2018a), '(The Impossibility of) Acting upon a Story that We Can Believe', *Rethinking History*, 22 (1): 105–25.

Simon, Z. B. (2018b), 'History Begins in the Future: On Historical Sensibility in the Age of Technology', in S. Helgesson and J. Svenungsson (eds), *The Ethos of History: Time and Responsibility*, 192–209, New York: Berghahn.

Simon, Z. B. (2018c), 'The Story of Humanity and the Challenge of Posthumanity', *History of the Human Sciences*, online first article, doi: 10.1177/0952695118779519

Tamm, M., ed. (2015), *Afterlife of Events: Perspectives on Mnemohistory*, Basingstoke: Palgrave.

Vattimo, G. (1987), 'The End of (Hi)story', *Chicago Review*, 35 (4): 20–30.

Vinge, V. (2013), 'Technological Singularity', in M. More and N. Vita-More (eds), *The Transhumanist Reader: Classical and Contemporary Essays on the Science, Technology, and Philosophy of the Human Future*, 365–75, Malden: Wiley-Blackwell.

White, H. (1973), *Metahistory: The Historical Imagination in Nineteenth-Century Europe*, Baltimore: The Johns Hopkins University Press.

Wolfe, C. (2010), *What is Posthumanism?* Minneapolis: University of Minnesota Press.

Part Two

Multiple Temporalities

5

Revolutionary Presence

Historicism and the Temporal Politics of the Moment

Hans Ruin

'Behold this gateway, dwarf!' I continued, 'It has two faces. Two ways come together here: nobody has ever taken them to the end [. . .]' They contradict themselves, these ways; they confront one another head on, and here, at this gateway, is where they come together. The name of the gateway is inscribed above it: 'Moment' (Augenblick).
Nietzsche, *Also sprach Zarathustra*

Introduction

In one of the introductory sections of Martin Heidegger's magnum opus *Being and Time* (1927), where the methodological framework for his existential analytic is presented, it is stated that the inquiry into Being 'is itself characterized by historicity' (Heidegger 2010: 20). As philosophy seeks to address the fundamental questions of metaphysics, it is thus led to recognize that philosophical thinking is itself historically situated. This does not only refer to the fact that the thinking human being is located *within* the stream of history, but that thinking *is* historical, and that it has to take this predicament into consideration and act upon it accordingly if it is to be carried out in an adequate way. Later in the book, Heidegger devotes an entire chapter to 'historicity' (*Geschichtlichkeit*), as one of the basic so-called *existentiales* of human existence or Dasein, describing it as the way in which Dasein *happens* through a *repetition* of what has been for a future. It is here that he also outlines the possibility of a presumably *authentic* way of living this predicament, where the temporality of the *moment* (Germ. *Augenblick*) as a qualified sense of *the present*, captures the fullest potential of historical existence, as also a practical-ethical task of responding to its own situation and to act as a 'kairological' critic, in other words as one acting in, from, and upon the moment (Heidegger 2010: 328, 338).

When history is viewed primarily as an objective chronological sequence of events, within which every individual life is also situated as a dynamic entity within space–time, it misrepresents not only the deeper temporal condition of individual human existence, but also history itself. It is not through the *knowledge* of history that human existence *is* historical; on the contrary, it is by *being* historical that human existence can also *know* history. Temporal-historical existence precedes temporal-historical understanding. This is the basic hermeneutical idea that Heidegger picks up from Dilthey and elaborates in the context of his existential-ontological understanding of historicity.[1]

Here I want to focus on one particular aspect of this complex analysis that is actualized by our current topic of historical time and 'presentism'. It concerns how the present is projected as an ontological, epistemological and ethical-political problem in the temporality of the *moment* or the *Augenblick*, literally the 'glance of the eye'. When seen from the perspective of the problem of presentism, Heidegger's analysis of historicity as culminating in the authentic temporality of the moment confronts us with a philosophical antinomy. If history as commonly understood is ultimately a secondary phenomenon in relation to the existential historicity of human existence – as concentrated in the authentic *Augenblick* – then the analysis could appear as an extreme version of presentism. If, on the other hand, it is only on the basis of such an enacted authentic temporality that it is possible to fully grasp the nature of historicity, then it is through this *Augenblick* that we must move in order to access the ontological roots of history and historicism as commonly understood.

In the motto above from Nietzsche's *Thus Spoke Zarathustra*, the protagonist of the story finds himself standing in a dream-like scene before the gate of an *Augenblick* in a confrontation with the 'spirit of gravity'. Towards the end I shall return to this strange allegory and to Heidegger's reading of how it culminates in a radical break and existential decision.[2] The political 'decisionism' articulated in different ways in the mid-war period – among both right revolutionary and left revolutionary thinkers such as Heidegger and Benjamin – may to some seem politically outdated. Yet, I believe that it is imperative – not least in our present situation – to learn from Heidegger's profound exploration of this inner revolutionary dimension of lived historical time.

The chapter begins with a brief survey of how the very concept of *the historical* became a philosophical battle-ground, in particular in the phenomenological circles in Heidegger's early years. It then moves to a more detailed analysis of the stakes involved in the 'moment' (*Augenblick*) as a way of thinking a present that is characterized by both fullness and fracture at once. As such it can be interpreted as both a philosophical-epistemic but also political counter-move to the effects of a socially, scientifically and technically construed present of the 'now' (*Jetzt*). The last part explores Heidegger's interpretation of Nietzsche, where the question of the temporality of the *Augenblick* leads up to the fate of what is seen as a nihilist modernity. Through this reading the *Augenblick* is presented as a hidden ligature in the inner construction of historical time.

Thinking the historical

From the second part of the eighteenth century, *history* and *the historical, as both Historie and Geschichte*, gradually obtain a new and philosophically more charged significance. After having designated simply what belongs to the past and the knowledge of this past, it starts to signal a mode of becoming of human being as well as a redemptive hope of self-understanding through a proper grasp of this development. The schema is anticipated already in Herder and brought to its full articulation in Hegel, whose phenomenology conveys the hope of a historically mediated self-explication of spirit. From that point onward, *history* becomes an intellectual battle-ground, with competing narratives of the inner logic of the historical fate of humanity, but also with competing views on the value of historical-developmental thinking as such, mirrored in the intense debates of the meaning and value of 'historicism' around the turn of the nineteenth century.

The dominant historicist conceptions of philosophy were criticized not only by the early proponents of analytical philosophy, notably Frege and Russell, but also by Husserl, who called for a more *systematic* and scientific way of doing philosophy. In the programmatic 1911 essay 'Philosophy as Rigorous Science', he explicitly spoke out against what he saw as current 'historicist' tendencies in philosophy, that ultimately lead to relativism and 'sceptical historicism' (Husserl 1965: 77).

At the same time, there were strong voices arguing for an even deeper engagement with the historical nature of thought. Husserl's essay is partly written in critical dialogue with Dilthey, who from his 1883 *Introduction to the Human Sciences* onward had sought to develop a method for the interpretative human sciences that included a sense of how the interpreting subject is always historically situated, while still seeking to avoid the threat of subjectivism and relativism. Dilthey's explicit goal was to accomplish for the human sciences what Kant had done for the natural sciences. Whereas the knowledge of nature concerns the possibility of having a knowledge of what is external to the human mind, the study of humanity in its historical expressions must be understood as an inescapable self-reflexive enterprise, where 'life knows life'. The problem of historicity concerns precisely this *intersection*, and how to conceptualize life as both a topic and condition of possibility in the study of history. Another significant voice was Nietzsche, who in his *Second Untimely Meditation* ('On the Use and Abuse of History for Life') had described life as characterized by memory and historical awareness that positioned it within a historically determined space, in either a *monumental*, an *antiquarian*, or a *critical* comportment. A few years later he spoke out in *Human, All Too Human* of the need for developing for the first time a truly historical philosophizing and of how the lack of 'historical sense' was the 'congenial defect of all philosophers' (Nietzsche 1984: 14–15).

Within the group gathered around Husserl these two seemingly contradictory views constituted part of the dynamism of the early phenomenological movement. On the one hand, there was a strong commitment to the basic sense of phenomenology as a new form of foundational first philosophy that could reach deeper into the roots of experience, consciousness and life than the different competing more epistemologically and logically oriented Neo-Kantianisms (to which Frege could also be said to belong). Heidegger even refers to it as an 'existential a priori'. On the other hand, the hermeneutic and critical sensibility of Hegel, Dilthey and Nietzsche pointed in the direction of an even more radical historical thinking. This productive tension comes out clearly in Heidegger's early Freiburg lectures, where he repeatedly returns to the issue of how to ultimately 'overcome the dichotomy between history and systematics'. In the end this goal leads him to opt for a conception of philosophy as 'historical knowing in a radical sense', which is the formulation he then uses in a seminal 1922 essay on the interpretation of Aristotle, often described as the blueprint for *Being and Time* (Heidegger 1989).

It is in this text that he articulates most succinctly the basic predicament of the interpreter as standing in a 'hermeneutic situation', where 'the past discloses itself only in proportion to the decisiveness and power of the ability to unlock which a present has at its disposal', and to 'repeat that which is understood in the sense of and for one's own situation'. The model deviates in at least one important respect from the Husserlian formula of mapping historical problems onto a systematic framework, because to this schema Heidegger adds that the *meaning of the present* and its supposedly systematic concerns can never be taken for granted. Just as the past becomes fully intelligible only by being mediated through the present, the present too becomes available to itself only as mediated through a history in which it exposes itself to a critical 'destruction' of its own inherited motives. It is this *circularity* of the fully actualized *hermeneutical situation* that captures the core of what he here sees as a genuinely *historical* thinking.

The 'hermeneutic situation' brings together the essential elements of historicity as a name for what it means to always *stand in the open exposure of a tradition*. History is no longer a name for what is simply *past*, but for what confronts life as both its foundation and its task to assume in interpretation and action. In 1922 Heidegger had not yet begun to use the actual concept of 'historicity' – *Geschichtlichkeit* – to designate this existential predicament. It appears in his writing only from the following year, and then as a direct result of his reading of the correspondence between Dilthey and his friend and interlocutor Paul Yorck von Wartenburg, published that same year (Dilthey and Yorck von Wartenburg 1923). It is a topic that Dilthey in one of the letters describes as 'their shared fundamental concern'. But it was especially the way that Yorck spoke of it that propelled this concept into a philosopheme of the highest importance from 1923 onward in phenomenological-hermeneutical circles, as demonstrated by the fact that he is in fact the single most quoted author in *Being and Time*.[3]

In one passage (quoted by Heidegger) Yorck states: 'Just as physiology cannot be studied in abstraction from physics, neither can philosophy from historicity, especially if it is critical' (Heidegger 2010: 402). Another important quotation concerns his criticism of the earlier school of historicists, notably Ranke, whom he accuses of having an 'ocular' approach to the past as only visualized forms that 'can never become realities'. Henceforth 'historicity' designates the inescapable historical situatedness of subjectivity, thinking and truth, indeed of life itself. But as such it also marks a *practical* challenge of authentically confronting its past as possibility for a future.

Historicity and authentic temporality

Chapter 5 in the second part of *Being and Time* remains the most extensive attempt to develop a phenomenological description of historicity as a basic existential condition and as itself the condition of possibility of historical experience or experience of what is historical. A standard answer to what makes something 'historical' is simply that it belongs to 'the past'. Yet, since the past is no longer present it is hard to see how the pastness of something could account for the experience of it as historical in the present. Heidegger then turns to the example of a specific artefact, as encountered in a historical museum. This is experienced as 'historical', he writes, not in virtue of itself being past, since it obviously exists here and now *in the present*. Instead it obtains this experiential feature of *pastness* and historicity in virtue of being perceived as belonging to a *world* that once was, in other words to Dasein as 'having-been'. It is this projected re-activation of a world no longer there and thus of a Dasein that has-been, *da-gewesen*, that accounts for its historical aura. In other words, the historicity of the object does not ultimately come from the object itself, but from a type of intentionality or concern (*Sorge*) that is characteristic of human Dasein as it projects itself towards a future so as to make Dasein as having-been appear again, in the form of *repetition* (*Wiederholung*) of an earlier existential possibility. It is this achievement or enactment of present and living Dasein that constitutes its historicity as one of its so-called existentiales. As such it also provides the existential foundation for *history* in the standard sense as a source-based account of the past.[4]

In the key section 74 Heidegger designates historicity as the general 'event-structure' – *Geschensstruktur* – of human existence and as an *a priori* of historical existence and experience. In and through this event of repetition, Dasein discloses its own possibilities for the future in terms of a 'heritage' that it takes over. Since life is always also a being-with-others, this constantly projected constitution of itself through the affirmation of an inheritance is carried out in a *shared* space of meaning. And in an ominous formulation, that recalls Dilthey's notion of 'generation', he writes that Dasein always acts and understands with its 'generation' and with its 'people'. This collective overtaking of an inherited possibility is designated as 'fate' and 'destiny', *Schicksal* and *Geschick*. In an italicized passage that concentrates the logic of this process he writes: '*Only being that is futural, is equiprimordially having-been, can hand down to itself its inherited possibility, take over its own thrownness and be in the Moment* (Augenblick) *of "its time". Only authentic temporality that is at the same time finite makes something like fate, that is, authentic historicity, possible*' (Heidegger 2010: 385).

The stakes involved in this dense passage are immense. In a conversation with Karl Löwith in Rome in 1936, Heidegger is said to have pointed precisely to the analysis of historicity in *Being and Time* as a key to his political involvement (Löwith 1986: 56). Löwith, who reports this remark in his memoirs, does not develop it further. One interpretation, that also corresponds with letters and diary entries from the relevant period, is that in opting for National Socialism in 1933, Heidegger felt that he was responding in an authentic way to the historical moment. It was a nationalist-communitarian intoxication that he shared with a large part of the German population. But beyond the endless debates around Heidegger's misguided political commitment to the National Socialist revolution, this correlation between history, politics and temporality of the moment also points to the more general phenomenon of what we could call a revolutionary political temporality. It is something that we find not only in Heidegger, but also in a leftist thinker like Benjamin. In the sixth of his 'Theses on the Philosophy of History', he writes: 'To articulate the past historically does not mean to recognize it "the way it really was" (Ranke). It means to seize hold of a memory as it flashes up at a moment (*Augenblick*) of danger.' And later on he continues: 'The danger affects both the content of the tradition and its receivers. The same threat hangs over both: that of becoming a tool of the ruling classes. In every era the attempt must be made to wrest tradition away from a conformism that is about to overpower it' (Benjamin 1968: 255).

Politically Heidegger and Benjamin represent two contrary orientations during the same historical period. Yet the philosophical-temporal framework within which they articulate the conditions and imperative to interpret and to act are strikingly similar, both in their anti-historicism and in their argument for a critical-destructive retrieval of the past in and for a future. And in both cases, it ultimately boils down to a decisive moment – an *Augenblick* – as the very joint in the fabric of historical time through which it is exposed, understood, retrieved and acted upon.[5] The *Augenblick* marks a mode of the present through which the very presentness of the present is placed in question. It is a mode of temporality that has folded into itself a temporal politics, or a politics of time, as well as a critique of a technologically engendered inauthentic sense of time. In order to explore this further we need to consider how Heidegger in *Being and Time* critically analyses the formation of the everyday sense of the present as 'now' (*Jetzt*).

Datability and the vulgar present

The last chapter of *Being and Time* is devoted to tracing the genealogy of the common conception of time. Here Heidegger describes how humans always 'count on' time, in an ongoing awareness of what has been and in an anticipation of what is to come, as a 'then' and 'now' and 'later'. This counting on time is always connected to tasks and to artefacts and thus to the basic condition of belonging to a world and a context of relations. He refers to it as 'datability' (*Datierbarkeit*), but he stresses that it should not be equated with actual dates and calendars (Heidegger 2010: 407). Instead it denotes a way in which human beings relate spontaneously to their environment as a temporal environment of then, now and later. To exist is to 'have' time as the possibility of acting upon the present for a future. This elementary temporality is always situated in a world in which the living find themselves. It is not an 'inner' experience of time that can be more or less adequately correlated to an objective 'outer' time. Humans have always begun 'counting on' time as a dimension of its involvement in the world. It is from within this environment of concern for a world that timescales and calendars can eventually be developed, as a way of dividing the day and as an instrument of orientation according to before and after. This analysis is firmly rooted in anthropological facts, of how temporal frameworks are commonly based on human activities and concerns and on the rhythm of day and night. The 'clock' has its existential origin in such a shared world of everyday doings and concerns. In a dense passage Heidegger writes: 'This means that with the temporality of Dasein as thrown, delivered over to the world, and giving itself time, something like a "clock" is also discovered, that is, a handy thing that has become accessible in its regular recurrence in a making present that awaits' (Heidegger 2010: 413). Since the time that is thus counted on and measured is a time of the shared world, we can also speak of it as a 'world-time'. But thereby is not implied that it is an entity to be found anywhere in the world. Rather, it is the way in which world is lived and manifested to those who inhabit it.

As long as humans describe time through the parameters that regulate their world, where the most elementary timescale is that of night and day and the natural movement of the sun across the sky, this spontaneous measuring and 'dating' of time is still closely tied to a lived environment or a life-world. But as humans are driven – by globalization, industry and communication – to invent more encompassing and precise time-standards and measurements, the measure itself will be inserted within an increasingly advanced technology, leading up to the present time-standard that is correlated to the frequency of the caesium atom. From within the existential interpretative model we can see how such time-technologies gradually emerge from a desire to organize larger social movements. But we can also sense how the time-technologies in and through themselves can provoke an experience of alienation with respect to an original domain of temporalizing and datability. Time is no longer primarily a way of being in a world, but the name for an objective entity consisting of infinitesimal now-points along whose axis human existence itself is projected as process and event. In order to capture the logic of this development, Heidegger exemplifies it with how we commonly use a watch. The principal gesture when looking at a clock is to say 'now', since the clock enables us to answer the question 'what time is it?' In other words, it gives a distinct name to the present now according to a shared means of measurement. The clock designates a now and thus makes the present present. Thus it makes time into something present-at-hand, be it in terms of day and year, hour and minute and second or nano-second. On the basis of such a shared measuring making-present the conception of time as a sequence of now-points is thus solidified.

Heidegger's analysis anticipates a social constructivist argument, according to which time (as we know it) is just a cultural construct for social ends. But his ultimate purpose is not to convey that time is something merely psychological, mental or cultural. His aim is rather directed towards the unsecuring or destabilizing of our common-sense understanding. In a flurry of quotation marks he states that: '"Time" is present neither in the "subject" nor in the "object", neither "inside" nor "outside", and it "is" "prior" to every subjectivity and objectivity, because it presents the condition of the very possibility of this "prior"' (Heidegger 2010: 419). In other words, the ontological region of time is indeterminate. It is misleading to say that time 'is' someplace in particular. It is also wrong to say that it is a (pseudo-spatial) fourth 'dimension', or that it is the 'form' or 'shape' of being. The world is given in a temporal mode, as past, present and future and thus as 'datability'. This is the given situation, on the basis of which clocks and calendars can be invented for the purpose of naming and organizing reality. What is important to understand, however, is how this original temporality of being-in-the-world can lead to a more or less adequate understanding of time. It is a characteristic tendency of human thinking to objectify and to make into manageable entities also the ontological conditions of its own existence. By understanding time as such an objective entity or domain, life gives itself an artificial mastery of time that also includes itself as temporal sequence and entity.

What is particularly noteworthy in this analysis is how it ties the idea of time and the present to a critical understanding of how the very technology by means of which humans seek to master time can also generate an alienation with respect to time. The technically induced understanding of time as a sequence of nows amounts to both mastery and loss. It disrupts the inner bond between temporality and what it means to inhabit and act in a world. The critique of historicism situates itself in the extension of this analysis, to the extent that historicism fosters a fantasmatic image of human history as played out along an objective axis where it is in principle possible to survey and recover any point in time from the perspective of the ideal time-less eye of the historian. The idea of historicity, as articulated already by Yorck and Dilthey and developed by Heidegger and echoed by Benjamin, concerns precisely the way in which only that being who him/herself is historical can also understand history through a momentaneous repetition of the past. It is only from within a lived temporality that time as a linear sequence of events can be construed. Such a critique, however, must pass through not only a critique of the technology by means of which time is controlled, measured and communicated. It must also pass through a critique of the very idea of the present as a now-point in time. But in order even to enter this domain, thinking must cut through the veil of its own conceptual constructions of time, in order to glimpse the existential condition of its own temporality. In his analysis of the structure of temporality Heidegger writes: 'Resolute, Dasein has brought itself back out of falling prey in order to be all the more authentically "there" for the disclosed situation in the "moment" (*Augenblick*)' (Heidegger 2010: 328).

The purpose of the critical analysis of the present is not to secure or make existence feel more at home, as if the original domain of time as existential temporality could somehow provide a safe haven from its socio-technological misconstrual. The *Augenblick* is not the name for an experience of temporal fullness or plenitude. Rather it designates a deeper immersion into the temporality of life and action as a place where human existence is *not* at home, but where it finds itself instead dislocated from its familiar framework. Heidegger states it clearly in that he stresses how the deeper structure of temporality is 'outside of itself' (Heidegger 2010: 329). Temporality is not a being but 'a temporalizing in the unity of its exstasies'. It is only with the so-called 'vulgar' or conventional understanding of time that time is seen as a 'pure succession of nows', and that the 'ecstatic character of primordial temporality is levelled down'. In short: the present of the moment (*Augenblick*) opens the way to a destruction of the present of the 'now' (*Jetzt*). It all hinges on the quality and nature of the present and on how it is lived and enacted.

I summarize what has been said so far. The expanded technological mastery of time together with the historicist framework for understanding the past converge in the production of the present as a time-slot or now-point in the sequence of a presumably endless sequence that stretches from the past into the future. This representation of time occludes the deeper historical and temporal condition of human life as itself a being that gives shape to time and that only *understands* history to the extent that it *engages* in history. Benjamin gives voice to a similar idea when he speaks of resisting the yoke of historicist time to become instead an agent of time. For both, it is a question of wrestling tradition away from a conformism inherent in its self-understanding and representation. When we consider the discussion around the different concepts of the present in this light, we can also grasp the real stakes involved in this terminological battle. The challenge is to discharge the coercive force of a given time-regime of ordered temporal progression of nows by entering the temporality of the *Augenblick* as the dislocated exterior and ecstatic temporality of both epistemological and political action. The struggle concerning the present is thus also a struggle concerning presentness as such and of how to think it beyond its technological-theoretical domestication.

The temporality of the *Augenblick* in Heidegger's – and that is true also of Benjamin's version – marks a counter-movement against technical and political homogenization of time. It is explicitly anti-chronological, and as such it constitutes a revolutionary temporality, or a temporality of revolutionary action. It works against the homogenization and chronologization of time that is presumably produced by synchronized communication systems and also by epistemic regimentation of historical time. It seeks to reveal their origin in life's datability. And by collapsing the objective time frame into this constitutive and dislocated present of the *Augenblick*, it also seeks to open itself up to its future transformations.

In current attempts to escape what is perceived as a shrinking horizon of presentism, some voices are gesturing towards big, deep, and long history as possible remedies for an increasingly myopic present. But whichever way we turn, and whatever distant historical evidence we bring to the table, we cannot escape the hermeneutical situation in which our historical imagination is shaped and from within which it seeks its orientation. If we do not think the temporal and existential condition of historical knowledge such gestures will easily shrink down to just another extension of the given historicist normative temporal framework to which Benjamin refers in his theses. The heightened temporality of the present implied by the notion of the *Augenblick* does not constitute a move into an irrational dimension of time, as opposed to a presumably rational-chronological framework. On the contrary, it locates itself at the edge of the temporal-historical imagination, insisting that we keep open the foundations of its own possibility also in our way of inhabiting this temporal domain. It invites us to question the technologically generated mathematical-chronological time frame in relation to the lived temporality. It thus enables us to see how history and historical awareness can also cover over human historicity or the historical in history.

In his later writings, Heidegger would gradually abandon the term *Augenblick*, in favour of *Ereignis*, or the 'event'. In his *Contributions to Philosophy (of the Event)*, written during the years 1936 to 1938 and published posthumously in 1989, he speaks intermittently of *Ereignis* and *Augenblicks-stätte*.[6] But in his most important work besides *Being and Time*, namely his extraordinary Nietzsche-interpretation that was first presented as lectures in the years 1936 to 1940 and then published in 1961, the philosophical stakes around the question of the *Augenblick* are raised to a maximum. In the final section I will analyse how Heidegger there approaches the enigmatic allegory from Nietzsche's *Zarathustra* of the gate of the *Augenblick* and the spirit of gravity that was recalled above. It brings together both the potential and the disturbing ambiguity of this revolutionary politics of time.

Nihilism and the redemptive politics of the *Augenblick*

In the section 'On the Vision and the Riddle' in Nietzsche's *Thus Spoke Zarathustra*, the protagonist tells a story of how he was wandering upwards in a desolate landscape, seeking 'elevation' while struggling with the 'spirit of gravity' in the form of a dwarf who whispers in his ear that everything 'must fall' (Nietzsche 2005: 134–8). Suddenly they find themselves before a gate on which the word is written: *Augenblick*. Zarathustra tells the dwarf of how in this present now-point the infinite past and the infinite future come together and confront one another. And since the world has lasted forever and will last forever it will have come back to this point again and again: 'And are not all things knotted together so tightly that this moment draws after it all things that are to come? Thus itself as well?' At this point Zarathustra hears a dog howling, and sees a young shepherd, into whose mouth a snake has crept. After having first tried to pull it out from the boy's mouth, Zarathustra screams at him to bite off the head of the snake. And as the boy bites and spits it out, he bursts out in joyous laughter: 'No longer shepherd, no longer human – one transformed, illumined, who laughed! Never yet on earth had a human being laughed as he laughed!'

Zarathustra presents this strange and disturbing story as a 'riddle' that requires an interpretation. In his monumental study of Nietzsche, Heidegger returns to this scene on several occasions, gravitating towards the enigmatic *Augenblick* around which the narrative is based as a site of both risk and redemption. He writes: 'It is not a matter of just any vision or just any riddle about something or other. It is a matter of that particular riddle with which Zarathustra comes face to face, *the* riddle in which being as a whole lies concealed' (Heidegger 1979: 37). In Heidegger's reading the dwarf represents a view of time as an endless circular sequence. He does not see what Zarathustra sees, namely how the past and the future come together and 'affront one another' (Heidegger 1979: 56). This is only accessible, he writes, to someone 'who does not remain a spectator, but who *is himself* the moment (*Augenblick*), performing actions directed toward the future and at the same time accepting and affirming the past [. . .]. To see the moment means to stand in it' (Heidegger 1979: 56–7). To Heidegger this is the most difficult aspect of the doctrine of the eternal recurrence, namely that 'eternity is in the moment, and that the moment is not the fleeting now (*Jetzt*)'. The moment marks the fusion of understanding and action, because only one who acts historically will have access to history. It is a revolutionary moment, because in and through this temporality, history and its conventional-normative orders and calendars are exposed to their possible reversal. It is thus also a volatile and potentially violent moment. Heidegger does not draw this conclusion explicitly, but it is implied by the logic of what follows. The 'most difficult matter', he writes, is also something that remains 'a sealed door to little men'. Yet these so-called 'little men' – the direct reference here is the figure of the dwarf in the story, but its real extension is indefinite – exist and they do not go away, on the contrary they too return: 'they cannot be put out of action; they pertain to that side of things that is dark and repulsive' (Heidegger 1979: 57).

One hundred pages later, he returns again to a detailed discussion of the mysterious encounter between Zarathustra, the dwarf and the shepherd. And here he is more explicit about what the serpent in the shepherd's mouth represents, namely 'drear monotony, ultimately the goallessness and meaninglessness of nihilism' (Heidegger 1979: 179). He continues to state that this nihilism cannot be overcome 'from outside', as when we 'replace the Christian God with yet another ideal, such as Reason, Progress, political and economic "socialism" or mere democracy'. The black snake of nihilism must instead be confronted by those who are prepared to 'bite into the danger'. This action is also a thought, since the thought can only take the form of an action. To *think* the gateway or the moment is equivalent to *enact* a decision through which 'prior history, the history of nihilism is brought to confrontation and forthwith overcome' (Heidegger 1979: 185). To properly think the moment, and thus to think the present in the form of an *Augenblick*, requires that we 'transpose ourselves to the temporality of independent action and decision, glancing ahead at what is assigned us as our task and back at what is given us as our endowment' (Heidegger 1979: 185). To think time, to think history, indeed to think eternity, is to think a moment as an action whereby we come into our own and thus assume the task of being-a-self (*Selbststein*).

To think the thought of the present is to engage the present and to bring it in confrontation with itself, thus fusing thought and action. In Heidegger's case this amounted to an involvement in the National Socialist revolution as rector for the University of Freiburg. For Benjamin, the attempt to think time and history from the viewpoint of an *Augenblick* as a constitutive temporal caesura was fused with his hopes for a socialist revolutionary transformation of the present. But irrespective of their different political choices, Heidegger's analysis can still serve as a means to explore how human existence on one level is called to respond not just to some specific historical challenge, but to the constitution of the temporal-historical framework as such. The gate of the *Augenblick* opens thinking to the inner dynamism of temporality itself, where decisions have to be taken that concern the overall orientation of the acting individual in time. To engage with this foundational situation is not equivalent to securing thinking and acting in any particular orientation. It is instead the challenge to descend towards the foundation of the temporal-historical ligature that holds historical time together. And here the concrete *engagement* in the present will emerge not just as a choice within time, but also of and with time as such.

Beyond Heidegger's particular understanding of the history of nihilism and his political choices, his analysis of the temporality of the moment and its connection to the historical offer us a rare view into the existential and political consequences of the formation of historical awareness as also a route to commitment and action. Its peculiar 'presentism' – its insistence on the constitutive role of a decisive *moment* – is also the key that opens the space of the historical situatedness of existence to its own inner instability and transformation. It gives access to an understanding of how every historical-chronological framework is a volatile construction and as such also open to its inner transformation.

The paradox or antinomy that was recalled at the outset can now be viewed from a wider perspective. It is true that the thought of the *Augenblick* in Heidegger – and also in Benjamin – designates an intensified present, thorough which the historical as such is reflected. As such it can be seen as a theoretical anticipation of the symptom today diagnosed as *presentism*. Yet at the same time, the whole problem of the *Augenblick* is directed precisely towards a critique of the present understood as 'now' (*Jetzt*), namely as a technically and epistemically construed segment of time that ultimately veils the underlying condition of existential temporality and historicity.

We can mobilize any number of historical archives, and we can expand the time-lines to the known corners of the universe. We can take in the full width of the predicament not only of humans, but of the Earth as such, which we now take to have existed for approximately five billion years, with an expected future of approximately seven billion years, but with a capacity to sustain biological life only for another hundred million years. But even reminding ourselves of these vast timescales does not take away the philosophical significance of confronting the underlying condition of our temporal being and belonging, because it is from this perspective that we also glimpse into the possibility of new orders of time and new historical narratives.

The *Augenblick* implies both closure and openness. It holds the potential for a radical-revolutionary politics as well as a critical assessment of technological presentism. Even though it implies a critique of the effects of processes of rationalization, it is not in itself irrational. Rather, it opens the door towards a hyper-rationality, since it takes aim at the very emergence and construction of temporal ordering as such, pointing towards the intersection of time, understanding and action. It discloses the human predicament as never quite at home in time combined with a technical desire to precisely to control and inhabit time.

In the end, it releases thinking from the ruse of full mastery of time, exposing it to the unyielding responsibility of always having to inhabit time anew.

Notes

1   This fundamental idea was to have a decisive impact on Ricoeur's and Gadamer's philosophical hermeneutics (and via the latter also Koselleck), and also on Derrida's deconstruction and Foucault's genealogy. For a recent survey of the genesis and legacy of this topic, see Ruin 2018. See also Ruin 1994a for a broader background. The specific topic of the *Augenblick* is also treated in Ruin 1998.

2   The story of the gate of the *Augenblick* and the encounter with the spirit of gravity is found in the beginning of part three of *Thus spoke Zarathustra*, in the section entitled 'On the Vision and the Riddle'.

3   For a more extensive analysis of Yorck and his contribution to historical thinking, see Ruin 1994b.

4   In Ruin 2019 I develop this analysis in the direction of a more explicit ontology of history as a 'being with the dead', where the Dasein 'having-been' is explicitly explored as the other no longer living. In confronting history, we confront, converse with, and care for the dead.

5   For the historical-etymological background to the word and topos of the *Augenblick* (from Paul and Kierkegaard), see chapter Five in Ruin 1994a and also Ruin 1998. Cf. also Falkenhayn 2003 and Ward 2008.

6   For an elaborated comparison between these two terms and their inner transformation, see Ruin 1994a, chapter 5 and also Ruin 1998.

References

Benjamin, W. (1968), 'Theses on the Philosophy of History', in his *Illuminations*, ed. H. Arendt, transl. H. Zohn, 253–64, New York: Schocken Books.

Dilthey, W. and Yorck von Wartenburg, P. (1923), *Briefwechsel zwischen Wilhelm Dilthey und dem Grafen Paul Yorck von Wartenburg 1877-1897*, Halle: Niemeyer.

von Falkenhayn, K. (2003), *Augenblick und Kairos: Zeitlichkeit im frühwerk Martin Heideggers*, Berlin: Duncker und Humblot.

Heidegger, M. (1979), *Nietzsche, Vol I–II*, transl. D. Farrell Krell, San Fransisco: Harper.

Heidegger, M. (1989), 'Phänomenologische Interpretationen zu Aristoteles. Anzeige der hermeneutischen Situation', *Dilthey-Jahrbuch*, 6: 237–69.

Heidegger, M. ([1927]2010), *Being and Time*, transl. J. Stambaugh, Binghamton: SUNY Press.

Husserl, E. (1965), 'Philosophy as Rigorous Science', transl. Q. Lauer, in E. Husserl, *Phenomenology and the Crisis of Philosophy*, 71–147, New York: Harper & Row.

Löwith, K. (1986), *Mein Leben in Deutschland*, Stuttgart: Metzler.

Nietzsche, F. (1980), *On the Advantage and Disadvantage of History for Life*, transl. P. Preuss, Indianapolis: Hackett.

Nietzsche, F. (1984), *Human, All Too Human. A Book for Free Spirits*, transl. M. Faber and S. Lehmann, Lincoln: University of Nebraska Press.

Nietzsche, F. (2005), *Thus Spoke Zarathustra*, transl. G. Parks, Oxford: Oxford University Press.

Ruin, H. (1994a), *Enigmatic Origins. Tracing the Theme of Historicity Through Heidegger's Works*, Stockholm: Almqvist & Wiksell.

Ruin, H. (1994b), 'Yorck von Wartenburg and the Problem of Historical Existence', *Journal of the British Society for Phenomenology*, 25 (21): 111–30.

Ruin, H. (1998), 'The Moment of Truth: *Augenblick* and *Ereignis* in Heidegger', *Epoche*, 6: 75–88.

Ruin, H. (2018), 'Historicity and the Hermeneutic Predicament: from Yorck to Derrida', in D. Zahavi (ed.), *The Oxford Handbook for the History of Phenomenology*, 717–33, Oxford: Oxford University Press.

Ruin, H. (2019), *Being with the Dead: Burial, Ancestral Politics, and the Roots of Historical Consciousness*, Stanford: Stanford University Press.

Ward, K. (2008), *Augenblick. The Concept of the 'Decisive Moment' in 19th- and 20th-Century Western Philosophy*, Aldershot: Ashgate.

6

Time Outside History

Politics and Ontology in Franz Rosenzweig's and Mircea Eliade's Reimagined Temporalities

Liisi Keedus

If any question why we died,
Tell them, because our fathers lied

R. Kipling, *War Epitaphs*[1]

'The study of history ... no longer holds the centre of my attention,' wrote Franz Rosenzweig (1886–1929), a young German Jewish philosopher in 1920, having returned from the Balkan front of the First World War (Rosenzweig 1999: 25). Before joining the army as a volunteer, Rosenzweig had completed a brilliant doctoral dissertation, *Hegel and the State*, under the guidance of Friedrich Meinecke, one of Germany's most esteemed historians. The work was an exercise in historically oriented philosophical research, as well as an expressed confidence in the modern state as the promise of transcendence from individualist subjectivity – as a higher and more superior reality. Now the young author himself called it a book that 'could no longer be written' (Rosenzweig 1962: xiii). Nothing seemed more grotesque to him than the Hegelian idea of rational history as a march towards progress, culminating in the modern state. Instead, history had come to mean war, violence and ruin; it was little else but a stage for an irrational and brutal struggle for power.

Indeed, 'we find ourselves once again in the pre-Hegelian position,' noted Mircea Eliade (1907–1986) in the immediate aftermath of the next World War (Eliade 1959: 140). He dedicated the final chapter of his first major theoretical contribution, *The Myth of the Eternal Return: Cosmos and History* (1949), to what he phrased as the problem of 'terror of history' – and the chapter resonated with his interwar political and literary obsession with rethinking historical time. The Hegelian concept of historical necessity had been practically applied to justify, if not be compliant in 'all the cruelties, aberrations, and tragedies of history' (Eliade 1959: 148). As a Romanian scholar and novelist, Eliade was keen to point out that while history may have once embodied a new kind of purely human freedom for major European powers, for secondary peoples, or 'nations marked by the "fatality of history"' it meant 'continuous terror' (Eliade 1959: 152) – 'sufferings and catastrophes' (Eliade 1959: 142) without either hope, consolation or meaning. Yet it was more than the senselessness or cruelty of recent events that Eliade sought to capture when highlighting the 'despair' that he argued had set on the human condition framed by historical consciousness. Perhaps even more importantly, Eliade's modernity was marked by an abysmal finitude, transience, and by what was in fact a failed promise of freedom – the fact that man was not the maker of history but simply subsumed by it – 'exhausted' by temporality in its new, entirely 'desacralised' and, hence for Eliade, barren existence. The price the West had paid for confining its horizons to the exclusively historical temporality was, in Eliade's, at least in this respect, Spenglerian narrative, its loss of rigour and creativity.

In several ways, Rosenzweig's and Eliade's critiques erupted and evolved within much broader currents of anti-historicism fuelled by the experiences of the newly dehumanized world after the Great War. The War had its roots, or so reasoned especially the younger generation (Wohl 1979), in the imperialism and industrialization of the nineteenth century. Yet the nineteenth century was also 'the century of history': in the more general sense because of the popularization of historical consciousness, especially national consciousness based on a sense of shared history, but also with its widely shared sense that temporality had an inherent meaning, purpose and direction (Koselleck 2004). Past versions of unchanging and universal natural law and natural right were increasingly contested as static and constructed, and replaced by organic understanding of individual human communities with their own unique dynamic of development – for the evaluation of which no universal viewpoint existed (Meinecke 1972). It was only its later critics that characterized this worldview in its various forms as 'historicist' and in this sense 'historicism' was by its birth an anti-term. For these mostly young critics, this modern replacement of transcendent truth and morality had translated into moral relativism wherein Might coincides with Right (Rosenzweig 1962: 88ff) and anthropocentric messianism that culminated in the global slaughter (Mosès 2008; Myers 2003). Moreover, like for Rosenzweig and Eliade, for their many contemporaries, endowing history with inherent linearity, coherence and meaning had resulted in a new and desperate emptiness of human time. This total history had devoured the individual man into the imagined mankind, it had also turned every single act or deed into a stepping stone inevitably subordinate to the next one to follow. The modern man still longed to be greater than his mortal life – but now it had come to mean submersion into and identification with the anonymous and ghastly flow of history (Benjamin 1969; Arendt 1961; Strauss 2013; Myers 2003).

Yet what makes Rosenzweig's and Eliade's critiques at least to some extent stand out, or unusual, in this wider stream of discontent with the previously dominant historical paradigm, was that they additionally adopted an outcast's perspective, as it were, on the flow of history, and, consequently, into their attempts to radically reimagine temporality. Rosenzweig was a German Jew, and his parents' generation had taken it for granted that their community was seamlessly integrated into German life and culture. Indeed, the young thinker himself had volunteered to join the army (Glatzer 1998). Now, this seemed like both an ill-placed illusion and a dangerous mistake for Rosenzweig and his like-minded Jewish peers who all rejected the previously inevitable seeming process of assimilation of the Jewish minority into the German nation – soon the dominant position among the young Weimar Jewish intellectuals (Myers 2003). Similarly, Eliade's formative experience as a Romanian was that of living at the margins of history. He also steered away from advocating his country's entrance into the progressivist history and historical consciousness, and turned this apparent weakness into a valuable resource instead.

Both Rosenzweig and Eliade used their experiences as outcasts as the basis of their criticisms of the idea that human existence is primarily historical and historically conditioned. But, in addition, they expanded on this experience theoretically, placing their communities as if outside, or even beyond history, and using this alternative relation to history as a basis of an alternative temporal ontology – which then in turn had a much wider reception than only within their immediate audience. Moreover, they also translated their experientially and politically grounded novel conceptions of time into methodological revolts against dominant historical approaches in the human sciences. In what follows, I will explore the ways in which these seemingly distinct concerns became synchronic in their thought, as well as suggest that these efforts resonated with their readership significantly beyond their specific scholarly fields. Also, while the anti-historicist revolt is more familiar from accounts of Weimar intellectual and cultural history (Gordon and McCormick 2013; Keedus 2015), I want to pave the way to an understanding that it is only a distinctively European narrative that can capture the full ramifications and legacies of this fundamental rupture in thought.

'It walks unperturbed through history': Rosenzweig's Jewish eternity

During the war, Rosenzweig abandoned the adherence of his youth to the idea of the unique and historic mission of the German nation and nationalism as historicism's political descendant. 'Nationalism expresses not merely the peoples' belief that they come from *God* [. . .] but that they go *to* God. But now peoples do have this belief, and hence 1789 is followed by 1914–1917, and yet more 'from . . . to's' (Rosenzweig, cited by Mosès 2008: 29). The consequences of the divinization of a nation were for Rosenzweig, like for many others, arrestingly plain to see, as were the implications of the Hegelian reasoning that the unfolding of history, including its wars, is not only the unfolding of necessity but also an expression of morality. Yet in his major philosophical work, *The Star of Redemption* (1920), Rosenzweig did not so much seem to be arguing that Hegel had misunderstood the course of universal history of emerging and decaying nations but rather suggesting that his reflections were arrestingly right (Mosès 2008: 35ff). Nonetheless, Rosenzweig saw a number of problems with this, of which I will briefly outline only two, as well as refused to grant this historicity totality or see it as the only temporality.

First, when modern communities had shed their faith in the Christian promise of eternity, the state became an attempt 'to give the peoples eternity in time'. Yet 'the State is the ever-changing form under which time moves to eternity step by step' (Rosenzweig 2004: 352). All the 'world nations', and this distinguishes them from the Jewish people, can preserve longevity beyond a generation 'only by safeguarding a place for (themselves) in the future' (Rosenzweig 2004: 317) and 'appropriate from its permanence a guarantee of their own permanence. Their will to eternity clings to the soil and to [...] the territory' (Rosenzweig 2004: 318). Land, however, is conquered, and as the people on it perish, even if the land persists, so 'the earth betrays the people' (Rosenzweig 2004: 318). In other words, there is an irreconcilable discord between the nations' hope placed in the teleological movement of time and their desire to preserve themselves in this change. On the one hand, nations are not only born but also devoured by the universal history, and the 'sweetness' of the sense of national belonging is inseparable from the 'bitterness' of the presentiment of its death 'however far off' (Rosenzweig 2004: 324). On the other hand, aside the external forces played out in wars, the internal dynamic of states is no less violent. Permanence within the state is just as elusive: the positing of law seems to halt the ceaseless alteration, yet 'since time cannot be denied, movement triumphs' (Rosenzweig 2004: 353). Without this change, a people would not be alive, yet the contradiction between the new and the old law is always solved by 'violence'. 'Therefore war and revolution are the only reality that the State knows' (Rosenzweig 2004: 553).

Second, Rosenzweig shunned the historicist idea of progression that, he argued, contained the secularized notion of redemption, which is self-contradictory as it would mean the completion of history, or the cessation of time. Further, its horizons and vision of the final condition are inevitably narrow and confined to the logic of the already existing convention – which it translates into *the* reality. The only time that it can imagine is irreversible, causal, continuous and linear, and while change and movement are the essence of history, these are composed of the mere quantitative accumulation of the very same logic. There is only a variety of combinations of the same reality, repetition of war and violence, with no imaginary space for radical alterity (Rosenzweig 2004: 235–44). Rosenzweig's criticism is evasive and scattered – and can probably be grasped only in contrast to his own concept of Jewish redemption – but Stéphane Mosès has helpfully captured its understanding of progress in terms of organic evolution, and in this sense as condemned hope (Mosès 2008: 49ff). There is hope inscribed in each human act that the final victory belongs to the Good, 'but the realization of that hope must inevitably be postponed from day to day, as a horizon that retreats indefinitively as we approach it' (Mosès 2008: 50). So on the one hand, this hope is limited to mere quantitative change, excluding any radical transformation, and on the other, the movement is towards both an endlessly retreating and an impossible goal.

However, in contrast to all the 'peoples of the world', Rosenzweig's Jews voluntarily render themselves to political infertility and thereby refuse to participate in the Hegelian cycle of triumph and fall of other nations. They live at the margins of history, which is first of all sealed by the fact that they don't have a homeland: it is over territories that wars are fought but from this too the Jews distance themselves (so while Rosenzweig was anti-assimilationist, he was by no means a Zionist, which has made his legacy in Jewish thought controversial). Instead, their community and its eternity are based on the significance of religion rather than politics for their identity, their experience of proximity to God, as well as a continuity of 'blood' and sense of electedness – and this communion is secured precisely by detaching themselves from politics, and thus from history (Rosenzweig 2004: 317–55). 'The Jewish spirit,' Rosenzweig emphatically declared, 'breaks through the shackles of time. Because it is eternal and aims for the Eternal, it disregards the omnipotence of time. Indeed, it walks unperturbed through history' (Rosenzweig, cited in Myers 2003: 103).

From the perspective of world history or history of other nations, the Jews could be seen to be renouncing life itself – 'the true eternity of the eternal people must remain always foreign and annoying to the State and to world history' (Rosenzweig 2004: 354). Yet for Rosenzweig this merely means distancing themselves from transience sealed by the flow of emergence and disappearance of nations. It also means that the Jews are the only community that survive this necessity: if temporal life is denied to them, it is 'for the sake of eternal life. [. . .] It cannot fully and creatively also live the historical life of the peoples of the world, it is always somehow between a worldly and a holy life' (Rosenzweig 2004: 323). From the perspective of historical time, the Jews are separated from each other and they lack a visible communion, yet it is through the creation and participation of their 'own eternity' that they ensure their continuance across and beyond time. Noteworthily, Rosenzweig granted this concept of timelessness at least potentially universalist implications, relating it to the promise of peace: 'The Jew is the only man [. . .] who cannot take war seriously, and therefore is the only genuine "pacifist"' (Rosenzweig 2004: 351).

What creates then this 'eternity not as the twelfth stroke of the world clock, but as that which coincides with the present of every hour' (Rosenzweig 2004: 325)? First, the living of Rosenzweig's Jews in a nonhistory is warranted by the religious tradition and its ritual life, resulting in 'a static temporality, structured year after year by identical cycles of religious holidays, a lived eternity [. . .] in the spaces of sacred time' (Mosès 2008: 44). In contrast to the historical times of secular chronology, already in the annual cycle of liturgical time, the Jews experience proximity to God, their community, their shared past and their awaited future – with all being simultaneously and really present. Historical time is not eliminated, but participating in symbolic time allows one to transcend it. For example, Exodus is not merely commemorated at Passover, or remembered as a *past* event in daily prayers, but celebrated each time as a *presently* occurring event and thereby renewed – and thus it is 'the cycle of the year (that) guarantees its eternity to the eternal people' (Rosenzweig 2004: 352). These festivities are traces of eternity in the otherwise monotonous flow of quotidian time, flashes of a radically different reality.

Second, in contrast to the hope for progress that places the final end to indefinite future, the promise of redemption inserts the future into the present (and the past). Redemption is the central concept in Rosenzweig's thought and he used it to articulate – not the relation between God and the world – the collective human initiative that is defined by a waiting for a better world and acts upon it (Rosenzweig 2004: 221ff). Unlike the hope for progress, this hope – which Rosenzweig called redemption – is not historical but symbolic. It is the miracle against all odds, a new beginning, an act or a stroke of lightning, the exception that defies the law, in other words, the moment when normal ways of human history are breaking down (Rosenzweig 2004: 271). Unlike the hope for progress, it is not a distant horizon but can appear unexpectedly at any time; there is no infinite path leading to it, but it is inherently interruptive; instead of an accumulation or improvement of the familiar, it is an intrusion asserting a radically and qualitatively new world (Mosès 2008: 49ff). This hope both represents radical alterity but in a way is at the same time lived and immediately present through rituals and symbolism – nonetheless remaining, as noted, a category articulating the relation between man and the world.

Rosenzweig's extraordinary dedication to practical and open-minded Jewish community work – in which he engaged despite debilitating illness that left him unable to talk or write and led to his untimely death at the age of 42 – may well be seen to exemplify and explain what he might have meant by this category of expectation defying, miracle-like alterity. To Rosenzweig, the Jewish experience of timelessness in any of the above senses was nothing that was simply there as present and available. To the contrary, it had been concealed from his own post-assimilationist generation and one of the ways to regain it was – not merely to wait and hope – but to seek it in the past yet untouched by history (Löwith 1942). This too was no simple task and, for this purpose, Rosenzweig founded what was to become an immensely popular Free Jewish Study House (*Freies jüdisches Lehrhaus*) in Frankfurt. The adult learning institution sought a path of return to one's Jewish roots through knowledge of their pre-modern sources, and reflection of their immediate impact on contemporary Jewish life – and notably, was boycotted by the Frankfurt orthodox Jewish community (Brenner 1996: 69–128).

The Study House was a strikingly multi- and interdisciplinary educational and cultural institution, as well as the driving force behind several prominent Jewish publications, including the nationally distributed and widely read monthly magazine *Der Jude*. The school also brought together intellectuals and social activists from the entire political spectrum, from the Left to the Right, but also from very different fields, such as law, politics, religious studies, sociology, philosophy, arts and aesthetics. Although there was considerable diversity between the instructors and their methods, Rosenzweig's purpose was to encourage pedagogical innovation. This could mean a variety of experiments, but one of the most conspicuous among them was the rejection of historical learning. Instead, Rosenzweig reportedly asked his students to begin instruction with whatever moved them in their daily lives, and then the class jointly explored the past Jewish sources that might be relevant for addressing these issues. The emphasis was on one's immediate emotional bond to the tradition and its untying from the mediation of historical knowledge (Brenner 1996: 69–128). Interestingly, Rosenzweig's source of inspiration for Jewish timelessness and how to practise it in one's own daily life was his frontline encounter with the Balkan and, later, other Central and Eastern Jews, whose metahistorical aloofness, even absence, from their political contexts and unmodern religiousness fundamentally differed from those of the assimilated German and French Jews (Mosès 2008: 44).

'Condemned to history'? Eliade's plural time

Against the historical consciousness of the West, Eliade similarly set what he would call 'anhistorical' cultures and nations, like the nations of the Balkans. He too deemed the latter as a sort of misfit both in the sense that, first, any teleological or holistic historical narrative seemed absent from their lives and, second, they had always been subject to history making by external, more significant powers. First, what Eliade called 'progressive history' justifies the 'historical nations' embarking on civilizing missions upon others. Second, it also forces experiences that are conflicting and dislocated within the narrative of progress – like those of Romanians, for whom it would have been nothing short of obscene to endow what had been forced upon them as 'continuous terror' with some inherent meaning – into oblivion, insignificance, even, in the historical sense, into inexistence (Eliade 1959: 139ff). To adopt the inherently hierarchical historical consciousness by these so-called secondary people would mean to be erased and engulfed by it, but also to internalize one's inferiority, dislocation and, perhaps even, senselessness.

Like Rosenzweig, Eliade embarked on a quest for a new vision of history that would move not only beyond the belief in humanity's progress, but also the spirit of assimilation and politico-cultural imperialism. On the one hand, Eliade's verbalism 'terror of history' was certainly rooted in the European apocalyptic mood that the occidental culture was at its dusk. This Spenglerian diagnosis also identified the modern historicist stance, described as retrospective, passive and relativist, as one of the causes of the West's loss of rigour, creativity and even vitality. The modern historical consciousness is marked by focus on change, desire for novelty, pleasure in the fleeting moment of the present, but it lacks exemplary models to follow and instead the empty notion of progress is taken as such a model (Wittkau 1992). We reject transhistorical norms and ideals to aspire to – which for Eliade were sources of creativity and meaning. On the other hand, as we saw, the young Romanian author's 'terror of history' expressed his judgement on the idea that some nations are more progressed than others (Eliade 1961b, 1959: 152n). Yet on neither front did he advocate a resigned position and like Rosenzweig was more original than following a simple narrative of decline, focusing his explorations, instead, on alternative experiences of temporality and the possibilities contained therein.

Already, at a very young age, Eliade had became obsessed with the problem of time and its non-Western and pre-modern perceptions. He was inspired by the combination of static and cyclical temporalities of his fellow countrymen, but additionally spent several years in India where he became particularly captivated by local multi-layered experiences of temporality. Anecdotally, when he returned he began experimenting with radically cutting sleeping hours so as to gain more time for study, and also embarked on his lifelong search through peasant symbolism and Indian religious practices for methods to manipulate psychosomatic time. His preoccupation with radically rethinking time is particularly conspicuous in his highly popular fictional work, where we see him as anything but resigning to Western conceptions of temporality (Călinescu 1988). His protagonists can shift temporalities from present to past in 'enchanted' and 'forbidden' locations, from profane to sacred times to retrieve loved ones lost in the war and depart again with them, or change their age through ordinary yet miraculous interruptions. While time is a central motif in his novels, it is neither conventionally linear nor continuous, but far more ambiguous, often imaginatively bordering the fantastic, where ordinary events and time all of a sudden form a bridge to the transcendent, the supernatural and the extraordinary. These interruptions are rare yet real openings to escape the inherent 'despair' that Eliade believed was inscribed into completely profane, historical time (Călinescu 1988).

Eliade did not reserve the possibility of transcending historical time only for fiction, far from it. 'How is it possible to resolve the paradoxical situation,' is the recurrent question of his later academic work,

> created by the twofold fact that man, on the one hand, finds himself existing in time, *condemned to history*, and, on the other hand, knows that he will be 'damned' if he allows himself to be exhausted by temporality and by his own historicity and that, consequently, he must at all costs find *in the world* a way that leads into a transhistorical and atemporal plane?
>
> Eliade 1982: 242–3

Dedicating much of his scholarly attention to exploring this question, Eliade preserved his youthful fascination for the 'cosmic Christianity' of his native Romania as one example of a culture and way of life underpinned by its 'heterogeneous' temporalities. Pre-Christian (in Eliade's judgement, Romanian Christianity had not shed its pagan elements) and non-Western cultures not only experienced time as such fundamentally differently, but most significantly for Eliade their 'profane time' remained entwined and enjoyed access to 'sacred time' (Eliade 1987: 71; Eliade 1958: 388).

For Eliade, sacred, symbolic time is the time of either, first, the taking place of a ritual when one steps into sacred time or, second, during the performing of a mythical model through which one passes into a sacred story or a myth, and thus also into a sacred time. The commonest example is that each New Year's Eve marks the recreation and the reordering of the world. It is a promise and a chance for a new life, both for an individual and a community, while at the same time preserving permanence and a sense of purpose amidst historical instability and arbitrariness (Eliade 1987: 85ff). Through symbols and rituals, men can participate in the 'eternal present of the mythical event' (Eliade 1987: 89), in the universal and timeless structure of the world. They speak of and direct the individual towards symbolic, poetical and mythical knowledge, they provide a connection between a person as a microcosm to the macrocosm, as well as give coherence to time – and so relieve men from the anxieties, arbitrariness and contingency of their historical situatedness.

While historical time is irreversible, Eliade's mythical time, like Rosenzweig's ritual time, is reversible and repeats the time of the beginnings. When one participates in this practice of repetition, one not only commemorates the time of the beginnings, but relives and participates in the sacred, in the most real mode of being. Profane time transforms into sacred time through recreating the primordial beginning, thus through memory, which is in turn creative action. Eliade's 'beginnings' are more immediately related to the sacred, transcendent, universal (Eliade 1987: 68ff). This ahistorical mode of temporality, Eliade insisted, is also associated with the impulse to create and creation is constitutive of the human condition, and it is therefore that the homogenously historical time of modernity undercuts the fertility of Western cultures (Cave 1993: 83).

It seems, nonetheless, that instead of Eliade's modernity having successfully and definitively 'desacralized' time, it has merely settled into a temporary confusion (Eliade 1987: 89, 201ff). Like Rosenzweig, Eliade seemed to suggest that the experience of symbolic and sacred time has not altogether vanished, but remained the 'ground and model of all human history' (Eliade 1967: 178), 'a paradigmatic history which man has to follow and repeat, in order to assure the continuity of the world, of life and society' (Eliade 1967: 180). In this sense, continuity between archaic mythological thought and modern life has not been completely broken, and both in his scholarly work and in his fiction, Eliade sought to disclose 'the nonhistorical portion of every human being' (Eliade 1961a: 13), the 'primordial' dimensions of existential and religious experience that 'belong to man as such, not to man as a historical being' (Eliade 1964: xiv). While the sacred is irreducible, it is not opposite or separable from the profane, it is contained in, defines and qualifies the secular (Eliade 1987: 68ff). The quotidian life reduced to homogeneous time may indeed be incomprehensible, void of meaning and even obscene, yet when it opens itself up to plural time, the everyday life too may be bursting with meaning – and for Eliade, the miraculous expresses itself through the unconscious, archetypes immerse through symbols present in our only apparently ordinary routines (Călinescu 1988: xiii–xiv).

Furthermore, Eliade also argued that myth and its social and spiritual functions are misunderstood if labelled as fiction, and ought to be examined instead as endeavours to 'reveal the *truth par excellence*' (Eliade 1967: 171). The human imagination is mythological by its very structure and mythologies are necessary both for individuals and communities for orienting themselves in the world and for intensifying individual and communal lives within larger universes of meaning. While in his later work Eliade did not explicitly explore the political and social implications of his argument – or in fact seems to leave these intentionally undeveloped – his interwar political writings centre on the problem of history and action (Eliade 1990). This is not to say that they fill the gap left in Eliade's later work but, rather, that they testify to the political thrust behind his lifelong engagement with rethinking human time.

In the late 1920s and 1930s, the young Eliade was an active and outspoken member of prominent and publicly ambitious intellectual groupings, such as *Generation '27* and *Criterion* – which both called for the 'rejuvenating' of culture and the nation. To this aim, the crisis of historical consciousness represented an unprecedented promise and opening instead of conveying a sense of threat. Eliade's articles in the daily newspaper *Cuvântul* set forth his vision of Romania that, rather than remaining a perpetual follower of the allegedly progressive and in fact imperialist and colonialist West, would explore its own specific 'path'. In the groupings' manifestos, *A Spiritual Itinerary* (1927) and *The White Lily* (1928), their affiliates announced themselves as 'anti-1848-ers', 'parricidal', 'autochthonous' and 'experiential': 'We were the first generation that was not previously conditioned by a historical objective to be achieved' (Eliade 1994: 38). Moreover, the 'young generation' ought to act without delay – they ought to create their own culture while there was still time. However, in the 1930s, Eliade's optimism turned into an active support for Romania's neoorthodox and fascist Legionary movement, and this has discredited his declared pursuit of the Romanian version of 'neither Left nor Right' or of some sort of a political new way (Boia 2011: 21–47, 90ff, 161ff).

In the newly traumatized world, pre-1914 notions of teleological history not only seemed eerily misrepresentative of modernity, but ideological accomplices of nationalism and imperialism as mainsprings of the War. The historical self-conception of Western man was no longer testifying to his greatness and creativity but bespoke the human ability to commit previously unimagined atrocities. The certitude of the historically self-constituting agent had entered the dusk of its credibility – and Rosenzweig and Eliade both found themselves in the already post-metaphysical, but also in the newly post-secular and post-humanist age. One of their shared responses was the attempt to articulate a novel anti-historical temporal ontology – one that was both within the reach of and tangible for the human condition but at the same time transcended it. This attempt required nothing less than exploding the perceived circular structure between the ontological framework based on history as continuity and causality, political ideology of progress, ethics of historical relativism and, additionally – as will be elaborated in what follows – epistemological claims of the historical nature of all knowledge.

The past without history: Rosenzweig's and Eliade's hermeneutic revolts

The Frankfurt Study House was one of the epicentres of a series of hermeneutic upheavals that rattled the German humanities and social sciences in the 1920s. Its extraordinary methodological innovativeness can largely be traced back to Rosenzweig's personal openness and encouraging stance towards experimentation in teaching and scholarship, but also to the extraordinary social engagement and interdisciplinarity of its many and very diverse lecturers. Regular instructors at the school included the educationist Ernst Simon, the sociologist Leo Löwenthal, the economist Franz Oppenheimer, the cultural critic Siegfried Kracauer, the psychologist Erich Fromm, the philosophers Leo Strauss and Martin Buber, the critic and women's rights' activist Bertha Pappenheim and the scholar of Jewish mysticism, Gerschom Scholem, among many others (Brenner 1996). Their interests and teaching of course varied, yet one of the recurrent patterns for several of them was their rejection of historical methods and the search for alternatives.

For example, while Rosenzweig's own pre-war dissertation, *Hegel and the State*, was in a number of ways a conventional Diltheyan exercise in German historical-philosophical scholarship, his subsequent teaching and writing, as well as directorship of the Study House, sought to break with the established tradition of German historical scholarship. The teaching at the school paid particular heed to engagement with the Jewish earliest sources – the distant past – yet consciously ignored the historical scholarship as distortive of the past (Rosenzweig 2002; Löwith 1942). In other words, its attraction to the distant past was at the same time a rejection of recent history and its historical methods. According to its critics, the historicist imperative to historicize and contextualize the pursuit of the truth and of faith was blind to their own belonging to a particular, history-centred era. It claimed the historical contingency of all truths, yet at the same time the universal applicability of that of its own – and thus contained not only a tension but possibly misdirected the approach to sources that were paradigmatically differently constituted (Keedus 2015). Thus instead of the previously dominant emphasis on the contextual interpretation, Rosenzweig and several other Study House scholars advocated a closely text-bound reading that underlined the intactness and autonomy of the textual sources. The meaning of the text was only obscured by references to its historical context; instead, the reader ought to be guided, for example, by the text's specific integral clues, its component parts: its narrative structure, style, language and use of metaphors (Myers 2003: 68ff).

Another ambitious project was Rosenzweig's and Martin Buber's translation of the Hebrew Bible into German. They avoided translating the text into a more familiar sounding literary German and instead made it as literal as possible, calling their work 'Verdeutschung' ('Germanification') of the text. Often this meant coining neologisms in German, breaking conventional grammar and syntax rules. They rejected the idea that one could somehow retell or present the content of the Bible in the modern language, omitting for example some of its mythical and dogmatic elements. This was to not only distort the message itself, but also to confine engagement with biblical texts within contemporary frameworks, and in this sense, limit their potential to expand one's horizons. Thus instead, the translation needed to preserve the text's 'uncanny' difference from modern mentality and confront the reader with an entirely different imagination – only in this manner opening a genuine possibility to see, feel and think beyond the contemporary convention. The holy text's 'command' upon the Jew entailed the promise of radical disruption of one's habitual reality and perception, and thereby of responding anew to these biblical sources, but this promise could only actualize through preservation of the sense of strangeness, dislocation and 'uncanniness' (Rosenzweig 2002). The category of 'uncanniness' has a more generally central place in Rosenzweig's thought (as well as for other Lehrhaus teachers), as he also used it to describe Jewish self-contained isolation and difference in the world (Blond 2010; Batnitzky 2000: 83ff, 99ff) – hence its preservation in past texts and rituals becomes at least doubly important.

Eliade, who has been called an 'antihistorian of religion' (Dudley 1976: 44–8) indeed explained his 'phenomenological' methodology in contrast to the 'historical' approach (Eliade 1963). While he claimed that his own work was cross-disciplinary, one of his reproaches against historical scholarship was still that it tended to erase the autonomy of the study of religion, subsuming it, for instance into the history of art, literature, general history and so on, until the subject matter has just about dissolved (Eliade 1955). It has been pointed out that Eliade's methodological anti-historicism is based on at least three uses of 'history' (Strenski 1973; Allen 1988). First, he reproached historians for presenting 'chronicles', an antiquarian recording of events or sets of events. Second, Eliade's 'historical positivism', with its alleged scientism and empiricism, omitted human intentions and meanings. Third, he believed historical study of religion was too immersed in specific cultural contexts to pay heed to what for Eliade were obvious 'transhistorical' and 'prehistorical' elements of the sacred and that, moreover, 'condition the lower or historical meanings' (Allen 1988: 549).

On the one hand, Eliade acknowledged that the sacred can only become manifest within a particular historical, spatial and cultural context. He even claimed that there 'is no such thing outside of history as a "pure" religious datum [...] Every religious experience is expressed and transmitted in a particular historical context' (Eliade 1968: 250). On the other hand, he was wary of thereby making religious experiences reducible to nonreligious domains of human life (Eliade 1958: xiii). Moreover, Eliade insisted that there is 'no religious form that does not try to get as close as possible to its true archetype, in other words, to rid itself of "historical" accretions and deposits' (Eliade 1958: 462). Focused on a study of cross-cultural resemblances in religious practices and phenomena, he insisted these cannot be explained by reference to a common historical origin. He argued that these were evidence for nonhistoric myths and symbols, for nonhistorical, ontologically transcendent structures and phenomena, such as archetypes. Thus while historical research is necessary, it remained for Eliade a secondary means for recognizing transhistorical structures and meanings. Strictly historical scholarship is unable to establish that religious phenomena are specific to certain historical periods or societies. At best, historical research can demonstrate that particular contexts are favourable for the manifestation of one or another type of religious phenomena or experience. 'So at some point the historian of religion must become a phenomenologist of religion, because he tries to find meaning. Without hermeneutics, the history of religion is just another history – bare facts, special classifications, and so on' (Eliade 1973: 101–6).

Rosenzweig wrote on a variety of topics, including Jewish education, religion, history and politics, yet it was the interdisciplinarity of the Jewish Study House that sealed the unprecedented scope of his legacy across disciplinary boundaries. Despite his too early death his thought and life work continued to inspire and engage thinkers from many fields (Anckaert, Brasser and Samuelson 2004), among whom were Walter Benjamin, Karl Löwith, Jacob Klein, Emil Fackenheim, Emmanuel Levinas, Jacob Taubes and Jacques Derrida, in addition to those mentioned as Study House instructors. Needless to say, Rosenzweig's reception moved through these scholars from interwar Germany to postwar Israel, the United States, and other European countries.

Eliade's reception has been similarly multidisciplinary and possibly geographically even wider. He spent several interwar and postwar years in Portugal and France, emigrating to the United States in 1956, where he established his reputation as the key figure in founding the field of history of religions or comparative study of religions. His academic work has been translated into all European and several Asian languages and while his universalist ambitions in comparative religions have been at the very least controversial, their global impact on cultural and gender studies, and also anthropology and even art history, has remained monumental.

Conclusion

Let us conclude with a tentative answer to the overdue question – why consider Rosenzweig and Eliade in tandem? After all, they thought and wrote in strikingly different contexts, partly in different times, had divergent scholarly and political aims, and even their attempts to rethink time are only partly convergent.

First of all, their respective discontents with a variety of historicisms – and concurring ontological, political and methodological mentalities – are exemplary of the wider tide of anti-historicism(s) across interwar Europe, the transnational reach of which is seldom considered. Of this reach, even without considering other thinkers with similar concerns elsewhere, speak their extraordinarily vast audiences and intensely interdisciplinary engagement with their scholarly work. Second, while themes such as fascination with the distant past and endeavours to access it without the mediation of 'history', interest in the supra-historical human condition, assertion of the fragmentation and discontinuity of the human world and time, and emphasis on defamiliarization in exploding conventions are more familiar from avant-garde arts, music and literature, both Rosenzweig's and Eliade's works are illustrative of inserting the avant-garde *topoi* in interwar scholarship. More specifically, we saw how they translated their experience of the contemporary crisis and political criticism of its causes into a novel ontology and methodological experimentation, weaving the former into the very fabric of the latter. Third, I further argued that what distinguished Rosenzweig's and Eliade's thought from the wider discontent with 'history' were their experiences as outsiders, on the basis of which they constructed not only an alternative relation to history but new, at least potentially universal, temporal ontologies. Fourth, Rosenzweig's and Eliade's proposals alike on rethinking human temporalities and constructing bridges between the past, present and future were doubtless unconventional and compelling, even if highly controversial. While today's 'presentism' is our very own challenge to answer, the two thinkers' boldness in criticism, language and imagination may nonetheless continue to inspire experimentation and questioning beyond the conventionally reasonable – especially as the subject matter itself, the human time, can only partly be confined within the language of *ratio* (as they too amply remind us). Lastly, their universalist quests for transcending temporal transience, for caesuras of eternity in midst of human time, appear themselves deeply contextually rooted. Nonetheless, potentially more illuminating than pointing at this tension as a matter of the past, would be to use Rosenzweig's and Eliade's work to reflect on the similar situatedness of our own theoretical approaches to historicity – on how these are rooted in our hopes and fears, as well as shaped by our aims and revolts.

Note

1   I thank Arthur Smith for sending these lines to me on the day when I was finishing this paper. The research for the first draft of the paper has received funding from the Mobilitas research grant (MOBTP18) and for the final draft from the European Research Council under Grant Agreement No. 757873 (Project BETWEEN THE TIMES).

References

Allen, D. (1988), 'Eliade and History', *The Journal of Religion*, 68 (4): 545–65.
Anckaert, L., Brasser, M. and Samuelson, N., eds (2004), *The Legacy of Franz Rosenzweig: Collected Essays*, Leuven: Leuven University Press.
Arendt, H. (1961), 'The Concept of History: Ancient and Modern', in her *Between the Past and Future: Six Exercises in Political Thought*, 41–90, New York: Viking Press.

Batnitzky, L. (2000), *Idolatry and Representation: The Philosophy of Franz Rosenzweig Reconsidered*, Princeton: Princeton University Press.

Benjamin, W. (1969), 'Theses on the Philosophy of History', in *Illuminations*, ed. H. Arendt, 253–64, New York: Harcourt.

Blond, L. (2010), 'Franz Rosenzweig: Homelessness in Time', *New German Critique*, 111 (3): 27–58.

Boia, L. (2011), *Capcanele istoriei. Elita intelectuală românească între 1930 și 1950*, Bucharest: Humanitas.

Brenner, M. (1996), *The Renaissance of Jewish Culture in Weimar Germany*, New Haven: Yale University Press.

Călinescu, M. (1988), 'Introduction', in M. Eliade, *Youth Without Youth and Other Novellas*, i–xxxix, Chicago: Chicago University Press.

Cave, D. (1993), *Mircea Eliade's Vision for a New Humanism*, Oxford: Oxford University Press.

Dudley, G. (1976), 'Mircea Eliade as the "Anti-Historian" of Religions', *Journal of the American Academy of Religion*, 44 (2): 44–8.

Eliade, M. (1955), 'Mythology and the History of Religions', *Diogene*, 3 (9): 96–116.

Eliade, M. (1958), *Patterns in Comparative Religion*, London: Sheed and Ward.

Eliade, M. ([1949]1959), *The Myth of the Eternal Return: Cosmos and History*, New York: Harper.

Eliade, M. (1961a), *Images and Symbols*, Princeton: Princeton University Press.

Eliade, M. (1961b), 'History of Religions and a New Humanism', *Journal of Religion*, 1 (1): 1–8.

Eliade, M. (1963), 'The History of Religions in Retrospect: 1912–1962', *Journal of Bible and Religion*, 31 (2): 98–109.

Eliade, M. (1964), *Shamanism: Archaic Techniques of Ecstasy*, Princeton: Princeton University Press.

Eliade, M. (1967), 'Cosmogonic Myth and "Sacred History"', *Religious Studies*, 2 (2): 171–83.

Eliade, M. (1968), 'Comparative Religion: Its Past and Future', in W. Ong (ed.), *Knowledge and the Future of Man*, 245–54, New York: Holt, Reinhart and Winston.

Eliade, M. (1973), 'The Sacred in the Secular World', *Cultural Hermeneutics*, 1: 101–13.

Eliade, M. (1982), *A History of Religious Ideas*, Vol. 2, Chicago: Chicago University Press.

Eliade, M. (1987), *The Sacred and the Profane: The Nature of Religion*, New York: Harcourt.

Eliade, M. (1990), *Profetism românesc*, Bucharest: Roza vinturilor.

Eliade, M. (1994), *Fragmentarium*, Bucharest: Humanitas.

Glatzer, N. (1998), *Franz Rosenzweig: His Life and Thought*, Cambridge: Hackett Publishing.

Gordon, P. and McCormick, J., eds (2013), *Weimar Thought: A Contested Legacy*, Princeton: Princeton University Press.

Keedus, L. (2015), *The Crisis of German Historicism: The Early Political Thought of Hannah Arendt and Leo Strauss*, Cambridge: Cambridge University Press.

Koselleck, R. (2004), *Futures Past: On the Semantics of Historical Time*, New York: Columbia University Press.

Löwith, K. (1942), 'M. Heidegger and F. Rosenzweig or Temporality and Eternity', *Philosophy and Phenomenological Research*, 3 (1): 53–77.

Meinecke, F. (1972), *Historicism: The Rise of a New Historical Outlook*, London: Routledge and Kegan Paul.

Mosès, S. (2008), *The Angel of History: Rosenzweig, Benjamin, Scholem*, Stanford: Stanford University Press.

Myers, D. (2003), *Resisting History: Historicism and its Discontents in German-Jewish Thought*, Princeton: Princeton University Press.

Rosenzweig, F. (1962), *Hegel und der Staat*, Aalen: Scientia Verlag.

Rosenzweig, F. (1999), *Franz Rosenzweig's 'New Thinking'*, ed. A. Udoff, New York: Syracuse University Press.

Rosenzweig, F. (2002), *On Jewish Learning*, Madison: The University of Wisconsin Press.

Rosenzweig, F. ([1920]2004), *The Star of Redemption*, Madison: The University of Wisconsin Press.

Strauss, L. (2013), *On Tyranny*, Chicago: University of Chicago Press.

Strenski, I. (1973), 'Mircea Eliade: Some Theoretical Problems', in A. Cunningham (ed.), *The Theory of Myth: Six Studies*, 43–52, London: Sheed and Ward.

Wittkau, A. (1992), *Historismus: Zur Geschichte des Begriffs und des Problems*, Göttingen: Vandenhoeck und Ruprecht.

Wohl, R. (1979), *The Generation of 1914*, Cambridge, MA: Harvard University Press.

7

Pictorial Temporality and the Times of History

On Seeing Images and Experiencing Time

Johannes Grave

At first sight, images are not of particular importance for any reflection on the nature of history and historical time. The past might seem more accessible or tangible when it is portrayed in a picture. But generally speaking, from a historical point of view images share with textual accounts and other documents the central problem that they only offer mediated representations of something that is no longer there. Each picture has been subject to choices, arrangements as well as formal and aesthetic decisions by its creator; thus, it does not directly render the past present but represents it in a limited and filtered way. Even though images might serve as sources and may be used to analyse personal or collective imaginations, they are considered as merely one of many groups of objects that we have in mind when we try to get access to the past.

Against this widespread theoretical indifference concerning images, the following thoughts are meant to argue for the assumption that the reflection on images or pictures on the one hand and theories of history on the other share some crucial problems and paradoxes. This intuition may seem a little bit more plausible in the light of a surprising empirical observation: Quite a few influential concepts or theories of history explicitly refer to pictures or to the notion of the image. When philosophers or historians think about history, time, temporality and experience they often choose images in order to exemplify their point of view. In some cases, the references to images go even further and shall help to find answers to central questions of the theory of history. By referring to Frank Ankersmit, Walter Benjamin and Georges Didi-Huberman I will try to elaborate on the question of whether there is any closer relationship between the theory of history and notions of the image. After having summarized some intuitions of these thinkers, I will sketch the outlines of a theory of images or pictures that contributes to our understanding of history and historical time. In order to do so I will refer to both images and pictures without differentiating between them at each point of my argument – in doing so, I pick up a productive ambiguity of the German notion 'Bild'. It will become apparent that the theory of history has to look at images (in the sense of the Latin word *imago*, which also includes mental images) as well as at pictures (in the sense of *pictura*) in order to be able to learn from image theories.

The questions that could tentatively be answered this way primarily concern our notions of time and temporality. In the following I try to argue that images and pictures invite us to rethink our understanding of historical time(s). They call our attention to a complex interplay of multiple times and help to grasp what it means to conceive of the past as something that may be absent and present at the same time.

Entanglements between theories of history and concepts of the image

Scholars interested in art history or in image theories may be surprised by the number of theoreticians that explicitly or implicitly refer to images when they develop and explain their concepts of history or, to be more precise, the way they understand the temporality of history. While some of these references seem to be merely anecdotal, others are closely linked to central arguments of the theoretical project. This already holds true for early theoreticians of history like Johann Martin Chladenius. For his notion of 'Sehepunkte', which serves to consider the perspectivity of different eyewitnesses and interpreters of historical events, is inconceivable without a concept of mental images (Völkel 2011). But perhaps references to images or pictures recently even have increased and attract more attention in times when the field of theory of history tries to transcend the limitations of narrativist approaches (see, e.g., Runia 2014: ch. 4). Among a vast and diffuse number of very different theories that in some way or other draw on the notion of the image I single out only three exemplary approaches.

Frank Ankersmit

Considering my first example, Frank Ankersmit, it is difficult to decide on the importance and relevance of his pictorial example. In his inaugural lecture at the University of Groningen, 'The Historical Experience' (Ankersmit 1993, 2012), Ankersmit included some remarks on a painting by the Venetian artist Francesco Guardi (Figure 7.1). With his major contribution, *Sublime Historical Experience* (2005: 266–75), Ankersmit picked up this example. He not only integrated an interpretation of the picture into his theoretical discourse, but chose to show a reproduction of the painting on the cover of his book. From an art historical point of view, this decision is rather surprising and startling. The *Capriccio con sottoportico e maschere di Pulcinella* (ca 1780–85, Bergamo, Accademia Carrara) exemplarily demonstrates Guardi's qualities as a painter of *capricci*, in other words, of fantastic pictorial arrangements of imaginary and real buildings (see Craievich and Pedrocco 2012: 177). But these *capricci* neither illustrate historical facts nor were they supposed to stimulate sublime feelings. Indeed, Ankersmit himself stresses that Guardi's painting above all evokes the experience of tedium and deep ennui. But, by doing so, the painting fits perfectly into the broader concept of 'historical experience' that is central for Ankersmit, who insists on a fundamental rupture between past and present. By contemplating Guardi's painting, Ankersmit experiences a feeling that is essentially strange to the modern or postmodern subject. This experience of strangeness itself is present and, at the same time, lets him feel our distance to the epoch of the Ancien Régime.

Figure 7.1 Francesco Guardi, *Capriccio con sottoportico e maschere di Pulcinella*, ca 1780–1785, oil on canvas, 42 × 29 cm, Bergamo, Accademia Carrara. Courtesy of Accademia Carrara.

With his much contested concept of 'historical experience' Ankersmit looks for a way to 'enter into a real, authentic and "experiential" relationship to the past [...] that is not contaminated by historiographical tradition, disciplinary presuppositions, and linguistic structures' (Ankersmit 2005: 4). By doing so, he seeks to answer the question of why we are moved by the past and on which grounds historical consciousness may emerge. Ankersmit defines 'historical experience' as something that is both ephemeral and inconspicuous. It is rooted in individual phenomena that are decontextualized, appear isolated and baffle familiar correlations of meaning. 'Historical experience', in his view, befalls us involuntarily like a sudden event. Therefore, it is not due to ingenious intuition or inspiration; instead, the subject is passively overpowered. Such moments of 'historical experience' often are provoked by unconscious incoherencies or by something strange within a familiar context. They provide, in Ankersmit's opinion, the rare chance to have a direct and unmediated experience of the past or, to put it in a more sophisticated way, to experience the 'contiguity' between subject and object. That's why Ankersmit associates 'historical experience' closely with authenticity. In my opinion, it is not by chance that this concept shows striking similarities to Roland Barthes' notion of *punctum*, which is something that 'pierces' and 'wounds' the observer, a 'personally touching detail that establishes a direct contact' (Stewart 2007: 6; see Ankersmit 2005: 424, note 95; Barthes 1981; Jay 2005: 390).

It's not my task to judge on the plausibility and persuasiveness of Ankersmit's notion of 'historical experience' or to point at open questions and possible shortcomings of this concept (see, e.g., Roth 2007, or Icke 2012). Instead, I want to stress its particular relationship to images. For Ankersmit primarily exemplifies this experience by referring to Guardi's painting. In his description and interpretation of the picture he not only concentrates on its iconography and the depicted scene but also turns his attention to Guardi's composition and the application of perspective. For the following it doesn't matter that, in my opinion, Ankersmit's analysis of the painting is not completely convincing. More important is the fact that he starts to face an unmediated 'historical experience' by stumbling upon incoherencies between that which is represented and the representation itself. It is the specific formal and figural arrangement of the painting that allows him to realize incoherencies and tensions which, in turn, provoke a temporal process of contemplation. As we will see, such incoherencies are typical of images and rooted within their fundamental properties. By no means has Ankersmit considered the idea that pictures could have a special status within his concept of 'historical experience'. But the example of contemplating Guardi's *capriccio* is deeply rooted in the particularities of pictures.

Walter Benjamin

On first impression, the second example I briefly want to introduce is completely different. In his *Arcades Project* (*Passagen-Werk*) Walter Benjamin not only occasionally builds on and refers to pictures, but he puts the notion of image at the core of his fragmentary theory. Within the framework of his theory of history Benjamin's concept of the 'dialectical image' is of essential importance in order to understand his historical materialism. On several occasions Benjamin formulates in a very dense manner what he means by 'dialectical image' and why this notion is crucial for our access to the past:

> It is not that what is past casts its light on what is present, or what is present its light on what is past; rather, image is that wherein what has been comes together in a flash with the now to form a constellation. In other words: image is dialectics at a standstill. For while the relation of the present to the past is purely temporal, the relation of what-has-been to the now is dialectical: not temporal in nature but figural [*bildlich*]. Only dialectical images are genuinely historical – that is, not archaic – images. The image that is read – which is to say, the image in the now of its recognizability – bears to the highest degree the imprint of the perilous critical moment on which all reading is founded.
>
> Benjamin 2002: 463 [N3,1][1]

The notion of image serves to overcome conventional forms of the production of meaning and to circumvent unilinear or unidirectional relations between past and present without leading towards a blending that results in blindness for their differences.

Conventional narration seems to be the hidden enemy that has to be avoided. The image, however, allows the what-has-been and the now to be co-present and tangible at the same time. They form a constellation that does not reduce one of them to being the cause or the result of the other. In another fragment Benjamin explains more specifically how such images emerge:

> To thinking belongs the movement as well as the arrest of thoughts. Where thinking comes to a standstill in a constellation saturated with tensions – there the dialectical image appears. It is the caesura in the movement of thought. Its position is naturally not an arbitrary one. It is to be found, in a word, where the tension between dialectical opposites is greatest. Hence, the object constructed in the materialist presentation of history is itself the dialectical image. The latter is identical with the historical object; it justifies its violent expulsion from the continuum of historical process.
>
> Benjamin 2002: 475 [N10a,3][2]

Dialectical images are not simply given (for instance by tradition); they are not detectable amongst the bulk of pictures of the past that survived until now. It's rather the process of historical thinking that can provoke the emergence of dialectical images if it is not reduced to purely chronological and causal relations. Without any doubt, Benjamin distinguishes between images and pictures. He clarifies explicitly that he does not primarily refer to paintings, drawings, prints, sculptures or photographs when he talks about 'dialectical images': 'Only dialectical images are genuine images (that is, not archaic); and the place where one encounters them is language' (Benjamin 2002: 462 [N2a,3]).[3] These images protect themselves against any reification and permanent consolidation.[4] Thus, they prevent an externalization of the past that is typical for any attempt to rationally master and control history.

Nevertheless, Benjamin's reflection on and thinking 'in' images is deeply influenced by his experiences with pictures. As Sigrid Weigel (2014) and Steffen Haug (2017), amongst others, have shown, Benjamin constantly worked with different types of pictures and took great benefit out of this practice. It is not by chance that Benjamin uses the notion of image to conceptualize an experience that combines the temporality of a sudden flash with the tension of simultaneously given 'dialectical opposites'. To put into a phrase: Benjamin's notion of image is not dependent on the tangible pictures, but the picture most probably served as a model, a paradigm to conceive the complex concept of 'dialectical images'. Intuitively it seems difficult to understand pictures as instances of dialectics and as temporal, ephemeral phenomena. But as Ankersmit's contemplation of Guardi's painting already indicates, there are indeed good reasons to conceive of pictures as settings for tensions and incoherencies that can only be realized by a strongly processual and dialectical mode of thinking.

Georges Didi-Huberman

Similar arguments can be found in the work of Georges Didi-Huberman who partly relies on Benjamin's ideas. As Didi-Huberman (2000, 2002) combines the perspectives of philosophy and art history he focuses on pictures, but in doing so he implicitly also develops a theory of history. Didi-Huberman argues against traditional ways of conceptualizing and practising art history. In his view, it is inadequate and misleading to take pictures as mere visual documents to gain positive knowledge about the past. Rather than 'taming' pictures by placing them in a chronological ordered and teleological directed history he wants us to regard them as objects that create or break time. For him anachronism is not a cardinal error which has to be avoided, but a main feature of pictures as historical phenomena. Depictions quite often refer to specific events, times or temporalities, but, at the same time, the process and moment of production is an integral and vital part of the picture itself and resonates in the process of viewing and contemplating it. This palimpsest of different time-layers even gets more complex if we consider the trivial fact that the beholder experiences the picture in the present – and often as it were for the first time:

> Before an image, however old it may be, the present never ceases to reshape, provided that the dispossession of the gaze has not entirely given way to the vain complacency of the 'specialist'. Before an image, however recent, however contemporary it may be, the past never ceases to reshape, since this image only becomes thinkable in a construction of the memory, if not of the obsession. Before an image, finally, we have to humbly recognize this fact: that it will probably outlive us, that before it we are the fragile element, the transient element, and that before us it is the element of the future, the element of permanence. The image often has more memory and more future than the being who contemplates it.
>
> Didi-Huberman 2003: 35

As the act of contemplating an image touches very different temporalities, each encounter with an image necessarily is 'an anachronistic enterprise' (Moxey 2013: 61). Didi-Huberman himself concludes: 'It is better to recognize the necessity of anachronism as something positive: it seems to be internal to the objects themselves – the images – whose history we are trying to reconstruct. In a first approximation, then, anachronism would be the temporal way of expressing the exuberance, complexity, and overdetermination of images' (Didi-Huberman 2003: 37).[5]

By slowly and partly uncovering the palimpsest of the image, Didi-Huberman unfolds the inherently complex and overdetermined nature of 'historical time' itself. Images are particularly striking cases for the complexity of the 'times of history', because they demonstrate in an exemplary manner the powerful 'survival' of forms and images (*survivance, Nachleben*). By picking up this concept, originally conceived of by Aby Warburg, Didi-Huberman (2002) calls our attention to phenomena that undermine and intersect the frontiers between distinct historical times and, against all odds, re-emerge at certain moments.

To a certain degree, Benjamin's and Didi-Huberman's approaches can be regarded as complementary. Whereas Benjamin resorted to the notion of image to answer fundamental questions of the theory of history, Didi-Huberman primarily addresses the specific visual experience of encountering a picture. In the context of our argument Didi-Huberman's observation is particularly interesting, because it indicates that the entanglement and layering of different temporalities within and in front of pictures has itself a fundamental temporal structure. We only experience the constitutive anachronism of images if we invest time while contemplating a picture. By doing so, we stumble upon incoherencies and tensions within time and history.

Preliminary conclusions

What about these three ways of historical thinking that – in spite of many fundamental differences – seem to converge in a shared interest in *both* history *and* the image? Are these convergences simply accidental, arbitrary and idiosyncratic? Or is it possible to identify specific features and qualities of images that make them particularly interesting and helpful for any reflection on history and its temporalities? Before having a closer look at images and their specificities, it will be helpful to briefly summarize some latent similarities of the theoretical positions that I have mentioned. In my opinion, they share – apart from their interest in images (or pictures) – one common argument: Challenging or exigent experiences of the past are inherently contradictory and conflictual. They necessarily imply tensions or even contradictions between different levels of experience and knowledge. Whereas in Ankersmit's notion of 'historical experience' unmediated access to the past (or 'contiguity') comes along with our knowledge of the fact that a historical phenomenon is temporally distant, Benjamin's concept of the 'dialectical image' points at moments when movement and standstill are coinciding and when that which has been and the Now form a constellation. With his notions of 'anachronism' and 'survival' Didi-Huberman regards history as an entanglement of multiple contradictory phenomena. It is not by chance that he also refers to dialectical tensions. Actually, he even tries to temporalize the notion of dialectics in order to avoid that it might be brought to an end by a final result. It's obvious that the three approaches are – in many respects – hardly comparable. But in their unique and different ways Ankersmit, Benjamin and Didi-Huberman revolve around the intuition that history is not given, manifest or accessible and that it cannot simply be subjected to a 'presentification'. Instead, historical experience implies an entanglement of that which has been with the Now, an interlacing of past and presence, thus, it is deeply characterized by tensions and contradictions.

It is this specificity of historical experience that entails its particular temporality: In order to fully realize tensions or contradictions, we need time. We might instantly be able to *conceptualize* the coincidence of opposites, but it is only by temporal processes that we can fully *experience* them. We have to focus on one position of this never-ending dialectics at one moment and concentrate on its opposite the next in order to be able to realize its contradiction. Therefore, historical experience stands out due to (1) its inherently contradictory nature and (2) its specific temporality that helps to unfold this fundamental tension or contradiction.

If we understand historical experience in this way, the use of pictures and the reference to images becomes more plausible. As images are characterized by a similar tension and comparable temporality they are particularly helpful paradigms to reflect on historical times. Thus, conversely, it is *not* the frequently overestimated alleged power of images to render the past or the distant present that makes them productive for the reflection on historical experience. I doubt that there are any images that give us the impression of returning to the past and, simultaneously, let us ignore the distance between our presence and the past. Images do not serve to overcome the peculiarities and complexities of the temporality of history. Instead they open up new ways to make these complexities accessible to theoretical thinking.

The temporality of pictures and its implications for historical experience

When historians refer to a picture they often focus on two aspects of its temporality. The picture is either taken as a historical source that – after critical examination – may provide some information about the past by representing, e.g., objects of everyday life or particular events; or it is understood as an expression of a collective memory and widespread imaginations. However, before pictures and images (in a broader sense) can address these rather specific points, they are already involved in different layers of time: Besides depicted events or situations they imply traces and 'resonances' of the process of production, the aging and deterioration of the picture carrier, processes of perception as well as the memories and expectations of the viewer (Grave 2014). Furthermore, the supposedly simple act of viewing takes its own time. The perception of pictures cannot be understood as the simultaneous view of a given visual entity, rather it takes places within the framework of its own temporality when the eye of the beholder follows predetermined traces or establishes new ways of exploring the depiction. Each act of perceiving pictures implies processes by which different elements of the given depiction are related to each other (Grave 2016). It is this process of perception that realizes the manifold temporal layers, which are implied in any image and that become relevant in any situation that takes places in front of pictures. The temporal process of perceiving pictures is highly dependent on contingent, situational and ephemeral factors; but it is nevertheless influenced by figural and formal properties of the picture in question. Each picture opens up possibilities of temporal experiences or limits the multiple ways in which the process of perception unfolds. The representational, formal, sensuous and material properties of pictures shape the potential temporalities of the reception process. The temporality of perception insofar as it is predetermined or influenced by the picture has to be taken into account both by art history and by image theories.[6]

For pictures this temporality is of crucial importance as they are generally concerned with a paradoxical entanglement of presence and absence: Inasmuch as pictures show things, people or events, they make visually accessible what is – spatially or temporally – absent. This peculiarity already becomes clear when we refer to the probably most basic definition of pictures that derives from its semantics: *picture* or *image of x*. Dealing with images we intuitively presuppose an object x to which the image refers. But by showing something else, the picture necessarily also shows itself. This specificity of the image has been conceptualized as its duality (Kulvicki 2014: 13). It distinguishes the image from other objects and, at the same time, implies a particular temporality of its perception. Images, especially pictures, are characterized by an 'ambiguous unity of image vehicle and image object' (Pichler and Ubl 2014: 116; see also Pichler and Ubl 2018) that bears the potential to provoke tensions and contradictions. For the picture can only represent something else by presenting itself to the gaze of the beholder.

In the light of Edmund Husserl's (1980: 28–34) terminology this problem can be grasped in a more differentiated way: While that which appears in the picture, the subject of the picturing or *image subject* (*Bildsujet*), is usually absent, the *physical image* (*Bildding*) with the materiality of the image carrier, the means of representation, colours etc., is vividly and materially present at the moment of perception. Between these two instances mediates the *image object* (*Bildobjekt*), i.e., the 'representing object' that appears in the image carrier and is by no means identical to the external subject that served as reference for the depiction. Unlike ordinary signs, the picture does not point away from itself, but lets a particular, only visible object, the image object, appear, which features, as Lambert Wiesing (2009) has suggested, a purely 'artificial presence'. Although this is a presence without substantial attendance, the viewing of what appears in the picture is accompanied by a perceptual consciousness of the present. According to Husserl, the image consciousness of the observer makes it possible to experience the image object as sensually present, without confusing it with the presence of the thing itself. If the viewer is aware of being confronted with an image, he does not make the mistake of inferring from the artificial presence of the image object to a physical presence of the depicted subject. When something becomes present and vivid in the image, then the presence of the appearance of something absent occurs: the *image subject* remains absent, but its appearance takes place in the presence of the beholder. This specific form of presence distinguishes the image from ordinary signs that do not make something appear, but point away from themselves in order to refer to something else.

Therefore, pictures are characterized by an inherent antagonism. They confront their viewers with at least two objects simultaneously: the represented object, which appears by the means of the picture, and the picture itself with its physical appearance. An overly conspicuous presence of the image as a bordered flat object with its own materiality threatens to divert the view from the depicted. And quite analogously, concentrating on what appears in the picture can cause the viewer to briefly forget to stand in front of it. This is why any image that in any way refers to something else – to real objects as well as to phantasms – intrinsically implies a conflict that cannot be finally resolved in perception. The observer cannot help but repeatedly decide to focus either on what is depicted or on the image as an object in its own right.

With his concept of seeing-in, Richard Wollheim has elaborated an image theory by which this undecided battle of attention seems to be pacified. Wollheim (1980: 205–26; 1987: 43–100) assumes that when we look at images, we simultaneously perceive both the object that appears in the image and the picture itself in its own thingness and materiality (see also van Gerwen 2001). But recent research has modified Wollheim's argument insofar as tensions and rivalries between the various aspects of the image are accorded greater importance (Maynard 1994; Levinson 1998; Nanay 2011). It therefore is by no means out of the question that the ambiguity of the picture can stimulate shifts of attention, focusing at one moment on the represented and at the next moment on the image as a separate material object. Especially works of art such as, e.g., Guardi's painting (Figure 7.1) often stimulate complex processes of viewing. Whereas first we might take a closer look at the architecture and the scene that is represented, somewhat later formal or material qualities of the picture like the open and sketchy brushstrokes may attract our attention.

The fundamental antagonism between the represented object and the picture as an object in itself can only be realized and experienced in temporally extended processes of perception which unfold the conflicting elements of the picture's dual nature. In a sense, pictures could be taken as the most prominent examples of a *coincidentia oppositorum* – a coincidence of opposing and conflicting perceptual potentials, which are simultaneously given but need to be unfolded within time. If our view on pictures is not disciplined and domesticated by external conventions, by methods or by a functionalization of seeing, the picture inevitably becomes an object of a particular temporal and – potentially – historical experience.

Concluding remarks

By briefly referring to Ankersmit, Benjamin and Didi-Huberman we saw that challenging experiences of history are inherently contradictory. The 'times of history' are charged with tensions. Instead of linear and homogenous conceptions of time, they call for new models of polychronic temporalities in order to cope with the complexity of the past and its complex modes of presence. Recent attempts to transcend the boundaries of representationalism and narrativism have raised a new interest in the notion of 'presence'. It is apparent that the past cannot be entirely present in an unproblematic, evident sense; but, at the same time, things or places that are still accessible to us might have been in touch with the past and may serve as a substitute for what is gone (Runia 2014: 49–83). Eelco Runia (2014: 72, 79–80) has coined the notion 'presence in absence' to capture this particular mode of presence – which by no means should be confused with the much broader and vague desire for presence that has been expressed, e.g., by Hans Ulrich Gumbrecht (2004).[7] Runia's notion, instead, encompasses objects that metonymically can serve as substitutes for the absent past. But it also includes 'the absence (or at least the radical inconspicuousness) that *is* there', in which 'the thing that isn't there is still present' (Runia 2014: 72).

Exactly the same, seemingly paradoxical phrase 'presence in absence' has been used by Alva Noë (2012: 82–113) to conceptualize the specific mode of presence that is produced by pictures. For him, '[p]ictures have a distinct presence-in-absence structure; they enable us to encounter the presence of what is in fact absent; they give us access to a world beyond our reach. And moreover, they give us a kind of sensual or perceptual access' (Noë 2012: 86). Also in this case, it is clearly not the physical picture itself that allows for full access to the depicted object. As with the 'presence in absence' that characterizes experiences of the past, it is only in the course of the viewer's engagement with the picture that the image object becomes present.

It takes time to experience 'presence in absence'. Both in our relation to the past and in our perception of pictures we invest time in order to unfold the inherent tensions and incoherencies that characterize 'presence in absence'. This particular temporality seems to be the shared peculiar characteristic of pictures and history. Therefore it seems to be no mere coincidence that theories of history quite often refer to pictures or images. In doing so, philosophers and historians turn their attention to particular objects that – by means of their 'duality' – perfectly fit into the complex temporality of history itself.

Notes

1 'Nicht so ist es, daß das Vergangene sein Licht auf das Gegenwärtige oder das Gegenwärtige sein Licht auf das Vergangene wirft, sondern Bild ist dasjenige, worin das Gewesene mit dem Jetzt blitzhaft zu einer Konstellation zusammentritt. Mit andern Worten: Bild ist die Dialektik im Stillstand. Denn während die Beziehung der Gegenwart zur Vergangenheit eine rein zeitliche ist, ist die des Gewesnen zum Jetzt eine dialektische: nicht zeitlicher sondern bildlicher Natur. Nur dialektische Bilder sind echt geschichtliche, d.h. nicht archaische Bilder. Das gelesene Bild, will sagen das Bild im Jetzt der Erkennbarkeit trägt im höchsten Grade den Stempel des kritischen, gefährlichen Moments, welcher allem Lesen zugrunde liegt' (Benjamin 1982: 578). On the philological and systematic context of Benjamin's notion of 'dialectical image' see Hillach 2000; Zumbusch 2004: 57–71, 281–305 and 2018.
2 'Zum Denken gehört ebenso die Bewegung wie das Stillstellen der Gedanken. Wo das Denken in einer von Spannungen gesättigten Konstellation zum Stillstand kommt, da erscheint das dialektische Bild. Es ist die Zäsur der Denkbewegung. Ihre Stelle ist natürlich keine beliebige. Sie ist, mit einem Wort, da zu suchen, wo die Spannung zwischen den dialektischen Gegensätzen am größten ist. De[m]nach ist der in der materialistischen Geschichtsdarstellung konstruierte Gegenstand selber das dialektische Bild. Es ist identisch mit dem historischen Gegenstand; es rechtfertigt seine Absprengung aus dem Kontinuum des Geschichtsverlaufs' (Benjamin 1982: 595).
3 'Nur dialektische Bilder sind echte (d.h.: nicht archaische) Bilder; und der Ort, an dem man sie antrifft, ist die Sprache' (Benjamin 1982: 577).
4 See Benjamin 2002: 473 (N9,7): 'The dialectical image is an image that emerges suddenly, in a flash. What has been is to be held fast – as an image flashing up in the now of its recognizability. The rescue that is carried out by these means – and only by these – can operate solely for the sake of what in the next moment is already irretrievably lost.' Benjamin 1982: 591–2: 'Das dialektische Bild ist ein aufblitzendes. So, als ein im Jetzt der Erkennbarkeit aufblitzendes Bild, ist das Gewesene festzuhalten. Die Rettung, die dergestalt – und nur dergestalt – vollzogen wird, läßt immer nur an dem, im nächsten Augenblick schon verlornen [sich] vollziehen.' See also Kramer 2010: 119: 'Einerseits verdankt sich das dialektische Bild einer aktiv-destruktiven Operation, andererseits stellt es sich ein. Sobald es vorliegt, wirkt es unterbrechend. Die Reflexion auf die Geschichte konzentriert sich auf einen entscheidenden Punkt, anstatt rastlos kausale Verkettungen in der Geschichte nachzuvollziehen. Darin liegt die Chance, der konstitutiven Nachträglichkeit der Geschichtsbetrachtung zu entgehen. [...] Die Auseinandersetzung mit einem dialektischen Bild könnte dagegen eine Vergangenes für ein Jetzt erobern. In diesen Bildern liegt nämlich etwas gebunden, was das Subjekt oder das Kollektiv betrifft, dem sie sich zeigen. [...] wo kein Fortschritt im Denken mehr stattfindet, bringt die Konstellation, in die das Denken eingebunden ist, mit dem Bild eine Zäsur, also eine Unterbrechung hervor.

An diesen Vorgang knüpft Benjamin utopisch aufgeladene Vorstellungen, wie die des messianischen Umschlags, der Rettung und des Erwachens.'
5   See also Didi-Huberman 2002: 16: 'L'anachronisme serait ainsi, en toute première approximation, la façon temporelle d'exprimer l'exubérance, la complexité, la surdétermination des images.'
6   The German notion for this particular temporality of the image, 'rezeptionsästhetische Temporalität des Bildes' (Grave 2014: passim), is hardly translatable.
7   For a critical reading of Runia's thoughts on presence see Kleinberg 2013.

References

Ankersmit, F. R. (1993), *De historische ervaring*, Groningen: Historische Uitgeverij.
Ankersmit, F. R. (2005), *Sublime Historical Experience*, Stanford: Stanford University Press.
Ankersmit, F. R. (2012), *Die historische Erfahrung*, Berlin: Matthes & Seitz.
Barthes, R. (1981), *Camera Lucida. Reflections on Photography*, transl. R. Howard, New York: Farrar, Straus and Giroux.
Benjamin, W. (1982), *Das Passagen-Werk. Erster Teil* (*Gesammelte Schriften*, vol. V.1), ed. R. Tiedemann, Frankfurt am Main: Suhrkamp.
Benjamin, W. (2002), *The Arcades Project*, transl. H. Eiland and K. McLaughlin, Cambridge, MA: Harvard University Press.
Craievich, A. and Pedrocco, F., eds (2012), *Francesco Guardi 1712–1793* (exhibition catalogue Museo Correr, Venice), Milan: Skira.
Didi-Huberman, G. (2000), *Devant le temps. Histoire de l'art et anachronisme des images*, Paris: Éditions de Minuit.
Didi-Huberman, G. (2002), *L'image survivante. Histoire de l'art et temps des fantômes selon Aby Warburg*, Paris: Éditions de Minuit.
Didi-Huberman, G. (2003), 'Before the Image, Before Time: The Sovereignty of Anachronism', in C. Farago and R. Zwijnenberg (eds), *Compelling Visuality. The Work of Art in and out of History*, 31–44, Minneapolis: University of Minnesota Press.
Grave, J. (2014), 'Der Akt des Bildbetrachtens. Überlegungen zur rezeptionsästhetischen Temporalität des Bildes', in M. Gamper and H. Hühn (eds), *Zeit der Darstellung. Ästhetische Eigenzeiten in Kunst, Literatur und Wissenschaft*, 51–71, Hanover: Wehrhahn.
Grave, J. (2016), 'Form, Struktur und Zeit. Bildliche Formkonstellationen und ihre rezeptionsästhetische Temporalität', in M. Gamper, E. Geulen, J. Grave, A. Langenohl, R. Simon and S. Zubarik (eds), *Zeit der Form – Formen der Zeit*, 139–62, Hanover: Wehrhahn.
Gumbrecht, H. U. (2004), *Production of Presence. What Meaning Cannot Convey*, Stanford: Stanford University Press.
Haug, S. (2017), *Benjamins Bilder. Grafik, Malerei und Fotografie in der Passagenarbeit*, Paderborn: Fink.
Hillach, A. (2000), 'Dialektisches Bild', in M. Opitz and E. Wizisla (eds), *Benjamins Begriffe*, vol. 1, 186–229, Frankfurt am Main: Suhrkamp.
Husserl, E. (1980), *Phantasie, Bildbewusstsein, Erinnerung. Zur Phänomenologie der anschaulichen Vergegenwärtigungen. Texte aus dem Nachlass (1898–1925)* (Husserliana, vol. XXIII), ed. E. Marbach, The Hague: Martinus Nijhoff.
Icke, P. P. (2012), *Frank Ankersmit's Lost Historical Cause: A Journey from Language to Experience*, New York: Routledge.

Jay, M. (2005), *Songs of Experience: Modern American and European Variations on a Universal Theme*, Berkeley: University of California Press.

Kleinberg, E. (2013), 'Presence in Absentia', in R. Ghosh and E. Kleinberg (eds), *Philosophy, History, and Cultural Theory for the Twenty-First Century*, 8–25, Ithaca: Cornell University Press.

Kramer, S. (2010), *Benjamin zur Einführung*, Hamburg: Junius.

Kulvicki, J. V. (2014), *Images*, London: Routledge.

Levinson, J. (1998), 'Wollheim on Pictorial Representation', *Journal of Aesthetics and Art Criticism*, 56: 227–33.

Maynard, P. (1994), 'Seeing Double', *Journal of Aesthetics and Art Criticism*, 52: 155–67.

Moxey, K. (2013), *Visual Time. The Image in History*, Durham: Duke University Press.

Nanay, B. (2011), 'Perceiving Pictures', *Phenomenology and the Cognitive Sciences*, 10 (4): 461–80.

Noë, A. (2012), *Varieties of Presence*, Cambridge, MA: Harvard University Press.

Pichler, W. and Ubl, R. (2014), *Bildtheorie zur Einführung*, Hamburg: Junius.

Pichler, W. and Ubl, R. (2018), 'Images Without Objects and Referents? A Reply to Étienne Jollet', *Zeitschrift für Kunstgeschichte*, 81(3): 418–422.

Roth, M. (2007), 'Ebb Tide' (review of *Sublime Historical Experience*, by Frank Ankersmit), *History and Theory*, 46 (1): 66–73.

Runia, E. (2014), *Moved by the Past: Discontinuity and Historical Mutation*, New York: Columbia University Press.

Stewart, K. (2007), *Ordinary Affects*, Durham: Duke University Press.

van Gerwen, R., ed. (2001), *Richard Wollheim on the Art of Painting. Art as Representation and Expression*, Cambridge: Cambridge University Press.

Völkel, M. (2011), 'Bild zur Ansicht. Die Entwicklung des Topos von der "Sichtbarkeit der Geschichte" in der Frühen Neuzeit', in H. Busche (ed.), *Departure for Modern Europe. A Handbook of Early Modern Philosophy (1400–1700)*, 602–12, Hamburg: Meiner.

Weigel, S. (2014), 'Von Blitz, Flamme und Regenbogen. Das Sprechen in Bildern als epistemischer Schauplatz bei Walter Benjamin', in L. Bader, G. Didi-Huberman and J. Grave (eds), *Sprechen über Bilder – Sprechen in Bildern. Studien zum Wechselverhältnis von Bild und Sprache*, 225–40, Berlin: Deutscher Kunstverlag.

Wiesing, L. (2009), 'The Main Currents in Today's Philosophy of the Image', in L. Wiesing, *Artificial Presence: Philosophical Studies in Image Theory*, transl. N. F. Schott, 8–23, Stanford: Stanford University Press.

Wollheim, R. (1980), *Art and its Objects. An Introduction to Aesthetics*, 2nd edn, Cambridge: Cambridge University Press.

Wollheim, R. (1987), *Painting as an Art. The A. W. Mellon Lectures in the Fine Arts 1984*, Princeton: Princeton University Press.

Zumbusch, C. (2004), *Wissenschaft in Bildern. Symbol und dialektisches Bild in Aby Warburgs Mnemosyne-Atlas und Walter Benjamins Passagen-Werk*, Berlin: Akademie Verlag.

Zumbusch, C. (2018), 'Vor- und Nachgeschichte. Bild und Zeit bei Walter Benjamin', *Zeitschrift für Kunstgeschichte*, 81 (2): 198–212.

8

Time as History in
Twentieth-Century Photography

Anne Fuchs

In his influential study *Regimes of Historicity* François Hartog (2015) explores the ways in which societies relate to their experience of temporality and time by what he terms 'regimes of historicity'. For Hartog regimes of historicity create distinctive 'orders of time' that reflect changes in historical consciousness and competing conceptions of history. For example, Christianity separated time into two eschatological spheres through Christ's Second Coming and the Last Judgment. By contrast modern time is characterized by what Reinhart Koselleck called the 'temporalization' of time (Koselleck 2002b: 121). For Koselleck it was only in the context of the Enlightenment and the French Revolution that history emerged as a truly dynamic category shaped and controlled by human actors. No longer preordained by God but the outcome of human action and thought, history became subject to 'criteria which could only be derived from an understanding of history itself' (Koselleck 2002b: 120). Koselleck explains further that a gap opened up between the people's experience of reality, on the one hand, and their horizon of expectation, on the other. Once the difference between the past, the present and the future was conceptualized, the future turned into the horizon of urgent human planning and action *par excellence*.

The temporalization of history also effected the acceleration of the experience of time in modern history: time 'continually seems to overtake itself' in the service of progress (Koselleck 2002a: 113). For Hartog (who extensively draws on Koselleck) it is precisely this modern order of past, present and future that is in crisis. He is concerned that in today's global world the 'production of historical time seems to be suspended' (Hartog 2015: 17).

> Perhaps this is what generates today's sense of permanent, elusive, and almost immobile present, which nevertheless attempts to create its own historical time. It is as though there were nothing but the present, like an immense stretch of water restlessly rippling. So should we talk of an end, or an exit from modernity, from that particular temporal structure we call the modern regime of historicity? It is too early to tell. But we can certainly talk of a crisis. Presentism is the name I have given to this moment and to today's experience of time.
>
> Hartog 2015: 17–18

For Hartog our presentist experience of time is, however, deeply pathological because it extends our present simultaneously into the future and into the past, thereby destroying our historical relatedness to both the past and the future as ontological categories. Burdened with its 'twofold memory of the past and the future', Hartog concludes, 'it is also shadowed by entropy' – presentism is therefore a 'monstrous time' (Hartog 2015: 203).

In her recent book *Ist die Zeit aus den Fugen?*, Aleida Assmann too diagnoses a reconfiguration of our relationship to past, present and future: she argues that the time regime of modernity ended in the late 1980s when the future finally lost its shiny gloss against the backdrop of the unparalleled violence of twentieth-century history and in the context of emerging ecological threats (Assmann 2013: 18). But Assmann evaluates the disappearance of the modern time regime in a very different light: even though the future as a horizon of ideological investment has collapsed, the present remains a site where social actors manage to construct and synthesize their experiences of the past and expectations of their future (Assmann 2013: 273). For Assmann, cultural memory is the key instrument in the handling of our temporal experiences as it provides us with indispensable cultural frames. Assmann's reading of the 'culturalization' of time thus de-ontologizes the very category of time in favour of a constructivist perspective that takes account of the genuinely human ability to recall the past and project expectations into the future (Assmann 2013: 277).

Time in photography

These opposing views of time *in* and *as* crisis serve as a springboard for the ensuing exploration of the representation of twentieth-century history in photography. Using a very small corpus of photographs that represent two pivotal moments in German twentieth-century history – the end of the war in 1945 and the summer of 1989 shortly before the fall of the Berlin Wall – this chapter examines the ways in which photography mediatizes the experience of time as history. Arguably, the modern media, above all photography and film, have done more to shape our mental image of twentieth-century history than the written word: Dorothea Lange's representation of the Great Depression in 'Migrant Mother' (1936), George Rodger's picture of a small boy walking down a road lined with dead bodies at the Bergen-Belsen concentration camp (1945), Alfred Eisenstaedt's 'Times Square Kiss' (1945), Joe Rosenthal's 'Raising the Flag on Mount Suribachi' (1945) or Nick Ut's representation of the violence of the Vietnam War in his iconic 'Napalm Girl' (1972) are examples of global icons that have influenced the public memory of twentieth-century history more than any historical account. Icons are rhetorically effective because they appear to speak for themselves. They repress their encodedness by providing 'an instant and effortless connection to some deeply meaningful moment in history' (Goldberg 1991: 135). Their global circulation prompts further remediations and recursive loops of recognition that transmute history into canonical symbols devoid of anchorage in local contexts. According to Robert Hariman and John Louis Lucaites's authoritative study on the subject, the impact of icons increases over time as the images remain in the public eye while almost all of the other documentation of the period disappears into institutional archives. And the more collective memory is constructed through the visual media, the more likely it is that the iconic photos will be used to mark, frame and otherwise set the tone for later generations' understanding of public life in the twentieth century.

Hariman and Lucaites 2007: 11

Hariman and Lucaites investigate whether the visual practice of photojournalism has shifted in the United States from promoting democratic citizenship to advocating (neo)liberalism; they are therefore less interested in the complex temporality of the photographic medium in and of itself. Until recently the latter issue has been primarily debated with reference to photography's indexical recording of a moment in time that was made possible by technical advances, above all the reduction in shutter speed. Roland Barthes famously argued that the indexicality of the photograph is irrefutable because analogue photography always captures a singular and non-repeatable moment of and in time. In his classic book *Camera Lucida* he observed that photography's ontological status resides in the indisputable 'has-been-ness' of the photograph, which in turn provokes the unsettling experience of the 'punctum', that is of a moment when the observer is disturbed by a detail in the image that she cannot account for (Barthes 1993: 43). Susan Sontag, the great sceptic of photography, also focused on the photography's indexicality:

a photograph passes for incontrovertible proof that a given thing happened. The picture may distort; but there is always a presumption that something exists, or did exist, which is like what's in the picture. Whatever the limitations (through amateurism) or pretensions (through artistry) of the individual photographer, a photograph – any photograph – seems to have a more innocent, and therefore more accurate, relation to visible reality than do other mimetic objects.

Sontag 1973: 5–6

While Barthes and Sontag approached the photographic image from the perspective of the recipient, André Bazin (1980) attempted to pin down 'The Ontology of the Photographic Image' by comparing film as a medium with photography. Bazin claimed that, while cinema produces images of objects in duration, photography embalms time. Whereas film always unfolds in the recipient's time and space, photography can only offer images of a frozen past.

However, in more recent times this established view has been revised by a wave of critics, including Jan Baetens, Alexander Streitberger and Hilde Van Gelder, who have rightly pointed out that the classic approach to still photography was largely owed to the exclusive focus on technical advances: the reduction of shutter speed and of development and processing time supported the dominant view of the photograph as an indexical moment in time (Baetens, Streitberger and Van Gelder 2010: vii). From this perspective, the photograph appears as a 'presentist' medium in Hartog's sense precisely because it freezes a moment that is devoid of duration and temporality.

In the digital age, however, the conventional view of the photographic image has been overturned. The difference between the moving image and still photography has collapsed because the same digital camera can be used to take film shots and photographs or to arrest, repeat or slow down filmic images. But further to these technological innovations, there are strong epistemological reasons for scrutinizing these fixed ideas about exposure time. As Greg Battye argues

> it is no more intrinsically reasonable to presume that a photograph depicts only the time it took to make the exposure [...], than it is to presume that a painting depicts only the time it took to create the painting. It's even more unreasonable to assert that viewing time – the period we spend looking at it, thinking about, and reacting to a photograph – is tied in any way at all to either exposure time [...] or even to any understanding of conception and production time.
>
> Battye 2014: 78–9

Recent debates therefore increasingly focus on photography as 'a complex social process, which is not just a technique, an art, or a way of picture-making, but also a dream, an idea, a political device, in short an object that is by definition hybrid and networked: things, people, technology, and institutions, both synchronically and diachronically, are intertwined and produce social meanings and interactions that evolve in time and through time' (Baetens, Streitberger and Van Gelder 2010: viii). Martin Lister approaches the temporal multi-layeredness of the photographic image by distinguishing between the 'time in a photograph' and the 'time of a photograph': while the first flows from technology and refers to the exposure time as well as 'the peculiar temporality which invests a photograph at the time of its making', the latter captures the meanings and uses of photographs that are engendered in the process of reception (Lister 2012: 49). 'Once the image is inscribed,' comments Lister, 'it opens up to our cultural, our imaginative and intellectual investments in photography – especially with regard to how we conceive of time, the relations of past, present and future, and hence to matters of historical time and the temporality of memory' (Lister 2012: 55).

It is precisely the latter dimensions that this chapter explores with reference to a few photographs that stage or anticipate decisive historical turning points in Germany's turbulent twentieth-century history. Each of these photographs brings into view a distinctive mode of temporalizing history, each has its own history of production and remediation, each employs a particular narrative structure and specific ways of symbolizing time.

The heroic view

An outstanding icon of the global war imaginary of the twentieth century is Yevgeny Khaldei's famous photograph of the three Russian soldiers hoisting the Soviet flag on the Reichstag in Berlin.[1] Immediately recognizable, this photograph appears to capture the lived moment when the Russian fighting troops declared victory over their enemy by raising their flag. The appeal of this photograph lies in the apparent spontaneity of a gesture, which is presented as an unrehearsed patriotic expression by common soldiers. However, as noted in various studies on the subject, the supposed evidential authority of this image is the effect of careful orchestration and staging by the photographer. Khaldei's photo of the raising of the Soviet flag on top of the Reichstag was not only completely staged at the time but also manipulated retrospectively (Volland 2008). The Russians had already taken the Reichstag on 30 April, but the picture was only shot on 2 May. When the negative was developed, it turned out that one of the Russian soldiers was wearing two wristwatches. One of these had to be edited out, as this was evidence of Russian looting and thus not publishable. Further to this manipulation, Khaldei dramatized the staged moment of victory by superimposing a negative with smoke on the flag image. This suggested that fierce battles were still being fought in the streets below. The victorious pose in Khaldei's image with the iconic flag and a downward view on a ruined cityscape is of particular importance for the visual counter-narrative that was later put forward by German rubble photographers. As we will see, German photographers responded to the victor's iconography by way of an alternative narrative that fostered a melancholy reading of history.

Perhaps we can approach the temporality of this photograph by making use of Lister's distinction of the time in the photograph and the time of the photograph. The time in the doctored photograph was meant to capture the grand moment when the Red Army and, by implication, the entire Soviet nation finally succeeded in their long struggle to defeat Nazi Germany in a collective heroic effort. But this picture marks the endpoint of a much longer narrative arc that stretches from the Nazi invasion of the Soviet Union in June 1941 to the complete destruction of the Wehrmacht's 6th Army at Stalingrad in February 1943, arguably *the* decisive psychological turning point in the Second World War. For the Russian viewers of the postwar period, Khaldei's image therefore stands for much more than the moment depicted: the symbolism of the image can only be fully understood with reference to the Russian experience of the entire Second World War. The time in the photograph, the moment when the flag is finally raised above the ruins of the Nazi capital, thus gains a meta-historical dimension: the heroic gesture suggests that, in the end, collective sacrifice and heroic effort will defeat evil. The fact that Khaldei and the Soviets mistook the Reichstag for a major Nazi building does not diminish the powerful narrative symbolism: the soldiers in the foreground who are raising the Soviet flag right in front of our eyes are shown to enact the final scene in a historical drama of gigantic proportions. It is of great symbolic importance that the ruination of the German capital is only perceptible behind the Soviet Flag and from a raised perspective: Khaldei's carefully orchestrated composition implies that historical retribution is just.

The fact that Soviet viewers of Khaldei's victory photograph were likely to conjure up images of the ruination of Stalingrad and other Soviet cities, adds a further facet to the image. And yet the time of the photograph is malleable and subject to changing horizons of reception: while for the Soviet postwar viewer and perhaps even the contemporary Russian viewer the picture allegorizes Russian heroism, the contemporary viewer who is aware of the engineered origins of the photograph is likely to ironize this meta-historical dimension. From the latter perspective, heroism reveals itself as a staged and ultimately faked pose.

The melancholic view

In 1949, Richard Peter, a Dresden photographer, published a photo narrative under the title *Eine Kamera klagt an* (A Camera Accuses) with a print-run of 50,000 copies, which quickly sold out (Peter 1949). The photo narrative is an example of rubble photography that documented the destruction of cities during the Second World War. Examples include Hermann Claasen's *Gesang im Feuerofen. Köln: Überreste einer deutschen Stadt* (Song from the Furnace: Cologne: The Remnants of a City) and Kurt Schaarschuch's *Bilddokument Dresden 1933–1945* (Dresden in Images 1933–1945), which contrasted a range of iconic Dresden buildings in 1933 with their state of complete ruination in 1945. However, it was Richard Peter's photo narrative that gained iconic status in the postwar German imaginary. Its publication was accompanied by a nationwide poster campaign that promoted it with the slogan 'A book for all Germans – available in all bookshops'. For many critics Peter's photo narrative is an example of the German postwar desire for exculpation by displacement of their guilt, an interpretation that is supported by the accusatory title of Peter's book whose contents are attributed to the objective work of the camera rather than to the viewpoint of the photographer whose name does not even appear on the cover (Glasenapp 2008: 100–32; Mielke 2007: 140–4).

The photo narrative contains 104 photographs of which 48 depict the ruined city. Even though the book attempts to embed the destruction of Dresden in a teleological view of history that culminates in the Communist rebuilding of society, the photographic emphasis is on the experience of ruination and on a melancholy view of history that, in the last analysis, is supra-historical and non-temporal.

Before demonstrating this in detail with reference to one of the most iconic images of the destruction of Dresden, it is necessary to touch on the narrative arc of the photo book. The opening two photographs show us Dresden by night followed by a panoramic view of the city's architectural silhouette that imitates the point of view adopted in Canaletto's famous paintings of the Baroque cityscape. The stark contrast between the opening representation of architectural splendour and the ensuing depiction of total ruination in page after page produces an apocalyptic allegory of human history that erases human agency: it is as if we are studying these images after the city's and our own death. Georg Simmel (1998) argued that the ruin is a form of decay that offers a harmonious union between man and nature. For Simmel the charm of the Romantic ruin resides in the fact that a man-made structure appears as a work of nature. In contrast to this Romantic idea, the sheer scale of the destruction of Dresden is evidence of an excessive violence that unhinges the notion of gradually passing time, which is implied in the Romantic notion of decay. The sheer amount of rubble, the mangled steelworks and machinery that are displayed in image after image creates the effect of a supranatural excess that simultaneously invites yet refuses adequate representation. In its serial representation Peter's photo narrative exudes a tremendous appeal that pulls the viewer in. And so it is that Peter's aesthetic of destruction bypasses the question of historical cause and effect in favour of a transhistorical reading of the dreadful wreckage of history.

Peter's powerful representation of the wreckage of history is bookended by the photographic celebration of a bright socialist future. The final photograph adopts an upward angled shot to capture a reconstruction worker who appears to be climbing on a ladder straight into the socialist heaven. In its composition and theme this photograph promises historical redemption through socialism; it also provides a visual translation of the first two lines of the GDR anthem: 'risen from the ruins, turning towards the future'. And yet, it is questionable that the long-term reception of the book was really motivated by this overt socialist message. The high print run to this day suggests that it was the central section with the serial representation of Dresden's ruination that appealed to Germans in both the East and West.

One picture in particular – the photograph of the ruined cityscape from a top-down view with a sculpture in the foreground has become the single most iconic photograph of the destruction of Dresden (Figure 8.1). So let us study this photograph and its handling of narrative time in more detail. The scene of destruction is dominated by the sculpture of *bonitas* (goodness) in the foreground, one of the allegories of civic

Figure 8.1 Richard Peter, *Blick vom Rathausturm* (View from the Rathaus Tower), 1945. Courtesy of Deutsche Fotothek.

virtues that adorned the tower of Dresden's town hall. The figure's melancholic gesture lends the time in the photograph a non-historical index: with her mournful expression, *bonitas* appears to display the ruination not just of Dresden but of all human history. Because the image is not framed by a margin, the ruination seems to extend far beyond the temporal horizon of the Second World War into the realm of allegory. Peter's pictorial composition thus translates the time in the photograph, the moment when the picture was taken in 1945, into the time of the photograph and the allegorical evocation of a never-ending history of destruction. The prominence of *bonitas* with her mournful gesture evokes the Romantic paradigm that, as Peter Fritzsche has shown, popularized an aesthetic of melancholy in response to the violence of the French Revolution (Fritzsche 2004). And so it is that Peter remediates an already established visual iconography in order to arouse a melancholic response and a backward-looking reading of history as a series of violent dispossessions. By adopting the perspective of after our own death, the image transcends the historical context in which the shot was taken: what we see here is not so much the consequence of the perpetration committed by Nazi Germany but the aftermath of an all-consuming transhistorical rage that annihilated Nazi perpetrators and innocent victims alike. As I have argued elsewhere, the serial representation of the ruination of Dresden in image after image and in other artworks allowed the German postwar audience to mourn and work through its losses affectively (Fuchs 2012: 32–42, 2015). For postwar Germans the time in the photograph marked a traumatic ending rather than a new beginning.

Arguably the career of this photograph was helped by the career of Kaldhei's picture of the hoisting of the flag on the Reichstag. There is a perfect symmetry between the two pictures: in both we see two ruined German cities from a raised position. In Khaldei's picture the soldier with the flag in the foreground makes the photo an indisputable icon of just victory; in Peter's photo the presence of *bonitas* turns it into an icon of absolute and excessive defeat. Khaldei's picture promotes human agency and the future-oriented view of Marxist historiography. By contrast Peter's photograph suspends the teleological narrative arc of his photo book in favour of an allegorical perspective after our own death. It is for this reason that Khaldei's picture is indexical and Peter's is not. Khaldei's image demonstrably references a particular moment in time (the moment of victory as the endpoint of a long history of suffering), as well as a particular place (the conquest of the Reichstag in the centre of Berlin). Although Peter's photo was taken at a particular moment in time and in a particular place (Dresden in April 1945), it evokes a destruction of excessive proportions that annihilates the very notions of historical anchorage in place and time. Lifted from its concrete historical context, Peter's photograph became a trans-historical and trans-geographical icon of the disastrous effects of all warfare, regardless of the chain of cause and effect.

The presentist view

My third and final example is taken from East German photographer Ulrich Wüst's photobook *Später Sommer/Letzter Herbst* (Late Summer/Final Autumn, 2016) which covers various East German locations and a trip to Moscow in the momentous summer and autumn of 1989. Going against the conventional representation of the fall of the Berlin Wall, Wüst's photo narrative does not depict the usual images of the Monday demonstrators in Leipzig, of ecstatic East Berliners arriving in the West or of jubilant Westerners making their way into the unknown East, of lines of pastel-coloured Trabants at the open border, of bewildered and bemused GDR officials. His photo narrative consists rather of a series of impressions that, with a few exceptions, appear as non-events. Wüst's photographs are remarkably grainy, distanced and difficult to read.

Wüst's photobook is divided into a prologue, five central photo series, and an epilogue. Each section carries a sparse title, dates and place names.[2] The photographs are arranged either as a single photograph per page or as developed contact strips or sequences of negatives: four photographs with perforation holes run across and over the edge of the double page. The perforated roll film foregrounds the materiality and historicity of analogue photography: roll film not only massively helped to speed up exposure times but it also recorded the chronological occurrence of the photographs. Wüst overturns these conventions: his pictures capture neither the acceleration of history in 1989 nor do they allow the viewer to produce an 'order of time' through chronological sequencing. Even though the photobook records journeys undertaken by Wüst in 1989, these journeys appear uneventful and inconclusive.

In the following I will analyse the temporality of the first image in the central section 'Spätsommer Kühlungsborn' (late summer Kühlungsborn), which consists of nine photographs that, as the caption informs us, were taken in September 1989 near Kühlungsborn, a popular holiday resort on the Baltic coast of the GDR. The first

Figure 8.2 Ulrich Wüst, 'Kühlungsborn', in his *Später Sommer/Letzter Herbst* (1989, published in 2016). © Ulrich Wüst.

photograph shows a small group that could be a family: a woman dressed in a light overcoat with a large handbag hanging from her shoulder is about to place a black suitcase on the beach (Figure 8.2). She is flanked by two men: the middle-aged man on her left wears a black leather jacket and a light pair of trousers; he carries a small suitcase while looking out to sea. The young man on the right – perhaps the couple's son – has rolled up his dark trousers above his ankles; in his right hand he holds a small travel bag with a white pair of trainers tied to its handle. He too is gazing at the sea.

Wüst's beach photograph clearly conjures up a speculative narrative arc that involves the liminal moments of arrival and departure. Liminal moments are consequential plot elements in narratives; they engender transitional instability, ontological uncertainty and the possibility of social and political disorder. The anthropologist Arnold Van Gennep first demonstrated that in closed, small-scale societies the liminal experience is managed by rites of passage which stage individual and collective progression through the cycle of life (Van Gennep 2004). Broadening the meaning of the concept, Victor Turner (1967) then argued that liminality served 'not only to identify the importance of in-between periods, but also to understand the human reactions to liminal experiences: the way liminality shaped personality, the sudden foregrounding of agency, and the sometimes dramatic tying together of thought and experience' (Thomassen 2009: 14).

Returning to Wüst's photo it is evident that the scene on the shores of the Baltic Sea is liminal, both in the temporal as well as the geographical sense. Even though we cannot tell with any certainty whether this group has just arrived or whether it is about to depart after a holiday at the Baltic Sea, the pictorial composition seems to suggest the latter interpretation: these people are looking out at the sea in the knowledge that they are expected to resume their mundane lives. However, the picture also exudes a sense of uncertainty about whether the transition to normalcy will succeed. It is as if these people are hoping for a change that lies beyond their reach. Set on the beach of the Baltic Sea, the geography of the composition is liminal too: the beach may evoke the expectation of a departure or the arrival of a ship from distant shores; it can also promise a radically different future or carry connotations of transcendence. For the German viewer the composition is perhaps reminiscent of Caspar David Friedrich's *Der Mönch am Meer* (*The Monk by the Sea*, 1808–1810). Friedrich's epochal painting depicts a single figure in a long garment in rear view on a dune overlooking the sea and the vast expanse of the horizon. The symbolism of Friedrich's painting derives from the vastness of the sky (which takes up more than three quarters of the picture) and the small scale of the human figure – the only vertical element in an otherwise horizontal composition. Wüst's photograph, too, makes do with only a small number of compositional elements. Apart from the beach, the sea, the sky and the three figures, only a pair of seagulls are to be seen, one resting on a post at the edge of the picture on the left, the other bobbing in the water to the right of the centre of the picture. As in the case of Friedrich's painting, the picture is composed of strict horizontal layers: the sky is separated from the bottom half of the picture by the sharp line of the horizon. However, while in Friedrich's painting the sky symbolizes Romantic transcendence, in Wüst's photograph this association is curtailed by the lack of any perspective depth. Wüst's figures stare at a horizon that, despite its breadth, appears opaque.

Wüst's photograph thus can be read as an allegorical representation of the longing for emigration and political freedom at the very moment when this was about to become possible. And so it is that the time of the photograph is intensely historical in Hartog's sense precisely because viewers superimpose their knowledge of the fall of the Berlin Wall and of the subsequent unification of Germany. However, the time in the photograph (as captured by the temporal caption 'September 1989') complicates the retrospective historicity: while the beach setting fuels the liminal expectation of some kind of transition from one state of affairs to another, the laden sky captures entrapment in a stagnating and extended present without a future horizon under the conditions of GDR socialism. Or to put it differently: within the decisive moment of the picture the future horizon remains closed off for the human actors in this setting.

Conclusion

Rather than merely embalming a particular moment in time, photography can indeed produce powerful visual narratives that allegorize history and operate at a meta-historical level in Hayden White's sense (White 1975). The photographs by Khaldei and Peter in particular turn the end of the Second World War into immediately recognizable global icons that provide an effortless connection to history. And yet, these photographs also induce in the viewer what Greg Battye terms a 'narrative-like feeling' (Battye 2014: 45), mobilizing cognitive frames that organize our experience of time as history. Instead of merely capturing one decisive event at a particular 'presentist' moment in time, these photographs come with longer narrative arcs that are activated in the process of reception. As Bence Nanay points out, 'even though a picture can depict one event only, it can represent more than one event. Thus, it is perfectly possible that a picture represents a narrative' (Nanay 2009: 121). In Khaldei's case, the time in the photograph stages a heroic moment in time; it evokes the history of the Second World War from the Nazi invasion of the Soviet Union to the end of the war in May 1945. However, from the perspective of the contemporary recipient who knows the history of the production of the image, the deliberate meta-historical representation of collective heroism is likely to be ironized.

While Khaldei's image dramatizes the reward of human effort by means of a theatrical visual rhetoric, Richard Peter's photo narrative sidelines human agency in favour of a totalizing representation of ruination: here history is not something that is subject to human agency but a destructive, violent and unforgiving ultra-human agent of sublime proportions. By prompting a contemplative reception through a visual iconography that draws on the melancholy tradition, Peter's photograph ultimately transports history onto a non-temporal plane that abandons historical cause and effect.

Finally, Ulrich Wüst's photo narrative *Später Sommer/Letzter Herbst* represents 1989 no longer as an electrifying moment of global historical change but as a highly precarious and uncertain liminal time. The belated appearance of the photobook more than twenty-five years after German unification creates reflective distance and an alternative view of history that displaces the global iconicity of 1989. Instead of dramatizing the acceleration of history, the photo narrative brings into view inconclusive movement through urban and non-urban landscapes that are difficult to read. The Kühlungsborn series at the centre of the book adopts a more representational language, but it too induces ontological uncertainty about the pathway and temporal order of history. The scene on the beach in particular captures the presentist outlook of these GDR tourists from the position of the future anterior. What this means then is that the time in the photograph and the time of the photograph keep collapsing into one another with the disturbing effect of cancelling historical time. When we study Wüst's picture we are no longer certain that the future has really overcome entrapment in presentism. Like the people in the picture we look at the horizon longingly but with a great deal of uncertainty that it holds the promise of change.

Notes

1   As the various versions of this image are widely available on the internet, they are not being reproduced here. See for example: http://100photos.time.com/photos/yevgeny-khaldei-raising-flag-over-reichstag (accessed 15 May 2018).
2   'Stadtflucht Berlin Prenzlau' (Escape from the City: Berlin Prenzlau) and 'Sommernacht Prenzlauer Berg' (Summer Night Prenzlauer Berg) were shot in August 1989; 'Spätsommer Kühlungsborn' (Late Summer Kühlungsborn) in September 1989; 'Oktober (1)' was shot in Leipzig in September, 'October (2)' in Berlin on 6 and 7 October, that is shortly before and on the fortieth anniversary of the GDR. While 'October (3)' was shot in Leningrad and Moscow in October, the epilogue carries no dates or locations at all: it contains two photographs of a GDR flag hanging from a domestic radiator underneath a net curtain with a floral pattern.

References

Assmann, A. (2013), *Ist die Zeit aus den Fugen? Aufstieg und Fall des Zeitregimes der Moderne*, Munich: Hanser.
Baetens, J., Streitberger, A. and Van Gelder, H., eds (2010), *Time and Photography*, Leuven: Leuven University Press.
Barthes, R. (1993), *Camera Lucida. Reflections on Photography*, transl. R. Howard, New York: Vintage Classics.
Battye, G. (2014), *Photography, Narrative, Time: Imaging our Forensic Imagination*, Bristol and Chicago: Intellect.
Bazin, A. (1980), 'The Ontology of the Photographic Image', in A. Trachtenberg (ed.), *Classic Essays on Photography*, transl. H. Gray, 237–44, New Haven, CT: Leete's Island Press.
Fritzsche, P. (2004), *Stranded in the Present. Modern Time and the Melancholy of History*, Cambridge, MA: Harvard University Press.
Fuchs, A. (2012), *After the Dresden Bombing: Pathways of Memory, 1945 to the Present*, Houndmills: Palgrave Macmillan.
Fuchs, A. (2015), 'L'horreur sublime de l'histoire: representations visuelles du bombardement de Dresde', in M. Preti and S. Settis (eds), *Villes en ruine: images, mémoires, métamorphoses*, 290–303, Paris: Louvre éditions.

Glasenapp, J. (2008), *Die deutsche Nachkriegsfotografie: eine Mentalitätsgeschichte in Bildern*, Munich: Fink.

Goldberg, V. (1991), *The Power of Photography: How Photographs Changed Our World*, New York: Abbeville Press.

Hariman, R. and Lucaites, J. L. (2007), *No Caption Needed. Iconic Photographs, Public Culture, and Liberal Democracy*, Chicago and London: The University of Chicago Press.

Hartog, F. (2015), *Regimes of Historicity. Presentism and the Experiences of Time*, transl. S. Brown, New York: Columbia University Press.

Koselleck, R. (2002a), 'Time and History', in his *The Practice of Conceptual History. Timing History, Spacing Concepts*, transl. T. S. Presner, 100–14, Stanford: Stanford University Press.

Koselleck, R. (2002b), 'Concepts of Historical Time and Social History', in his *The Practice of Conceptual History. Timing History, Spacing Concepts*, transl. T. S. Presner, 115–30, Stanford: Stanford University Press.

Lister, M. (2012), 'The Times of Photography', in E. Keightley (ed.), *Time, Media and Modernity*, 45–65, Basingstoke: Palgrave Macmillan.

Mielke, C. (2007), 'Geisterstädte: literarische Texte und Bilddokumentationen zur Städtebombardierung des Zweiten Weltkrieges und die Personifizierung des Urbanen', in A. Böhn and C. Mielke (eds), *Die zerstörte Stadt: mediale Repräsentationen urbaner Räume von Troja bis SimCity*, 125–80, Berlin: Transcript.

Nanay, B. (2009), 'Narrative Pictures', *Journal of Aesthetics and Art Criticism*, 67: 119–29.

Peter, R. (1949), *Eine Kamera klagt an*, Dresden: Dresdner Verlagsgesellschaft.

Simmel, G. (1998), 'Die Ruine', in his *Philosophische Kultur. Über das Abenteuer, die Geschlechter und die Krise der Moderne. Gesammelte Essais*, 174–85, Berlin: Wagenbach.

Sontag, S. (1973), *On Photography*, New York and London: Doubleday.

Thomassen, B. (2009), 'The Uses and Meanings of Liminality', *International Political Anthropology*, 2 (1): 5–27. Available online: http://www.moodlevda.lt/moodle/pluginfile.php/2205/mod_resource/content/0/8%20Thomassen%20-%20Uses%20and%20meanings%20of%20liminality.pdf (accessed 30 June 2018).

Turner, V. (1967), *The Forest of Symbols. Aspects of Ndembu Ritual*, New York: Cornell University Press.

Van Gennep, A. (2004), *Rites of Passage*, transl. M. B. Vizedom and G. L. Caffee, London and Henley: Routledge and Kegan Paul.

Volland, E. (2008), 'Die Flagge des Sieges', in E. Volland and H. Krimmer (eds), *Jewgeni Chaldej: Der bedeutende Augenblick. Eine Retrospektive*, 112–23, Leipzig: Neuer Europa Verlag.

White, H. (1975), *Metahistory. The Historical Imagination in Nineteenth-Century Europe*, Baltimore and London: Johns Hopkins University Press.

Part Three

Material Temporalities

9

Heritage and the Untimely

Torgeir Rinke Bangstad

A single family house from Olderfjord and a barn from Indre Billefjord in Northern Norway have been re-erected *ex situ* at Norsk Folkemuseum's open-air museum in Oslo for the 125th anniversary of the museum in 2019. The barn and the house were built during the so-called Reconstruction era (ca. 1945–1960). Both buildings have been disassembled board by board and shipped in large containers to the museum where they will accommodate a permanent exhibition on the scorched earth retreat in 1944 and the post-Second World War reconstruction in Northern Norway. The buildings are from Finnmark, a county where only very few fishing hamlets and remote farms survived the systematic destruction of buildings carried out by retreating Wehrmacht forces in the winter of 1944.

The purpose of this chapter is to explore the sense of time in reconstruction architecture with regards to its preservation in the twenty-first century. I will argue that timeliness was an important ideal for reconstruction architecture in the sense that it aspired to a distinct material articulation of the requirements of the postwar era. Moreover, I claim that timeliness is also important in forms of historic preservation where the primacy of style historical origins in the material fabric contributes to a sequential notion of historical time. In contrast to these attempts to co-relate historical time and material form, I will employ the notion of the untimely to discuss the difficulties of unequivocally determining the historical identity of buildings. The notion of the untimely works against the idea of objects' proper time and against the fixed object-position where material form and historical age coincide as a distinct style. I will demonstrate that the notion of the untimely allows us to approach material transformation of the Olderfjord house at the crowded intersection of different rhythms, paces and times. I will expound the issue of temporality in architectural heritage through an exploration of the materially untimely.

The second aim of the chapter is to contrast the material articulation of untimeliness with presentism in heritage theory, which sees heritage as derived from, if not confined to, an increasingly self-absorbed present. The chapter shows how material remains store memories of past events, and demonstrates how such retentions, like other memories, occasionally find their way back into the present in unsolicited ways. The notion of untimely brings attention to the multitemporal properties of objects and builds on the idea that the past and the present are not defined by the singularity of one specific age that is wholly incongruent with what follows or precedes it. Instead of determining unequivocally whether heritage is *of* the past or the present, this will be an attempt to show how untimely things sometimes traverse such neat temporal partitions.

Purifying time: On the modern construction of timeliness

The German term *zeitgemäss* (timely) was important for nineteenth-century writers as a synonym of 'modern, progressive, up-to-date', which suggested temporal propriety by suiting a time and being fully of it (Harris 2008: 11). Similarly, the timely was employed in the first half of the twentieth century as a form of shorthand for architecture which responded to requirements of the day and aptly absorbed cultural and technological advances in society. Modernist architects in the interwar period considered the timely to be an ideal in attempts to attain a purer form of architecture in terms both of its construction materials and design. More specifically, the timely in architecture was opposed to historicist mimicking of historical styles and the alleged chaos of different stylistic influences in the late nineteenth and early twentieth centuries. The artistic historicism was a natural antagonist for the modernist movement, which regarded it as regressive and nostalgic and without independent, creative power (Assmann 2013: 179).

According to the influential Norwegian modernist architect, Johan Ellefsen, giving a lecture in 1927, the stylistic confusion of nineteenth century historicism necessitated a form of ascetic, aesthetic liberation: 'The result was a pursuit for timeliness, simplification, clarity and unity in ambition' (Ellefsen 1927: 166). Comparing historical styles to animal species Ellefsen (1927: 165) claimed that 'a style dies as a new mentality, a new mode of living or a form of construction is introduced'. It was no longer the arts that would approximate and express the time and its mentality most lucidly, but technology *qua* art enabled by the foresight of scientists and engineers. The idea of historical progress imparted by Ellefsen and many of his contemporaries suggested that the steady improvement of technology, like the aeroplanes and automobiles of his day, ensured that only the most suitable technological and cultural forms would endure. Consequently, to conceive of something as timely meant that it was closely aligned with the requirements of the day and that a check was put on stylistic excess. Creative urges were subordinated to this duty of timeliness. Ellefsen praised standard houses as one way to arrive at a more accomplished architecture. By subjecting the architectural form to testing and continual improvement like cars manufactured in factories, a process of refinement would yield an appropriate architecture and the excessive and redundant would not stand the test of time. The problem for Ellefsen was that the past, and the nationwide enthusiasm for the history and heritage of the newly independent country (the union with Sweden was dissolved in 1905), was literally obstructing a favourable reception of these modern ideas. More importantly, this modernist notion of the timely suggested that the new could flourish only by superseding the old.

In 1923 the renowned architect Ludwig Mies van der Rohe claimed that '[a]rchitecture is the will of the age conceived in spatial terms' (van der Rohe 1990: 74).

The idea of a form of architecture that would articulate the culture and character of the age has a long pedigree in art history and is seen in relation with the German romanticist ideas of *Zeitgeist*, which has also been tremendously influential in architectural historiography (Payne 1999; Whyte 2006; Lending 2007; Hvattum 2009). The question of what constitutes a style appropriate to a specific age has haunted architectural thinking since the early nineteenth century. Architecture was and is often still treated as reified *Zeitgeist*, an embodiment of specific attitudes prevailing at a given time in history. The notion of the architecturally timely also reflects a similar expectation. The new era would by necessity give rise to a unique style, which according to many modernists was 'pure' where the eclecticism of nineteenth-century historicism had been 'chaotic'.

The attempt to identify and attain a timeliness in architecture is arguably also practised in historic preservation. The Norwegian term for timely, *tidsmessig*, is hardly in use in the common tongue anymore, indeed the word itself now seems somewhat outlandish and anachronistic. However, it has been claimed that the preservationist understanding of authenticity covers some of the same semantic ground, but in relation to historic buildings rather than contemporary architecture (Rustad 2009). Authenticity is a predominant concept in heritage and museum practices to assess whether objects genuinely belong to the time, place or artistic oeuvre that is assumed or claimed. Whereas authenticity is a concept used to evaluate different components in historic buildings, the notion of timely pertains to contemporary buildings and their compliance with the cultural climate of an era. Despite their differences, these terms express an affinity for seeing material culture as a genuine articulation of a culture at a given point in time – past or present. They also deal with ways of adequately approximating the characteristic properties of a historical period in material terms.

Attempts to find the appropriate form of housing in which to accomplish the large-scale postwar reconstruction of Norway also involved attempts to transcend the momentary, the fashionable and the ephemeral. The Norwegian Prime Minister, Einar Gerhardsen (1946: 1), claimed that architects and designers faced with the challenging task of rebuilding proper housing in the country should resist whims of fashion and momentary ideals and that such excess should be reserved for more abundant societies. Due to scarcity of resources, it was crucial that new construction methods minimized the use of building materials. It was also considered vital that new domestic buildings improved living conditions from the pre-war situation. A timely architectural form would have to be robust and ductile enough to incorporate the specific and local without resorting to mere imitation. In 1940 the Committee for War Reparations (Krigsskadetrygdens gjenreisningsnemd) laid out the principles for the rebuilding of domestic housing in Norway after the war and stated that: 'The houses will have to satisfy the requirements of good architecture and, in a timely form, reflect regional building traditions' (Krigsskadetrygdens gjenreisningsnemd 1940: 18). The timely was both decidedly of the age and at the same time able to absorb the regional tradition in a form appropriate for the dawn of the new age.

The scale of the destruction and the overwhelming sense of broken continuity with the pre-war tradition complicated this work. It is estimated that approximately 12,000

private houses were demolished or torched in Northern Norway as the Wehrmacht
moved west and fire squads were ordered to demolish all buildings east of Lyngen in
Troms county to slow down the advance of Soviet forces (Jaklin 2016). In early October
German forces withdrew from the Murmansk front through Kirkenes. Soviet troops
entered Finnmark on 22 October and seized the town of Kirkenes on 25 October. The
scorched earth tactics of retreat was ordered on 28 October and continued throughout
the winter of 1944 and 1945. More than 50,000 civilians were forced to evacuate. The
rebuilding of Nord-Troms and Finnmark would go on until the late 1950s, and today
fishing hamlets, towns and the countryside are dotted with the square wooden houses
of the reconstruction era.

In the project entitled Finnmark 1956 carried out by Norsk Folkemuseum, the
museum exhibition in the relocated reconstruction buildings sheds light on daily life
during Nazi German occupation of Norway (1940–1945) and on the tremendous
hardships endured by civilians in the forced evacuations and the scorched earth policy in
the north. As a national museum that specializes in *ex situ* preservation of historic
buildings and vernacular architecture, Norsk Folkemuseum has made attempts to make
its collections more geographically and historically representative. Finnmark 1956 will
include buildings from the regions in Northern Norway, which have, until now, been
absent from the buildings exhibitions. As heritage considered, reconstruction architecture
is so ubiquitous in Nord-Troms and Finnmark that it hardly warrants the appellation of
heritage in peril. The incentive to carry out the project should rather be attributed to a
nationwide process of recognizing the unprecedented experience in the northern regions
where the scorched earth retreat caused destruction on a massive scale. Finnmark 1956
reflects a twofold aim, which corresponds both to the modern desire for a more complete
collection of regional building traditions as well as a late modern politics of recognition
where the traumatic experiences and difficult heritages are increasingly acknowledged.

This twofold character of the exhibition begs the question of the temporal orientation
not only of this exhibition, but of architectural heritage in museums more generally. In
what follows I will discuss the museum as a proto-modern institution for the safeguarding
of objects against the destructive forces of time, and the recent presentist claim that
heritage results increasingly from the interest and ambitions of our present day and age.
Heritage, I claim, is too often treated as the fallout of the transition from modern
progressive history to a postmodern depthlessness, from one history to no history, from
progressive history to temporal flattening (cf. Massey 2005: 78). I argue that the untimely
complements these ideal types of heritage as futurity *or* presentism, past *or* present, by
attuning the analysis to the time of things. The wide variety of heritage practices are
covariant also with particular properties and temporalities of different classes of objects.
Different objects require approaches that respond to the specific pace of material
transformation, the rate of decay and the different timescales of preservation. The
ephemerality of an abandoned postwar domestic building is profoundly different from
the durability of Mesolithic rock art and their individual timescales beg widely different
questions, which in turn condition heritage practices. So instead of identifying the
abstract temporality of heritage, I want to argue that the time of things presents not as
subsets either of modernist timeliness or presentist self-absorption, but as local
articulations of multiple temporalities that unfold over time as things change.

Folk museums from monuments of modernity to heritage and presentism

Museums are often claimed to take artefacts out of the ordinary flow of time and preserve them for future generations by conferring a degree of stability upon them that would otherwise not occur. The museum institution was once described by Michel Foucault (1986: 26) as a place 'of all times that is itself outside of time and inaccessible to its ravages'. The birth of modern museums both reflect and alleviate the sense of historical rupture. As the first museum in Norway to combine ethnographic collections with open air exhibitions of vernacular buildings, Norsk Folkemuseum in Oslo corresponds with the Foucauldian idea of museum as a particularly powerful modern chronotope. The founding of the museum in 1894 was precipitated by the alleged peril of traditional culture. The influx of mass-produced goods into rural communities and the transition to a more diverse work life undermined traditional craftsmanship and customs of autarkic, rural households. The underlying mechanism that caused a sense of urgency in this kind of museum work was the growing awareness of history as a momentous, forward-moving force, which would cause irreversible change in traditional peasant societies (Eriksen 2014). In what was perceived as an increasingly volatile present, the enduring artefacts of rural folk life acquired both affective and economic value. Folk museums that were established as memorials of traditional culture became monuments of modernity, according to Anne Eriksen (2014: 108), who regards them as exemplary expressions of the modern regime of historicity and historical consciousness. The growing historical awareness of the profound difference between past and present, yielded a new way of approaching traditional artefacts and vernacular architecture. Fuelled by a widespread sense of loss, the artefacts were approached historically and, irrespective of their actual age, their rural origins made them into exemplars of a non-descript 'past', 'tradition' or 'national culture' (Eriksen 2014: 110).

Folk museums are still testaments of the sense of irrevocable and accelerating historical change that brought them into existence as caretakers of the vanishing past in the age of industrialization, but their temporal scope has been broadened to include buildings from the past 70 years. Current collection practices are however far more restrictive compared with the heyday of the folk art movement. The transition, however, from a modern to a presentist framework for understanding our relation to the past has been understood as the extent to which heritage is shaped by interests in the present, effectively making the past a derivative of the present. Eriksen (2014: 147) claims that heritage is temporally flattened, or not even primarily about the past; rather it is a system of sites, buildings and objects brought into the present in terms of property, owned by states, groups or even individuals committed by a sense of moral obligation or political interest. Heritage as a late twentieth-century phenomenon 'above all addresses the relationship between the object and its present owner' (Eriksen 2014: 149). It is the interest of the heirs that determines the heritage and as a consequence it is seen as decidedly presentist. In contrast to antiquities or monuments where age and historical consequence defines their value, heritage value is defined in the present by those who are willing to act as its heirs (Eriksen 2014: 149).

Heritage is often treated as a symptom of presentism. The academic response to the heritage boom of recent decades has been to explore its political, cultural and economic motivation in the present. Several studies in the field have dealt with how contemporary discourses and institutionalized practices render certain pasts valuable and meaningful, while ignoring or actively repressing others. Accordingly, heritage is often seen as a result of deliberate selection of elements with which present societies wish to identify (Harrison 2012: 4). A presentist notion of heritage starts with the cultural recall in the present and argues that heritage reflects the present more than it represents the past. 'What makes these things valuable and meaningful [. . .]', Laurajane Smith states in her influential book, *Uses of Heritage*, 'are the present-day cultural processes and activities that are undertaken in and around them' (Smith 2006: 3). Steve Watson and Emma Waterton (2010: 89) assert that '[h]eritage is thus very much a thing of the present rather than the past to which it constantly alludes', given that objects which notionally belong to the past are still owned and used in the present. Barbara Kirshenblatt-Gimblett (1995: 369) has also stressed this presentist aspect of heritage on several occasions, maintaining that 'heritage is a new mode of cultural production in the present that has recourse to the past'. For other authors, cultural heritage refers to an 'ongoing reconfiguration of the past as dictated by the needs of the present' (Burch 2005: 212–3). The past itself is placed resolutely in square brackets.

These perspectives from cultural heritage studies suggest a kinship with the work of François Hartog in the sense that heritage is understood as a cultural expression where the meaning of the past derives increasingly from the present (Tamm 2015: 1). Heritage also plays a central role in Hartog's (2005, 2015) discussion of presentism, which he argues is a new attitude towards time that differs in several respects from the modern, progressive and future-oriented conception of historical time. Memory and heritage are key concepts employed by Hartog in characterizing how contemporary societies relate to the past. He claims that the contemporary era is engulfed by an expanding and perpetual present, which makes it difficult to resolutely and positively consider the passing of time as a progression from past, through present and into the future. Heritage is both a symptom of and a response to presentism (Hartog 2015: 191). Central to the notion of presentism is the sense of unease caused by an uncertain future and the inability to fully break with the past, to the effect that the present becomes omnipresent, a regime of historicity enfolded by the unending 'now'. Heritage is mobilized in times of crisis as a way of both acknowledging and alleviating ruptures in time, but, as Hartog contends, it is difficult to settle on one definite meaning of the term heritage (Hartog 2015: 189). Hartog's conceptualization of heritage relies on Krzystof Pomian's notion of 'semiophores' understood by Hartog as signs of the type of relation to time that a society decides to establish, or 'visible objects endowed with meaning' (Hartog 2015: 152). Heritage is seen as a sign of our specific relation to time, which is characterized both by our fear of letting the past slip away as well as our reluctance towards meeting the future head on. Hartog states that memory and heritage 'testify to the uncertainties in, or the crisis of, the present order of time' (Hartog 2015: 11).

Presentism is characterized by a twofold obligation that acts retroactively as a sense of debt and the duty to remember, and is ahead of itself in the manner of responsibility and precautionary thinking: 'This double indebtedness, toward the past and the future, but derived from our present and weighing upon it, is another hallmark of our contemporary experience' (Hartog 2005: 202). It is a mode of relating to time that results from unease and precaution, rather than attesting to an organic continuity with the past, or that progresses by placing the past resolutely in the rear-view mirror. Consequently, heritage calls to mind the proverb, grasp all – lose all. For neither is heritage able to foster an organic relationship with the past as immersed in daily life, nor is it capable of attaining a proper historical distance to the past. Heritage deals with a past that 'the present cannot or does not want to relinquish entirely' (Hartog 2015: 152).

This presentist rendition of heritage presents us with a paradox. For, on the one hand, it seems as if the present is in possession of powerful tools to control and sanction specific understandings of the past through heritage. On the other hand, the recent, almost indiscriminate application of the term – an eclecticism which 'turns everything into heritage' (Hartog 2015: 189) – means that the concept has been pushed to its limits and that our era is besieged by memory and heritage. The inflation of heritage and memory is treated as symptomatic of the end of the modern regime of historicity and the associated inability to squarely dissociate past from present. I claim that if we consider this not as a failure to attain critical distance, but as a way to recognize the manifold ways that the past exerts pressure on contemporary life and practice, we may attribute the broader and more eclectic understanding of heritage to a growing recognition of the past as still ongoing. This is the potential I wish to explore by bringing attention to how disjointed time, or a time out of joint, can live on in organic matter and in time assert agency. The questions raised to explore this potential are of a different kind. Instead of identifying an overarching sense of historical time, one might start by questioning the assumption of a unitary temporality that endows heritage objects with meaning. As untimely, objects are seen as 'polychronic assemblages that are temporally out of step with themselves and their moment' (Harris 2008: 10).

Unsolicited heritage and the precarious achievement of stability

The faltering of the modern conception of time as a linear, sequential process from past to present and future, has, claims Hartog, been replaced by a new presentist regime of historicity even though there are cases where regimes overlap or where interferences occur (Hartog 2015: 107). Despite these overlaps or interferences, the idea of a regime of historicity is that of a homogenous, stable and all-pervasive structure (Jordheim 2014). In this sense heritage is a genuinely new and wide-ranging phenomenon that attests to the collapse of, or crisis in, the modern conception of historical time. Still, it may be argued that the idea of heritage in presentist thought as a present-day cultural construct also serves to reaffirm the profoundly modern notion of the past as left behind and available only through different forms of cultural recall in the here and now (Olsen and Pétursdóttir 2016: 38). The result is that the past seems optional rather than an inevitable and 'thrown' condition of any present (Olsen and Pétursdóttir 2014: 22). One of the problems with the concept of presentism in this context is that it does not acknowledge the haunting dimension of traumatic pasts or the notion of a past that will not pass, so central to memory studies and philosophy of history in recent years

(Assmann 2013: 257–8; Lorenz 2010: 70). The presence of the past is also materialized in our surroundings. The rich material afterlife of the Second World War illustrates a prolonged and unwanted occupancy (Olsen and Witmore 2013). Leftover barbed wire, blown up gun turrets and military telegraph cables protruding from the ground are not only material memories of war, but objects that continue to emit the echoes of military zones, fortifications and no-go areas for decades after wars end. This kind of material afterlife in our surroundings affects not only our movements and heightens a sense of trespassing, it also conditions future action and the stratigraphic layering of the landscape for years to come. As a form of unsolicited heritage, the rich and recalcitrant material afterlife in our immediate surroundings does not align well with the split between a passive past and an active present.

Our ways of making sense of and relating to time might also be affected by things that cross temporal borders and chart a different course from the one we had anticipated. The notion of the untimely is closely related to the idea of materials unfolding over time, and particularly the idea that material processes cause things to 'slide out of joint from their expected object-positions' (Domínguez Rubio 2016: 62). Theories of the untimely also point to the flaws of understanding objects as positioned by the singularity of one particular moment in time. Jonathan Gil Harris has employed the concept of the untimely in his study of Shakespeare and Renaissance material culture, and one key insight of this work is the sense in which an object can 'prompt many different understandings and experiences of temporality – that is, of the relations between now and then, old and new, before and after' (Harris 2008: 4). Here the past is not cancelled by the present in a temporality of simple, linear succession. For Harris, one ambition of developing a theory of untimely matter is rather to ask how 'the past is alive in the matter of the present' (Harris 2008: 12). By calling attention to the untimely and hybrid realities of untimely matter, Harris also reserves the potential for things to articulate a different experience of temporality where past and present become entangled, or exist as conjunctions that combine active elements from different times (Harris 2008: 145). In contrast to the modern understanding of the timely, which sought to distil a material expression fit for the age, the untimely disrupts the identity of positioned objects through a more complex articulation of past–present relations.

The work of the untimely

It might seem strange to suggest some kind of affinity between the untimely and heritage, or to consider the possibility of experiencing the untimely through heritage. More than anything, the form of objecthood in the heritage realm is characterized by the representational role appointed to objects on display, meaning that their form is expected to reflect the character of a distinct period, people or place and that we invest a lot in their material stability, which we regard as integral to maintaining cultural memory and a sense of identity. In museums the object often becomes an index of a geographical and temporal origin, which it is expected to represent faithfully. Likewise, in the project Finnmark 1956, the practice of 'territorializing time' and 'historicizing space' to depict 'the story of the people of place x and time y' is instrumental in the selection process (Dicks 1999: 352). The house from Olderfjord will be restored to its near-original form to reflect how it would have looked in 1956. As soon as a definite temporal threshold is established, certain things will seem out of place, out of season and untimely and will be left out of the final museum exhibition altogether. As a chronotope, Finnmark 1956 guided museum conservators upon entering the abandoned house in Olderfjord to determine what kind of building materials, interiors, household appliances and furniture they would bring along to the final exhibition. Authenticity, in turn, becomes a function of this chronotope in the sense that objects which were present in that place at that time, are considered indispensable, while more recent additions to the household are disposable.

A theorization of the untimely applied in a heritage context would have to consider the possibility that the heterodox time of things and their active pasts exceed the historical periodization where objects are fully of one time. It would also question the assumption that objects unequivocally belong to one period, which they in turn represent. A theory of the untimely invokes the multitemporal layers of things where older historical layers may materially condition recent additions, and where new layers will change the constitution of something that is already there. Museums are not beyond the ravages of time, they are working hard to maintain the specific and recognizable object-positions of artefacts, which are changing incessantly to the despair of preservationists. Fernando Domínguez Rubio (2014: 621) has claimed that processes of entropy and change inherent to all objects – their materials expanding and contracting, their colours fading or yellowing, their surfaces bulging and cracking – might compel us to rethink 'museum collections as collections of processes rather than as collections of "objects"'. Taking the temporality of museum objects into closer consideration, he recognizes that stable objects are in fact 'precarious achievements' (Domínguez Rubio 2016: 65). For Domínguez Rubio the distinction between objects and things is crucial to understand the practice of stabilizing artefacts. Things are understood as materials unfolding over time, in contrast to objects that describe *positioned* things, subordinated to a specific category of value and meaning, 'a particular moment, a position, in the life of some-thing' (Domínguez Rubio 2016: 62). Objects, in other words, are more uniform in terms of their temporality, by being determined by a particular set of values and meaning prevailing at a given point in time.

But how would this sense of unfolding things translate to heritage in practice and how is this multiple temporality expressed in things that are becoming positioned as recognizable objects of one specific time and place? In one of the rooms of the Olderfjord house, the interior walls had been painted bright pink at some point after 1956 and it was determined by conservators that the wall panels should ideally be restored mechanically or chemically to their original state – a brown, transparent linseed oil paint, which revealed the texture of the wooden panels underneath. An alternative to restoration would be to replace the original wall panels with replicated boards made *ex situ* in Oslo, which would create an exact copy of the visual profile of the original boards. If the pink paint proved difficult to remove, it would not only require a lot of time and manpower, it could also risk altering the visual appearance of the original wooden panels. Reconstructed panels would severely compromise the authenticity of the historical interior as these were not native to the chronotope Finnmark 1956.

Nevertheless, transformations in the material fabric occasionally work to the advantage of conservators. As two different paint systems with different properties interact on the same surface over time, it may create the untimely effect known as craquelure. Oil paint dries by absorbing oxygen from the surrounding environment and in this process the surface stretches. Oxidation continues even after the paint has dried and when the oxygen eventually meets the underlying older layer it causes additional strain on the top layer. If the surface level is already strained to the max and the underlying layer has not hardened properly, the result is that the more recent layer disintegrates. This is what happened in the Olderfjord house where the original layer of brown linseed oil continued to expand after the pink coat of paint was added. Together with exposure to the sun and fluctuating temperatures across the seasons, this meant that the pink paint peeled off and could easily be removed to reveal the coveted 1956 layer (Figure 9.1). The original wall panels were labelled and carefully placed in

Figure 9.1 The cracked pink layer of paint being removed from a sample of the interior wall. Conservation department at Norsk Folkemuseum, March 2018. Photo: Torgeir Rinke Bangstad.

containers bound for the museum in Oslo. In this case it was the tension between different layers which caused the surface to crack. Understood as a response to specific material properties, historic preservation is here seen not as forcing one definite expression unto a passive, material substrate, but as working with the specific properties of the material at hand and picking up on the already ongoing transformation. Minor events and decisions in the past are still determining the present leeway of action. This process involves contingencies and happy accidents, which cannot easily be attributed to either the intentional preservation strategy or inherent qualities of a static object. It is a process where different temporal layers, seasonal variations and material properties interact over time to condition the potential and limits of preservation.

In our analysis this is significant because it reflects the sense in which past and present layers are not materially isolated as autonomous entities, rather they condition each other and affect each other's duration. The important thing to stress in this regard is that each historical layer has a distinctive tempo, which converges with other time spectrums to create these untimely effects. The material transformation affects the range of options available to preservationists several decades later. What Domínguez Rubio writes about the constantly changing face of the Mona Lisa is equally true for mundane, domestic architecture in the Norwegian Arctic; it is not an object made at one point in time but a *slow event*: 'Thus, when we look at the Mona Lisa today we should remember that we are not looking at a completed event, but at a particular moment of an event that is still taking place' (Domínguez Rubio 2016: 66). If we extend this notion to heritage objects on a more general level, we recognize that past events are still taking place in their very fabric and changing their constitution even if preservationists invest a lot of time and effort in maintaining a stable object-position.

Prevailing notions of heritage in museums emphasize its tranquil existence at a safe distance from the destructive forces of time, but often forget that past occurrences continue to shape the object-event right in front of our eyes. The object itself engenders both constraints and potentials in the present based on past events as well as the different durations of the constituent material elements. These effects cannot be recreated retroactively, but should be attributed to the material lifetimes from past to present and future. What we encounter in a museum's objects are not passed pasts, but the temporarily arrested moment of ongoing events. Craftsmen and artisans often insist that rather than imposing form on inert, raw material, they work with living material and follow its movement, tensions and elasticities (Ingold 2012). In our case this is particularly valid, as the tension between historic layers presented as cracks in the surface and made it possible for conservators to simply respond to the movement that was already ongoing. In and of itself this allowed the restoration of the fragile condition of timeliness that the building once aspired to when material expression embodied its age.

The pace of reconstruction and 'glacial time'

Reconstruction architecture was developed through a search for a simple, affordable and modern form of housing. A typical reconstruction house was a fairly simple, single family unit with gable roof, a near square floor plan and one and a half or two floors. The houses were uniform in style and the scale of the reconstruction effort required central, universal standards as a way to assure quality housing. Most buildings were based on standard house plans, and these blueprint house types were disseminated in periodicals and plan books. However, the inclination of central government to plan everything far in advance also met with an urgent desire to get the job done with the resources people had at hand. In the immediate postwar years it was difficult to get hold of wood, nails, cement, bricks, paint and everything else that was needed to build a house.

Figure 9.2 The house in Olderfjord prior to disassembling, May 2016. Photo: Torgeir Rinke Bangstad.

The construction of the house in Olderfjord commenced in 1950 and it was completed in 1951. The foundations were cast in cement without reinforcing steel bars and mixed with stones to reduce building costs. Because they were laid on a clayey plot of land, over time they started to give in under the weight of the house, which would have become increasingly inhospitable due to the structural damage. In recent decades the building was used irregularly as a weekend cottage, before it was permanently abandoned in the early 2000s. In contrast to most reconstruction houses in the community, the Olderfjord house had retained its overall fundamental properties over time without any major alterations (Figure 9.2).

The intersection of hectic postwar reconstruction and the slow-grinding, subterranean flux at work in the ground beneath the house as a sort of 'glacial time' (Urry 1994: 140), has created a kind of proto-museal capsule frozen in time, which matches the ambition to depict Finnmark anno 1956. But the impression of a house caught at a standstill in time belies the tremendous amount of energy and movement that has been active over the years to forge this peculiar anachronism. The faultlines where a slow material transformation met with the frenzied pace of postwar reconstruction are a fruitful point of departure for understanding the untimely, of how a house is not of one, but of many times and durations.

To keep using the Olderfjord house as a primary residence would have involved heavy investment to keep pace with the times and to reverse the collapse of the building's foundations. As a rule, reconstruction houses in Northern Norway have been extended, changed, refurbished or otherwise transformed so that the simple and timely architectural expression is amended by new layers that express both rising levels of income and buildings being refitted in accordance with individual tastes and personal preferences. The notion that buildings reflect the spirit of the times and change in accordance with broader social and cultural change is still not quite satisfactory in this case, as it tends to neglect the specific elements of houses that endure over time and transform on their own accord and not as articulations of broader, cultural shifts. One of the advantages of the theory of untimeliness is that it suspends the sequential thinking and alerts us to the intersecting rhythms in a building and how its multitude of interlaced pasts present a rich, material biography where zeitgeist is only one section among many others.

Norsk Folkemuseum was on the search for a reconstruction house that could represent the specific cultural traits of the postwar years and also reflect the characteristics typical of a reconstruction house. They found a good candidate in the house from Olderfjord, which had not undergone any substantial, structural alterations since it was first built apart from the addition of a veranda (Figure 9.3). I have argued that this case reflects the ways in which minor events in the past actively and continuously shape the historical trajectory of a particular building and how the movement of matter exceeds the human ability or the resources available to keep it firmly in place as a distinct and timely object. My encounter with the abandoned house in Olderfjord was also an encounter with what was once a more definite object with a clear identity and purpose, which had slowly given way to the unruly character of its material components.

Figure 9.3 The Olderfjord house being re-erected *ex situ* at Norsk Folkemuseum at the Bygdøy peninsula in Oslo, March 2018. Photo: Torgeir Rinke Bangstad.

The times of things

The Olderfjord house may be treated as a crowded intersection of different natural and cultural rhythms, which continue to shape the building long after its human abandonment. The house is also an assemblage of things unfolding over time according to their own peculiar material bent. Things engender specific, local temporalities where the past lives on and, on occasions, asserts an agency of its own in the present. Normally it is the changing social and cultural conceptions of certain categories of objects under different historical epistemes and regimes of historicity that have received most attention in heritage research. As semiophores, heritage objects are treated as signs of our relation to the past and as symptoms of the crisis of a modern regime of historicity that is being superseded by a pervasive presentism of indebtedness and precaution. But even within one predominant mode of relating to and making sense of time, the time of the thing is not one but many. The rich, ongoing material history of the Olderfjord house cannot be attributed to temporal identities parcelled out as isolated cultural periods. While preservationists have sophisticated means to recover and isolate individual temporal traits of objects, they also work with living materials that are prone to change and to articulate past events in the present through its many unpredictable folds. The practice of heritage preservation has been understood in this chapter less as the unidimensional human process of valuation enforced on inert and compliant matter of the past, and more as a response to complex material processes that also have leverage in determining the form, course and duration of heritage. The tensions between different historic layers and between cultural and material rhythms may even occasion a curious form of self-preservation. The untimely quality of materials unfolding over time became apparent as the postwar architecture was joined by seasonal change, expanding layers of paint, sliding clay, frost, rot and material fatigue. These ongoing material processes articulate the past of the building while also continuing to form its legacy in ways which can never be recreated or predicted accurately. At the sight of unfolding things that also effectively *make* heritage, we recognize the inherent limitations in designating the one proper time of untimely things.

Acknowledgements

I am indebted to the staff at Norsk Folkemuseum who generously took the time to talk to me and allowed me to be around both 'in situ' in Porsanger and 'ex situ' at the museum as Finnmark 1956 materialized. Thank you.

References

Assmann, A. (2013), *Ist die Zeit aus den Fugen? Aufstieg und Fall des Zeitregimes der Moderne*, Munich: Hanser.

Burch, S. (2005), 'The Texture of Heritage: A Reading of the 750th Anniversary of Stockholm', *International Journal of Heritage Studies*, 11 (3): 211–33.

Dicks, B. (1999), 'The View of Our Town From the Hill: Communities on Display as Local Heritage', *International Journal of Cultural Studies*, 2 (3): 349–68.

Domínguez Rubio, F. (2016), 'On the Discrepancy between Objects and Things: An Ecological Approach', *Journal of Material Culture*, 21 (1): 59–86.

Ellefsen, J. F. (1927), 'Hvad er tidsmessig arkitektur?', *Byggekunst*, 13: 161–70.

Eriksen, A. (2014), *From Antiquities to Heritage: Transformations of Cultural Memory*, New York: Berghahn Books.

Foucault, M. (1986), 'Of Other Spaces', transl. J. Miskowiec, *Diacritics*, 16: 22–7.

Gerhardsen, E. (1946), 'Innsats', *Bonytt*, 6: 1.

Harris, J. G. (2008), *Untimely Matter in the Time of Shakespeare*, Philadelphia: University of Pennsylvania Press.

Harrison, R. (2012), *Heritage: Critical Approaches*, London and New York: Routledge.

Hartog, F. (2005), 'Time and Heritage', *Museum International*, 57 (3): 7–18.

Hartog, F. (2015), *Regimes of Historicity: Presentism and Experiences of Time*, transl. S. Brown, New York: Columbia University Press.

Hvattum, M. (2009), 'Stedets tyranni', *Arkitektur N*, 91 (4): 40–51.

Ingold, T. (2012), 'Toward an Ecology of Materials', *Annual Review of Anthropology*, 41 (1): 427–42.

Jaklin, A. (2016), *Brent Jord 1944–1945. Heltene. Ofrene. De skyldige*, Oslo: Gyldendal.

Jordheim, H. (2014), 'Multiple Times and the Work of Synchronization', *History and Theory*, 53 (4): 498–518.

Kirshenblatt-Gimblett, B. (1995), 'Theorizing Heritage', *Ethnomusicology*, 39 (3): 367–80.

Krigsskadetrygdens gjenreisningsnemd (1940), 'Regler for gjenoppbygging etter krigsskade med støtte av Krigsskadetrygden', *Byggekunst*, 22: 18–19.

Lending, M. (2007), *Omkring 1900: Utkast til en norsk arkitekturhistorisk topikk*, Oslo: Pax forlag.

Lorenz, C. (2010), 'Unstuck in Time. Or: The Sudden Presence of the Past', in K. Tilmans, F. v. Vree and J. Winter (eds), *Performing the Past: Memory, History, and Identity in Modern Europe*, 67–104, Amsterdam: Amsterdam University Press.

Massey, D. (2005), *For Space*, London: Sage Publications.

Olsen, B. and Pétursdóttir, Þ. (2014), 'An Archaeology of Ruins', in B. Olsen and Þ. Pétursdóttir (eds), *Ruin Memories: Materialities, Aesthetics and the Archaeology of the Recent Past*, 1–27, London and New York: Routledge.

Olsen, B. and Pétursdóttir, Þ. (2016), 'Unruly Heritage: Tracing Legacies in the Anthropocene', *Arkæologisk Forum*, 35: 38–45.

Olsen, B. and Witmore, C. (2013), 'Sværholt. Recovered Memories from a POW Camp in the Far North', in B. Olsen and Þ. Pétursdóttir (eds), *Ruin Memories: Materialities, Aesthetics and the Archaeology of the Recent Past*, 162–90, London and New York: Routledge.

Payne, A. A. (1999), 'Architectural History and the History of Art: A Suspended Dialogue', *Journal of the Society of Architectural Historians*, 58 (3): 292–99.

Rustad, R. (2009), '"Hvad er tidsmessig arkitektur?": En undersøkelse av arkitekturens diskursive rammer gjennom tre arkitektkonkurranser og tre tidssnitt', doctoral thesis, Norges teknisk-naturvitenskapelige universitet. Available online: http://hdl.handle.net/11250/231095 (accessed 20 April 2018).

Smith, L. (2006), *Uses of Heritage*, London: Routledge.

Tamm, M. (2015), 'Introduction: Afterlife of Events: Perspectives on Mnemohistory', in M. Tamm (ed.), *Afterlife of Events: Perspectives on Mnemohistory*, 1–26, Basingstoke: Palgrave Macmillan.

Urry, J. (1994), 'Time, Leisure and Social Identity', *Time and Society*, 3 (2): 131–49.

van Der Rohe, L. M. (1990), 'Working Theses', in U. Conrads (ed.), *Programs and Manifestoes in the 20th Century*, 74–5, Cambridge, MA: MIT Press.

Watson, S. and Waterton, E. (2010), 'Reading the Visual: Representation and Narrative in the Construction of Heritage', *Material Culture Review*, 71: 84–97.

Whyte, W. (2006), 'How Do Buildings Mean? Some Issues of Interpretation in the History of Architecture', *History and Theory*, 45 (2): 153–77.

10

'Let's Get Rid of That Old Stuff!'
Family Heritage Objects in France at the Age of Presentism

Jean-Pierre Legendre and Laurence Ollivier

When François Hartog states that our changing attitude towards the past is a symptom of presentism, he uses as an example the iconic symbols of French heritage: historical monuments and museums (Hartog 2018). Hartog highlights that this category of heritage is now considered as a 'safe haven in times of crisis' and that it essentially reveals our fear of the future (Hartog 2003: 253). But French heritage is not limited to monuments and museums. It also includes a huge amount of objects which are privately owned. Today, the values these things embody and people's attitude towards passing them on to future generations are also symptomatic of the deep and fast-moving changes that have reshaped our society. One cannot fail to see that the approach to the things which surround us is above all indicative of the growing importance of the present in our daily life.

In the mid-1960s, Georges Perec wrote a sociological novel where objects played a major role. *Things* (French: *Les choses*) reflects an entire generation's search for a way of life and a place in which to live it (Perec 1965). The novel depicts the aspirations and doubts of a young couple that has pulled up stakes in the provinces and moved to Paris. Espousing values promoted in the magazine *L'Express*, the couple attempts to construct a pleasant living environment consonant with the values of the social class to which they aspire. They like old things that they pick up in second-hand stores, but their preference goes to objects and furniture that are in fashion, which is to say that may soon be out of fashion. The author of *Les choses*, Georges Perec, was a Holocaust orphan. He inherited nothing from his parents, who were lost to him when he was five. He held not a single memory of them. The importance of objects, and of the absence of transmission, underlie all of his writings.

It has long been demonstrated by anthropologists that objects are playing an important social and cultural role in contemporary societies (Appadurai 1986). In this regard, things that surround people have been extensively studied, for example in the United States and in the UK (Csikszentmihalyi and Rochberg-Halton 1981; Dant 1999), but also in the case of Sweden (Murphy 2014), Russia (Roberts 2017) or Japan

(Daniels 2010). But oddly enough, unlike their colleagues from other countries (and unlike Georges Perec), French anthropologists seem to have undervalued this topic. In their studies of everyday surroundings, they seem above all interested in objects when they are 'exotic, unique, or ancient' (Kaufmann 1997: 111). As for transmission, it effectively lies at the heart of the work done by French anthropologists, but they tend to concentrate far more on the intangibles (knowledge, traditions) than on material culture (Berliner 2010). Very few studies focus on the way objects are transmitted (Chevalier 1996), even though tangible heritage, as Pierre Bourdieu approached it, is fundamental to the process of cultural heritage (Jourdain and Naulin 2011).

Acquisition and transmission: A matter of social classes

France is home to one of the greatest collections of heritage objects in the world. Their accumulation dates back to the Middle Ages and the Renaissance, when French nobles began acquiring chests and armoires to store their linens, and sideboards and credenzas to display their valuable tableware in an attempt to offer visual proof of their social prominence. The sight of these prized belongings and of the portraits of illustrious family members that surrounded them was intended to impress visitors with not just their high social standing but also with the fact that their lineage extended far back, which enhanced their prestige further still. The social ascension of the members of the urban bourgeoisie dates from the end of the Middle Ages (Pernoud 1962), which is also when they began imitating the lifestyle of the nobles and furnishing their homes accordingly. Rural areas, which did not share in the economic benefits that the cities enjoyed, were at first largely bypassed by this phenomenon. It was not until the seventeenth century, when a veritable 'rural bourgeoisie' emerged, that this newly constituted class began acquiring furniture and objects whose value was consistent with their newfound social status (Gairaud 1990: 9).

The nineteenth century witnessed the triumph of the bourgeoisie, which supplanted the aristocracy as the dominant social class. But this was also the moment when the French began cultivating an exalted view of their past. This period saw the first real history of France, which was the work of Jules Michelet, in 1833. In 1882, the laws championed by Jules Ferry that made primary education mandatory helped spread this new attitude throughout the population. As opposed to being lauded as individuals of modest family background who have succeeded, exemplified by the American myth of the self-made man, France's *nouveaux riches* felt the need to inscribe their ascension within a lineage that had its place in History. They would marry the penniless descendants of aristocratic families (Souriac 1996: 156) and even fabricate family crests of their own design. These were the newly minted bourgeois of brazen ambition and a desire for a prestigious family background whom Honoré de Balzac depicted in the novels of *The Human Comedy* (de Balzac 1842–1848).

The bourgeoisie had played a major role in the Industrial Revolution and enriched itself in the process. But industrialization brought with it standardized manufactured goods that were widely sold in the large department stores that began appearing at this time. The bourgeoisie reacted to assembly-line uniformity by purchasing antiques and centuries-old furniture as a way of evidencing their uniqueness and distinguishing themselves from the working classes, who could afford only the new, mass-produced items. The desire of the well-off to furnish their apartments with the material culture of centuries past was undoubtedly influenced by the prevalent taste of the Romantics for things ancient, but the acquisitions made by these *nouveaux riches* also reflected their desire to gain legitimacy by demonstrating that they were part of a long history, that of old bourgeois families or, better still, the nobility (Charpy 2007: 111). Guy de Maupassant described the bedroom of the famous writer Émile Zola thus: 'A Henri II bed stood in the middle of a huge room where light filtered in through antique stained-glass church windows. Antique fabric was everywhere, embroidered pieces of old silk and secular altar ornaments' (de Maupassant 1883). Nineteenth-century antique dealers and auctioneers were besieged by customers looking to buy furniture and antiques with little regard for the period they came from, which often resulted in motley collections. In 1836, Alfred de Musset remarked that, 'the apartments of the rich were veritable cabinets of curiosities, with Greek and Roman items displayed alongside others from Gothic times, the Renaissance, and the seventeenth century' (de Musset 1840: 33–4).

The upper classes' taste for antique furniture lasted well into the twentieth century, and even reached down into middle classes that had prospered during the economic boom of the 1950s and 1960s. The phenomenon swelled with the profusion of summerhouses that began appearing in France in the 1950s (Renucci 1984), for many of them were furnished with antiques to give them the look of old family homes. Working-class people could not afford antiques, but they tried to leave a material inheritance to their children in the various ways their means allowed. For example, instead of having their portrait painted by an artist, the lower classes began having their picture taken by professional photographers, whose services had become accessible to the greater part of the population by the end of the nineteenth century. For the very first time, working-class people had a picture of themselves they could hand down to their children, their wedding photo, which preserved the memory of the family's history. Regardless of social class, heirlooms were handed down from one generation to the next. Many French families are still in possession of the furniture, tableware, silverware or jewellery originally acquired by their ancestors. Their value was not simply pecuniary, for they held the memory of their ancestors and the family history. In the nineteenth century, the mementos marking family events (communions, marriages, deaths) were occasionally placed in veritable reliquaries in the form of bell-shaped glass display cases (Charpy 2007: 107). Until recently, everyone seemed to recognize the importance of passing on to the next generation the whole of a family's heritage belongings. It was a way of inscribing possessions along a grand temporal arc and thereby expressing family history in terms of lineage (Mortain 2003).

Heritage transmission undermined

This attitude towards heirlooms, which for so long seemed impregnable, has now been undermined. People no longer see heirlooms as the material witnesses to a family's past, and are generally far less interested in passing them on to their descendants. In the past, people would part with family possessions only when circumstances like grave financial difficulties forced them to do so. To give them up was even accompanied with a degree of shame. Today, the situation has radically changed: people have no qualms whatsoever about selling everything they have inherited, usually for a fraction of its value. Sales are transacted through shopkeepers – antique dealers, second-hand or consignment store owners – in auction houses, or online, through sites like eBay. This situation has increased over the last few decades because of lifestyle changes. Relatively settled lifestyles, which allowed people within the limits of their means to acquire heritage objects to pass on to their heirs, became less common with the great migration to the cities of the twentieth century and gradually lessened the possibility for heritage transmission. With an increasing number of individuals relocating and families breaking up, people found themselves forced to restructure their lives, sometimes more than once (moves, divorces, etc.). Starting at the end of the Second World War, and above all following the first oil crisis of the early 1970s, people's search for jobs is also scattering them more and more across the country. Family homes are evolving into shared vacation sites, with family members staying there over the holidays to return to their roots. But when major repair work needs to be done, they are often led to sell these houses, frequently with the whole of their contents (Rey-Lefebvre 2016). The transmission of objects across generations has for the most part come to an end. As the auctioneer Bernard Piguet put it, 'In the past, heirs would fight over grandma's secretary. Today, no one wants it. They sell it off cheap' (Dumont 2015).

A French TV show entitled *A Treasure in your Home* (French: *Un trésor dans votre maison*) offers an excellent example of this change in attitude. The programme has been running on the M6 channel since September 2010, and features an auctioneer, Emmanuel Layan, and the show's host, Jérôme Anthony. The two men try to help people who wish to sell at auction some of their family possessions, which are often antiques. Almost invariably, when people are asked why they wish to sell these objects, they offer the same responses: either they are planning on redecorating their house or they need the money to pay for a vacation trip or a major celebration. Heirlooms that sometimes reach back across many generations are sold off, often very cheaply, to satisfy a need that is both immediate and fleeting; for celebrations and trips last a matter of hours or weeks, and in a few years the new decor will have aged and will need to be redone. In a way that is typical of presentism, the instant gratification of ephemeral desires has triumphed over the will to pass family heirlooms on to the generations to come.

No object, however personal, has been spared, neither the linen embroidered with a married couple's initials, nor the locket with a loved one's hair, nor the orange blossom wedding garland that has been preserved under glass since the nineteenth century. People have lost all interest in these commemorative pieces. Now, they end up at best as the bric-a-brac of second-hand goods dealers, at worst, on the junk pile. Photographs, often bound in albums, had served as the repository of family history since the nineteenth century. They bore witness to a family's social evolution and to its various relocations; they held the memory of those who had passed away and allowed people to make comparisons between newborns and family ancestors. They were the thread that connected the various episodes of the family history. Photo albums, which had been handed down across generations along with notes identifying the people in the pictures, have now ceased serving this purpose. One finds them in flea markets with increasing frequency. And whereas a while ago only nineteenth-century photographs were being offered for sale, it is not unusual today to find 'family photos that could almost be from our generation' (Pillet 2007). They have become anonymous articles of commerce, devoid of meaning, just really good, or not so good, photographs. The advent of digital photography has effectively rendered the family album obsolete. Today, photos are rarely printed out. They are saved on computers, tablets, cell phones, and external servers (the cloud). Given how susceptible to loss and damage digital data are, there is the very real risk that a lot of family photographs stored in this way will eventually disappear (Checola 2010). And with them will disappear a part of a family's history.

The collapse of the antiques market

The change in attitude towards family heritage objects has not come without economic consequence. It has resulted in massive numbers of old objects and pieces of furniture suddenly being offered up for sale. Their numbers have been steadily growing while demand for them has experienced a decline. The younger generation is simply not interested in buying old furniture. They find it outdated, dusty, dark and cumbersome and they much prefer a more modern style. The imbalance between supply and demand has had immediate repercussions, with prices dropping markedly during the final years of the twentieth century (Benhamou-Huet 1996). This was especially the case for seventeenth- and eighteenth-century furniture, which had until then been considered the most worthy of interest and a secure investment. In 1976, for example, a Louis XV desk in good condition was worth between 14,000 and 15,000 francs, the equivalent of 10,000 euros today, taking into account the inflation rate (Romand 1976: 140). That same piece of furniture now sells for 1,500 euros, or one sixth of its value of forty-two years ago. The drop in price has been even sharper for seventeenth-century pieces. A buffet from that period went for between 14,000 and 28,000 francs in 1976, that is, between 9,500 and 19,000 euros in 2017, allowing for inflation (Romand 1976: 29). Today, it sells for between 500 and 800 euros, about one twentieth of its value of forty-two years ago. The same holds true for old pieces of pewter, china or glass that were once highly valued by collectors. An engraved stemmed glass from the mid-nineteenth century sold for 250 francs in 1990, today's equivalent of sixty euros. You can buy one now for ten euros, which is to say one sixth of its value of twenty-seven years ago. Only very high-end antiques of exceptional quality still find buyers willing to pay high prices. Those museum pieces are coveted by a small number of wealthy collectors, but they represent only a tiny part of the antique market (Gallifet 2007).

By the beginning of the twenty-first century, the drop in prices had provoked a veritable crisis in the antique profession, which had been thriving since the early 1800s. The speed and extent of the phenomenon came as a surprise. After nearly two centuries of stability, prices plummeted in the space of a mere few years. Antique dealers specializing in seventeenth-, eighteenth- and nineteenth-century furniture, who represented the great majority of professionals, saw their clientele shrink and their profits dwindle. Many shops were forced to close. Some dealers went into bankruptcy, others chose to retire, but could not find buyers for their businesses. The landscape of the art and antiques market underwent fundamental change as well. Following the Second World War, in several major metropolitan areas in France, antique dealers opened stores close to each other in specific neighbourhoods, even on specific streets, like the *Village Suisse* and the Paul Bert Serpette market in Paris, Notre Dame and Bouffard Streets in Bordeaux, and Auguste Comte Street in Lyon. The euphoria the antique trade was experiencing during the economic boom of the 1960s and 1970s led real estate promoters to induce a large number of dealers to set up shop under one roof and create a sort of antique mall. This was how Paris's *Louvre des Antiquaires* came into being in 1978: over 5,000 square metres spread over five floors, located directly across from the Louvre museum and housing 250 art and antique dealers (de Wavrin 2012). Its success was such that, ten years later, a similar complex, la *Cité des Antiquaires*, opened in Lyon: 130 shops spread over 5,800 square metres on two floors (Brionne 2017). The crisis the trade went through during the early part of the twenty-first-century took a disastrous toll on both of these undertakings. The number of shops in the *Louvre des Antiquaires* declined steadily: from 250 in 1978, to 220 in 2000, to 138 in 2009, 69 in 2010, 47 in 2012 and only 10 in 2015 (Guérin 2015). The same fate befell the *Cité des Antiquaires* in Lyon, with the 130 shops open for business in 1989 dropping to a mere forty-two in 2017, when it shut down (Largeron 2017). During the same period, antique stores began disappearing in the downtown areas that had traditionally been home to them. In Lyon, in the 1980s, Auguste Comte street and those adjoining it had formed a veritable 'antiques district'. By 2017, the fifty shops it once included had shrunk to twenty (Dalas and Faivre 2016). The businesses that have taken their place have nothing to do with the past. They are rather the epitome of early twenty-first-century consumerism, and offer for sale designer furniture, fully equipped kitchens, home decorations, jewellery and brand name clothing. The situation is much the same in the area around Notre Dame Street in Bordeaux, which saw its sixty or so antique shops reduced to about twenty in the space of forty years (Rousset 2017). Nor did the crisis spare the Paul Bert Serpette antique market in Paris, where sales have dropped by 20 to 50 per cent and many owners have been forced to close (Bommelaer 2009). To fill the empty spaces, rental prices have been slashed, even for the most sought-after locations (Alix 2010). Furniture restorers have been similarly affected, with many of them going out of business due to lack of clientele. 'Antique furniture isn't restored any more; it's sold off cheaply and sometimes just thrown away,' said Thierry Wagner, who has been working in furniture restoration since 1978 (Granat 2011).

At first, the recession did not seem to affect the 'heavyweights' in the field, like the major auction houses (Christie's France, Sotheby's France, Drouot) and the high-profile antique fairs such as the Biennale des Antiquaires in Paris. Auction houses thought they could fend off the danger by restricting themselves to high-end antiques. Christie's Paris now accepts only one out of every ten pieces submitted for auction, and none of a value of less than 2,000 euros. The strategy has not, however, prevented an increase in the number of pieces that find no buyer (Dumont 2015; Robert 2016). The legendary Hôtel Drouot, which works with seventy-five Paris-based auctioneers, has seen its annual sales languish between 375 and 378 million euros these last few years whereas they were up to 482 million in 2011 (Azimi 2015; Crochet 2016). As for the Biennale de Paris, the last two fairs were disastrous, with 30,000 visitors in 2016 and 32,000 in 2017 as opposed to 75,000 in 2014 and 90,000 in 2012 (Azimi 2017).

Presentist furniture: The 'IKEA generation'

Given the way in which heritage objects used to be passed down generations, it would have been difficult to imagine that even these household items would become fungible, and yet the tendencies that have taken root over the last few decades have accomplished exactly that. With antique heritage pieces no longer in fashion, more and more people are now buying new furniture. And whereas until the middle of the twentieth century newly built pieces were produced in limited numbers, today's furniture is churned out in industrial quantities and put on the market in numbers heretofore unimaginable. The largest and best known of these companies, IKEA, offers the most compelling example: it has already sold more than 45,000,000 of its *Billy* bookcases (Belot 2013). And because it sells home furnishings worldwide, it has helped create a uniformity of lifestyle never before seen. It is now possible to speak of an 'Ikea generation' in countries as distant from each other as France and the United States (Destouches 2017).

The massive numbers further indicate that the speed at which furnishings are being replaced is constantly on the rise, propelled notably by magazines devoted to interior design, like *Côté Maison*, *Idéat* and *Elle Décoration*. These magazines so frequently promote a 'new look' in home decor that redecorating almost seems an obligation. They present interior design as a seasonal undertaking, highlighting for example the fashionable colours (Soudant 2015), the materials that generate a seaside ambience (Perreau and Gireaudet 2017) or some new 'ethnic chic' style (Trouvat 2015), which, clearly, will almost certainly be replaced by some other 'must' in not that long a time. On their part, manufacturers prompt homeowners to create an interior of their own design by using mass-produced, prefabricated units. The results, which are personalized yet conform to the standards promoted by magazines, also offer the possibility for subsequent remodelling through the purchase of new modules. For example, kitchen cupboard doors can easily be replaced with new ones of the most up-to-date style and/or colour. Retail prices are kept sufficiently low to entice consumers to keep buying new pieces, even if the 'old' ones are barely a few years old and in good condition. Furniture and home decorations are no longer valued for their durability; they are seen as disposable goods, easily replaced.

Every year, IKEA prints 220,000,000 copies of its catalogue for 41 countries (Belot 2013). For many people, it is a veritable bible for interior redecorating, and the constantly changing models that appear in the catalogue are an invitation to buy. But the Swedish manufacturer also gets people to open their wallets by discontinuing certain lines, such as that of their modular storage units. In 2014, for example, IKEA ceased offering its *Expedit* bookcase for sale, even though it was extremely popular with vinyl record enthusiasts. IKEA replaced it with the *Kallax* model, which is built somewhat differently (its thinner side panels take up a bit less room overall) but offers the same amount of storage space. The change may appear minor, but it effectively forces *Expedit* owners to replace all of their shelving if they want to add on to what they already have without sacrificing a uniform look (which is especially evident when the units are placed side by side). This has not gone down well with vinyl record enthusiasts. They created a Facebook page entitled 'Save the *Expedit*' that quickly garnered more than 19,000 'likes' (Ganneval 2014).

The great majority of consumers seem to have accepted the fact that furnishings are short-lived, which has served as justification for the flimsiness of the products today's manufacturers make and sell. Up until the 1960s, a piece of furniture rested on a solid wooden base that assured its longevity. Today, most furniture is made of particleboard with a very thin veneer and holds up far less well. It rarely withstands, for example, the disassembling and reassembling necessitated by a move. Low-grade materials are in themselves an impediment to passing possessions on to future generations. Who would want to bequeath to his or her children or grandchildren objects of inferior quality that fall apart so easily? This kind of disposable furniture is built only for the present; its remarkable popularity with consumers is another example of the intrusion of presentism in our daily life.

New antiques: The 'vintage' furniture

There exists an alternative to disposable furniture that has been the object of a certain infatuation for the last ten years or so: 'vintage' furniture. Vintage normally refers to a wine's age, but today it has also come to refer to a style that was popular in the period between 1950 and 1980. The taste for vintage goods that developed in the 1990s focused initially on clothing: first a return to the garb of the 1950s, then to the styles of the 1960s and 1970s. It subsequently spread to other postwar objects such as Formica-top kitchen tables and counters and Danish or Swedish design furniture. A style that had long been an object of disregard was suddenly attracting buyers. Vintage pieces had become the 'new antiques', and suddenly an entire period of recent history found itself in the limelight. The tastes of a great many buyers now went to the ceramic ware, glassware, lamps and furniture made in the 1950s, to the compact, practical, aesthetic and functional objects that had been designed and manufactured during the period of optimism known in France as the Thirty Glorious Years (1945–1975), back when advances in technology heralded a future that could only be radiant. The bright colours and dynamic shapes of vintage pieces would seem to have retained some of the optimism and expectation of happiness which characterized that time. The clientele for them is made up of urban-based, educated, well-off, middle-class 30-year-olds that the French ironically refer to as 'bohemian bourgeois' or 'bobos' (Polloni 2010). They are staunch supporters of sustainable development and are motivated by the noble desire to limit waste by bringing used goods back into circulation. Vintage furnishings and furniture, beyond their now fashionable look, thus have the added advantage of a very small carbon footprint.

These 'new antiques' from the 1950s, 1960s and 1970s can be found in second-hand shops and flea markets where they increasingly compete, as it were, with far older pieces. Many antique dealers have opportunistically converted to vintage, and altogether ceased dealing in goods from the seventeenth, eighteenth and nineteenth centuries. A phenomenon that had been marginal in France in the 1990s now dominates the antique trade. This is the case for the Paul Bert Serpette market in Paris, which, with its 350 shops and 12,000 square metres, is the capital's largest. Out of a total of 269 dealers listed on its website in January 2017, at least 171 (63.5 per cent) describe themselves as specializing in the twentieth century, mostly in vintage pieces dating from 1950–1980. Only eighty-five of them (31.6 per cent) specialize in the nineteenth century, and only seven (2.6 per cent) in the seventeenth and eighteenth centuries.[1] The situation is much the same at the flea market in Lyon-Villeurbanne. It is considered the second largest antique market in France and the fifth largest in Europe, with 500 dealers spread over an area of nearly 55,000 square metres. A 5,000 square metres covered market houses fifty-three shops that deal exclusively in antique furniture. Twenty-six of them (49 per cent) offer vintage furniture from 1950 to 1980, fifteen of them (28 per cent) a mix of vintage and older pieces that mostly date from the nineteenth century and early twentieth, and just twelve of them (23 per cent) offer nineteenth- or, more rarely, eighteenth-century furniture.[2]

In addition to these established businesses, vintage objects and furniture are increasingly being traded at fairs. The first of its kind was the *Puces du Design* (Design Flea Market) that was organized by an impassioned visionary named Fabien Bonillo in 1999, at a time when vintage was not yet as fashionable as it is today. Its first edition brought together, for just one day and as a street fair, fewer than a dozen dealers. But with the increasing interest in vintage, this fair has grown steadily. It now includes a hundred dealers and, in 2016, was held inside the Parc des Expositions in Paris (de Santis 2016). The success of the *Puces du Design* fair spawned others. The *Salon du Vintage* opened in 2008 in Paris, and was soon duplicated elsewhere in France, for example in Nice, Aix-en-Provence, Nantes, Strasbourg, Rennes and Bordeaux. Others would follow – *Tendance Vintage*, *Vintage Legend*, *Rock and Roll Vintage*, the *Metropolitan Vintage Show* and the *Wonder Vintage Market* – and all of them met with success. The *Puces du Design* welcomes 30,000 visitors a year, the *Salon du Vintage* in Paris, some 40,000 over 5 days, which is to say, for the latter, more than the prestigious *Biennale des Antiquaires* for a similar period. It should be noted, though, that there is a growing tendency to mix authentic vintage pieces from the 1950s, 1960s and 1970s with those of recent fabrication. The 2018 *Puces du Design* was divided into two sections: one for 'real' vintage pieces and one for newly crafted objects and furniture of a contemporary design.

While vintage objects and furniture are principally associated with the middle class, the phenomenon has reached into the upper classes in France as well, albeit in an adapted form in keeping with their social status. It has now become important for the wealthy people to acquire the work of some of the famous designers from the second half of the twentieth century, whose creations have become veritable 'design icons' and are considered works of art and displayed in museums. They have now made their way into the homes of the rich, replacing the seventeenth-, eighteenth- and nineteenth-century furniture that people simply sell off. The more prestigious of these works serve to exemplify their owners' refined taste, but they also demonstrate especial prominence, for they can fetch prices that run extremely high. For example, a 1954 *Trapèze* table by Jean Prouvé recently sold for 1.2 million euros (Poplavsky 2018). And yet, for most of these affluent buyers, it matters little whether objects were made while their creator was alive or reissued more recently. Age is no longer of importance. As a social status marker, what counts most is image. You have to have a *Pipistrello* lamp by Gae Aulenti, or an LC4 chair by Le Corbusier, or a Charlotte Perriand bookcase, Harry Bertoia chairs or Gio Ponti lamps. As Matthieu Sausverd, who deals in design pieces, noted, 'these pieces serve as status symbols. A Le Corbusier chair in the living room is as much a sign of social standing as a high-end Audi car' (Godfrain 2016). Clearly, all these objects have come down to us from the past, but whereas the legitimacy of the bourgeois rested on a family heritage that was centuries old, today the period from 1950 to 1970 is considered old enough. These objects are all indicative of a contracted perception of time. People's roots remain planted in a mythicized past, but that past is now very close to the present. It is more a matter of childhood nostalgia than of the desire to have one's place in an age-old family history.

New things that look old

Given the success vintage and design furniture have enjoyed, both for reissues and originals, present-day manufacturers of household furnishings have had to adapt, and have done so in different ways. IKEA has launched its *Argang* collection, which includes reissues of twenty-nine of its top sellers from 1950 through 1970. In 2008, Ligne Roset began producing a reissue of its CM 141 desk and its Ursuline secretary, both of which were designed by Pierre Paulin in 1954 (Keyvan 2015). Discount chain stores (Alinea, Cdiscount, Conforama, But, Duhome, Fly, Gifi) have chosen simply to imitate the classics of design furniture and to introduce enough minor changes to avoid being sued for copyright infringement. One can now buy brand new low-cost copies of the Eames armchair (whose model was created around 1950) from several different manufacturers who market them under fancy names like Dogewood, Drive, Forum, Gala, Lund, Nina, Oslo and Paga. As for the Tolix chair designed by Xavier Pochard, you can now purchase various more or less faithful replicas of it called Aix Rot, Kennedy, Lix, Liverpool, Loft, Marcelle, Maxime or Wadiga, at altogether reasonable prices. These imitation Tolix chairs cost only 35 euros, as compared with the 230 euros that a genuine reissue sells for. The result has been the creation of some kind of 'neo-vintage' furniture that all people can afford, not just those of the middle and upper classes. Be it the originals from 1950–1970, official reissues, or low-cost 'neo-vintage' imitations, vintage furniture and its derivatives are an everyday presence in the lives of French people across the social spectrum.

Manufacturers, who are always on the lookout for new marketing ploys, have begun riding the vintage wave by adapting other products to the tastes of the times and by creating a wide range of other 'neo-vintage' models: digital cameras fitted with film-era camera boxes, or 'neo-retro' cars that are inspired by the mythical models of the 1950s, like the Fiat 500, the Volkswagen Beetle or the Citroën 2CV. The watchmaking industry has similarly jumped on the bandwagon, even with its luxury lines: for example, Tudor has put out a Black Bay collection based on a diver's watch from the 1960s. Bell and Ross has done the same with an aviator's watch from the 1940s, even if the brand name was only created in 1994 (Quignon 2013; McNish 2017). At the same time, vinyl records have been enjoying a major renaissance. Whereas in 2009 they represented just 30 per cent of the sales of independent record shops in France, that figure has now climbed to between 70 and 80 per cent (San 2013). Even chefs have heeded the vintage call by resurrecting long-forgotten family recipes from the 1950s and 1960s, such as cheese soufflés and duck *à l'orange* (Lizambard 2014).

This 'neo-vintage' is not only a fashion phenomenon, it is one of the consequences of the 'new regime of historicity' that is focused on the present; a present which is 'generating day-by-day the past [...] that it needs' (Hartog 2003: 157). In the case of 'neo-vintage', clever marketing strategies have deflected a mythical past (the Thirty Glorious Years) and have fused it with the present.

Conclusion

The last twenty years have seen profound changes in the way French people deal with family heritage objects. Practices that lasted through to the end of the twentieth century have lost currency, for the younger generations are simply not interested in antiques and antique furniture. Passing on inherited or acquired family possessions had been driven by a desire to maintain the family history. It spoke of the need for a link between the past (ancestors) and the future (descendants). That this link has now been broken is highly significant. One of the causes surely lies in the advent of consumerism, which brought with it, among other things, the notion of disposable goods, whose limited lifespan is in itself an obstacle to handing objects down across generations. But the root cause is above all to be found in the way today's society perceives its relation to the past, the present and the future. The last third of the twentieth century was in this regard a time of major upheaval. The 1970s were witness to the end of the optimism of the Thirty Glorious Years and the beginning of an economic crisis, to the rise of mass unemployment and the collapse of utopian dreams. Having failed to extract ourselves from these conditions, we find ourselves incapable of imagining the future. We are now living under the reign of presentism, with the present as our sole horizon, 'with neither future nor past' (Hartog 2003: 157). In a society that gives priority to the present moment, there is no place for the desire to inscribe oneself in the long line of a family history, which explains why young people have no inclination to live amid the furniture of their ancestors.

In 2017, 67 per cent of French people believed that their country was in decline (Nodé-Langlois 2017). That people are so wary of the future may well be the source of the vintage phenomenon that has so profoundly transformed the antiques market in France, which had dealt until recently in pieces from the seventeenth, eighteenth and nineteenth centuries. The infatuation with clothing, objects and furniture from the 1950s, 1960s and 1970s (either the originals or 'neo-vintage' copies) is a return to a reassuring past, a time when unemployment was unknown and when the future was that place where dreams would be fulfilled; a time when 'things were better'. In fact, even though the vintage and 'neo-vintage' phenomena are anchored in the past, they are essentially typical of presentism, for they exemplify our inability to think in terms of the future.

The changes in the way French people deal with heritage objects is all the more remarkable in the light of the seeming immutability it had known from the beginning of the nineteenth century onwards. This particular break with the past is but one symptom of a major societal transformation. Others are already well known to us, such as the ever-increasing demands of a consumer society that favours the ephemeral (Hartog 2003: 156). Clearly, we are now unable to view ourselves in the long term. We find ourselves, at least for now, condemned to live our lives under the reign of presentism, which has come to include even the objects that surround us.

Notes

1   The internet search was carried out on the Paul Bert Serpette website in January 2018.
2   The survey was carried out on the Lyon-Villeurbanne flea market in October 2017.

References

Alix, Ch. (2010), 'Les Puces ça eut marché', *Libération*, 19 March. Available online: http://www.liberation.fr/societe/2010/03/19/les-puces-ca-eut-marche_616016 (accessed 6 November 2017).

Appadurai, A., ed. (1986), *The Social Life of Things: Commodities in Cultural Perspectives*, Cambridge: Cambridge University Press.

Azimi, R. (2015), 'L'activité de Drouot en replis', *Le Monde Economie*, 30 June. Available online: http://www.lemonde.fr/economie/article/2015/06/30/l-activite-de-drouot-en-repli_4664249_3234.html (accessed 12 February 2018).

Azimi, R. (2017), 'La biennale Paris à la recherche de son lustre perdu', *Le Monde Economie*, 11 September. Available online: http://www.lemonde.fr/economie/article/2017/09/09/la-biennale-paris-a-la-recherche-de-son-lustre-perdu_5183248_3234.html (accessed 12 February 2018).

de Balzac, H. (1842–1848), *La Comédie Humaine*, Paris: Furne.

Belot, L. (2013), 'Ikea, la mondialisation vue de l'intérieur', *Le Monde*, 25 July. Available online: http://www.lemonde.fr/vous/article/2013/07/25/ikea-la-mondialisation-vue-de-l-interieur_3453536_3238.html (accessed 6 November 2017).

Benhamou-Huet, J. (1996), 'La grande braderie des meubles anciens', *Les Echos.fr*, 15 March. Available online: https://www.lesechos.fr/15/03/1996/LesEchos/17108-110-ECH_la-grande-braderie-des-meubles-anciens.htm (accessed 12 February 2018).

Berliner, D. (2010), 'Anthropologie et transmission', *Terrain*, 55: 4–19.

Bommelaer, C. (2009), 'Aux Puces, la crise réajuste les prix', *Le Figaro.fr*, 10 February. Available online: http://www.lefigaro.fr/culture/2009/02/10/03004-20090210ARTFIG00359-aux-puces-la-crise-reajuste-les-prix-.php (accessed 12 February 2018).

Brionne, I. (2017), 'La Cité des Antiquaires va fermer', *Le Progrès*, 14 June. Available online: http://www.leprogres.fr/lyon/2017/05/14/la-cite-des-antiquaires-va-fermer (accessed 7 November 2017).

Charpy, M. (2007), 'L'ordre des choses. Sur quelques traits de la culture matérielle bourgeoise parisienne, 1830–1914', *Revue d'Histoire du XXe siècle*, 34: 105–28.

Checola, L. (2010), 'Les données numériques à l'épreuve du temps', *Le Monde*, 30 March. Available online: http://www.lemonde.fr/technologies/article/2010/03/30/les-donnees-numeriques-a-l-epreuve-du-temps_1326207_651865.html (accessed 12 February 2018).

Chevalier, S. (1996), 'Transmettre son mobilier', *Ethnologie Française*, 26, 115–28.

Crochet, A. (2016), 'Bilan des ventes aux enchères 2016', *Le Quotidien de l'Art*, 21 December. Available online: https://www.lequotidiendelart.com/articles/10126-numero-special-bilan-des-ventes-aux-encheres-2016.html (accessed 12 February 2018).

Csikszentmihalyi, M. and Rochberg-Halton, E. (1981), *The Meaning of Things: Domestic Symbols and the Self*, Cambridge: Cambridge University Press.

Dalas, P. and Faivre, W. (2016), 'Rue Auguste Comte, la fête est finie pour les antiquaires', *Tribune de Lyon*, 29 June. Available online: http://www.tribunedelyon.fr/?actualite/societe/46338-rue-auguste-comte-la-fete-est-finie-pour-les-antiquaires (accessed 7 November 2017).

Daniels, I. (2010), *The Japanese House, Material Culture in the Modern Home*, Oxford: Berg Publishers.

Dant, T. (1999), *Material Culture in the Social World*, Buckingham: Open University Press.

Destouches, J. (2017), 'Appartenez-vous à la génération Ikea?', *Femme Actuelle*, 6 January. Available online: https://www.femmeactuelle.fr/deco/news-deco/appartenez-vous-a-la-generation-ikea-35559 (accessed 12 February 2018).

Dumont, E. (2015), 'Le marché de l'art broie du noir', *Bilan, la référence suisse de l'économie*, 12 October. Available online: http://www.bilan.ch/economie-plus-de-redaction/marche-de-lart-broie-noir (accessed 7 November 2017).

Gairaud, Y. (1990), *Le guidargus du meuble régional*, Paris: Les Editions de l'Amateur.

Gallifet, L. (2007), 'Ventes aux enchères. Les nouvelles tendances du marché de l'art', *Paris-Match*, 8 April. Available online: http://www.parismatch.com/Vivre/Argent/Olivier-Choppin-de-Janvry-133381 (accessed 12 February 2018).

Ganneval, R. (2014), 'Ikea dérange les amateurs de vinyle', *Libération*, 20 February. Available online: http://next.liberation.fr/musique/2014/02/20/ikea-derange-les-amateurs-de-vinyles_981775 (accessed 12 February 2018).

Godfrain, M. (2016), 'Le Corbusier, Perriand, Eames, des designers plein d'avenir', *Le Monde.fr*, 19 October. Available online: http://www.lemonde.fr/m-design-deco/article/2016/10/19/le-corbusier-perriand-eames-des-designers-pleins-d-avenir_5016204_4497702.html (accessed 12 February 2018).

Granat, A. (2011), 'Le marché du meuble ancien en crise', *Tout pour les femmes*, 31 March. Available online: https://www.toutpourlesfemmes.com/archive/le-marche-des-meubles-anciens-en-crise (accessed 12 February 2018).

Guérin, J.-Y. (2015), 'Le Louvre des Antiquaires à Paris va fermer', *Le Figaro.fr Immobilier*, 3 April. Available online: http://immobilier.lefigaro.fr/article/le-louvre-des-antiquaires-a-paris-va-fermer_9c8a58e8-da1d-11e4-ac96-7c96fd3ca975/ (accessed 7 November 2017).

Hartog, F. (2003), *Régimes d'historicité. Présentisme et expériences du temps*, Paris: Le Seuil.

Hartog, F. (2018), 'Patrimoine, histoire et présentisme', *Vingtième Siècle: Revue d'Histoire*, 137: 22–32.

Jourdain, A. and Naulin, S. (2011), 'Héritage et transmission dans la sociologie de Pierre Bourdieu', *Idées économiques et sociales*, 166: 6–14.

Kaufmann, J.-C. (1997), 'Le monde social des objets', *Sociétés Contemporaines*, 27: 111–25.

Keyvan, C. (2015), 'Mieux que le vintage, le néo-vintage', *Madame Figaro*, 6 October 2015. Available online: http://madame.lefigaro.fr/deco-design/mieux-que-le-vintage-le-neo-vintage-260415-96318 (accessed 7 November 2017).

Largeron, D. (2017), 'La Cité des Antiquaires de Villeurbanne fermera ses portes fin août', *Lyon-Entreprises*, 15 May. Available online: http://www.lyon-entreprises.com/News/L-article-du-jour/Le-terme-de-50-ans-d-histoire-la-Cite-des-Antiquaires-a-Villeurbanne-fermera-ses-portes-fin-aout-i81322.html (accessed 7 November 2017).

Lizambard, M. (2014), *Toute la cuisine vintage*, Paris: Solar.

de Maupassant, G. (1883), *Emile Zola*, Paris: Quantin.

McNish, W. (2017), 'Montres vintage, décryptage', *Haute Horlogerie Journal*, 9 May. Available online: https://journal.hautehorlogerie.org/fr/montres-vintage-decryptage/ (accessed 8 March 2018).

Mortain, B. (2003), 'Des grands-parents aux petits enfants: trois générations face à la transmission des objets', *Recherches et Prévisions*, 71: 45–61.

Murphy, K. M. (2014), *Swedish Design, an Ethnography*, Ithaca: Cornell University Press.

de Musset, A. (1840), *La confession d'un enfant du siècle*, Paris: Charpentier.

Nodé-Langlois, F. (2017), 'Les français sont les plus pessimistes au monde face à la mondialisation', *Le Figaro.fr*, 6 February. Available online: http://www.lefigaro.fr/conjoncture/2017/02/06/20002-20170206ARTFIG00002-les-francais-sont-les-plus-pessimistes-au-monde-face-a-la-mondialisation.php (accessed 8 March 2018).

Perec, G. (1965), *Les choses: une histoire des années soixante*, Paris: Julliard.

Pernoud, R. (1962), *Histoire de la bourgeoisie en France*, Paris: Le Seuil.

Perreau, C. and Gireaudet, S. (2017), 'La nouvelle déco bord de mer', *Côté Maison*, 22 June. Available online: http://www.cotemaison.fr/inspirations/diaporama/deco-bord-de-mer-chic-chambre-maison-salon_22330.html (accessed 12 February 2018).

Pillet, F. (2007), 'Photos jetées, photos trouvées, photos recyclées', *Edit Revue*, 28 June. Available online: http://www.edit-revue.com/?Article=186 (accessed 11 February 2018).

Polloni, C. (2010), 'Qui sont les bobos?', *Les Inrockuptibles*, 4 September. Available online: https://www.lesinrocks.com/2010/04/09/actualite/societe/qui-sont-les-bobos-1131952/ (accessed 12 February 2018).

Poplavsky, A. (2018), 'Nancy-Paris: Jean Prouvé affole les enchères', *L'Est Républicain*, 9 January. Available online: http://www.estrepublicain.fr/edition-de-nancy-ville/2015/05/21/jean-prouve-affole-les-encheres (accessed 12 February 2018).

Quignon, C. (2013), 'Le business du vintage: rétro c'est trop', *Libération*, 6 January. Available online: http://www.liberation.fr/futurs/2013/01/06/le-business-du-vintage-retro-c-est-trop_871965 (accessed 11 February 2018).

Renucci, J. (1984), 'Les résidences secondaires en France', *Revue de géographie de Lyon*, 59: 29–40.

Rey-Lefebvre, I. (2016), 'Les maisons de famille, des héritages encombrants', *Le monde*, 13 August. Available online: http://www.lemonde.fr/m-le-mag/article/2016/08/13/les-maisons-de-famille-des-heritages-encombrants_4982262_4500055.html (accessed 8 March 2018).

Robert, M. (2016), 'A Paris, Christie's leader sur l'art contemporain, Sotheby's sur l'Asie', *Les Echos.fr*, 8 July. Available online: https://www.lesechos.fr/08/07/2016/lesechos.fr/0211106691676_a-paris--christie-s-leader-sur-l-art-contemporain--sotheby-s-sur-l-asie.htm (accessed 12 February 2018).

Roberts, G. H., ed. (2017), *Material Culture in Russia and the USSR. Things, Values, Identities*, London: Bloomsbury Academic.

Romand, D. (1976), *L'argus des meubles*, Paris: Balland.

Rousset, J. (2017), 'Bordeaux: la chine en pleine révolution', *Sud-ouest*, 22 January. Available online: http://www.sudouest.fr/2013/01/22/la-chine-en-pleine-revolution-942037-2780.php (accessed 7 November 2017).

San, L. (2013), 'Pourquoi le disque vinyle fait un retour en grâce', *France Info*, 17 October. Available online: https://www.francetvinfo.fr/culture/musique/pourquoi-le-disque-vinyle-fait-un-retour-en-grace_437718.html (accessed 12 February 2018).

de Santis, S. (2016), 'Les Puces du Design à la Porte de Versailles', *Le Figaro.fr*, 14 November. Available online: http://www.lefigaro.fr/sortir-paris/2016/11/14/30004-20161114ARTFIG00208-les-puces-du-design-a-porte-de-versailles.php (accessed 12 February 2018).

Soudant, H. (2015), 'Tendance peinture: quelles couleurs pour 2016?', *Côté Maison*, 15 December. Available online: http://www.cotemaison.fr/peintures-carrelages-papier-peint/peinture-couleur-quelle-tendance-pour-2016_26280.html (accessed 12 February 2018).

Souriac, R. (1996), *Histoire de France 1750-1995*, Toulouse: Presses Universitaires Mirail.

Trouvat, E. (2015), 'Le style ethnique chic? On vous explique!', *Elle Décoration*, 26 February. Available online: http://www.elle.fr/Deco/Pratique/Astuces/decoration-ethnique-chic (accessed 12 February 2018).

de Wavrin, I. (2012), 'Le Louvre des Antiquaires débute sa métamorphose', *Le Quotidien de l'Art*, 18 December. Available online: https://www.lequotidiendelart.com/articles/1626-le-louvre-des-antiquaires-debute-sa-metamorphose.html (accessed 7 November 2017).

11

Death and Archaeology in the Present, Tense

Shannon Lee Dawdy

If we are at the 'end of history', then can the death of archaeology be far behind? This is a wrong-headed question. I will show why via a critique of anti-presentism. Then I will go somewhere more interesting. Namely, how cultural attitudes towards our individual deaths can be understood as a cosmological miniature of the dominant temporal paradigm (a cultural formation). How we think about and treat death is tangled up in our experience of the present, our projections of a collective future, and the way we write about the past. And death is changing rapidly: does this represent a 'crisis of time' (Hartog 2015: 16)? In this chapter, I will start with an anthropology of history and end up at an archaeology of the contemporary.

Some problems with presentism and the end of history

What happened leaves traces, some of which are quite concrete – buildings, dead bodies, censuses, monuments, diaries, political boundaries – that limit the range and significance of any historical narrative. This is one of many reasons why not any fiction can pass for history: the materiality of the sociohistorical process (historicity 1) sets the stage for future historical narratives (historicity 2).

Trouillot 1995: 29

Many scholars have been making pronouncements about the 'end of history' and the 'tyranny of the present'. What is meant by this? Unfortunately, many things. For one thing (I'll call it Problem Number One), it is often not clear whether they mean Trouillot's Historicity 1 or Historicity 2, or some confused blending of the two (another way to gloss the difference is 'traces of the past' versus 'historiography'). Most seem to mean the end of historicity 2, History with a capital 'H', or the grand narratives of domesticating events into a developmental trajectory. The writing of History abets Enlightenment ideas about progress, which are implicated as much in Marxian analysis as in racist evolutionary thought and aggrandizing nationalism. Historical writing of this era, a particular 'regime of historicity' in Hartog's (2015) language, was as much about inscribing the future as predicting the past. It was, in a word, teleological. Foucault's (1982) critique attempted to bring an end to this kind of History. Because it is a fiction woven through gaps and silences. Because it is so often an iteration of state power. But thus far Foucault has failed to revolutionize the deeply conservative field of History.

Or the entrenched ideological attraction of teleological discourse. A case in point is another well-known author who tried to kill off history from a completely different perspective. With *The End of History and the Last Man* (1992), Francis Fukuyama attempted to write one of the grandest narratives of the late twentieth century. Following the Hegelian tradition, which presumes a universal world history unfolding, this political scientist pronounces that the end is coming in the form of a perfected stage of development – there's nowhere else (better) to go after most of the world is governed by liberal democracies and the free market. Fukuyama firmly believes that human history (that is, Historicity 1, the past) follows an evolutionary course and although he worries about the dangers of uncontrolled technology, his political stance doesn't so much end history as it ends the future. It is already known. No surprises are possible. This is Problem Number Two – even those who pronounce 'the end of history' really mean the end of the future, which is confusing. In *Specters of Marx*, Derrida (1994) analysed Fukuyama's rhetoric as an essentially Christian eschatology (the world will finally be united as a Holy Empire of non-nations) and an anxious attempt to kill Marx and end any possibility of communism by simply declaring it a thing of the past. Fukuyama's narrative is a kind of textual super-modernity (Augé 1992; González-Ruibal 2008) rather than postmodernity.

Somewhere in between lies François Hartog's (2015) *Regimes of Historicity*. While being a 'historian of history' who synthesizes the work of others (primarily that of Reinhart Koselleck and Paul Ricoeur), Hartog most of the time seems to mean Historicity 2 – or the way that we Western-style academics narrate events of the past. He starts with Homer and works his way up. But what remains entangled is how the experience of time – its duration, its speed, its repeatability, its depth – is reflected in how we write history. *Temporality* would have been a better translation into English than historicity for many of his examples. The gap between experience and narrative seems to be almost non-existent for Hartog. Thus, there seems to be no significant distinction between the perspective of the historian and the experience of other actors. History (Historicity 2) and its cultural milieu (its anthropology) are one and the same. Although I'm going to call this Problem Number Three (the occlusion of everyday temporality and narrativity), this perspective has its merits. It does not enshrine the historian with a privileged, omniscient experience of time denied to the rest of us.

Hartog's account narrates the by-now familiar depiction of modernity as characterized by speed and acceleration. Anthropologist Thomas Eriksen (2001) in his book, *Tyranny of the Moment*, documented the speed-up of time that has been growing exponentially since at least the Industrial Revolution, and its deleterious effects on human relations. He says, 'acceleration affects both the production of knowledge and the very mode of thought in contemporary culture' (2001: 148). Eriksen expresses an apocalyptic sense of temporality that is shared by the French architect and philosopher Paul Virilio, geographer David Harvey and theorist-at-large Frederic Jameson. That is: that we live in an era in which time is compressed and broken up, through our telecommunications, travel and modes of work into tiny, manic fragments such that we have lost even modernity's sense of progressive linearity. Eriksen and Virilio go so far as to say that time itself stops and melts into an eternal present. According to Virilio, dromocracy, or a political economy where speed is power, is creating 'a society that has no future and no past, no extension and no duration' (1997: 28).

Frederic Jameson writes in an article titled the 'The End of Temporality' (presumably playing with Fukuyama) that 'the new rhythms are transmitted to cultural production in the form of the narratives we consume and the stories we tell ourselves' (Jameson 2003: 704). He then proceeds to analyse the Keanu Reeves and Sandra Bullock Hollywood blockbuster film *Speed* as a cultural production that captures what Eriksen would call the tyranny of the moment and what Virilio would call dromocracy. Virilio's (2004) work is coloured by a dystopian romanticism, a sense that not only experience, but materiality and space itself, are being emptied out by the virtual, and by speed. The means (vehicles) matter more than the ends (cargo) and we are losing sight of where we are going. We have lost the future.

What is helpful from this anxious literature is the serious attention to tempo (speed) over progression, especially as evidenced by an anthropology of experience that documents how media, digitized communication, transportation, warfare, artificial lighting, etc. affect our experience of time. What is not so helpful (Problem Number Four) is the simplistic division of time into past–present–future that really doesn't get us very far towards a cultural phenomenology of time. When these authors note the planned and ever-faster obsolescence of commodities, the way that even unprecedented events like 9/11 are immediately mediated and archived, or the ways that technology (especially cell phones) keeps us always reacting and rarely planning, they are not describing a society living in the present. What they are actually describing is a form of temporality chopped into little bits – pieces of data – that are moved around in space–time in different configurations. It would be more accurate to say we have become a compulsively archival society that does anything *but* experience the present because we are so busy recording and creating a past as a resource for the future. Sometimes the bits (digital images, emails, but also material items like plastic cups) are put quickly and permanently into the past – archiving as oblivion, discard. Sometimes the data bits are collected precisely because you plan on using them in the future – for utilitarian purposes, or planned nostalgia (the Facebook function that recycles posts on their anniversary captures this archival function perfectly – it is both retrospective and prospective). The past is, if anything, more accessible to more people than ever before. Further, a great deal of labour and life activity is oriented not so much towards the present but a near-future (the next thing on our to-do list, the weekend, etc.). This is, in fact, a common observation of contemporary consumer society about which many people have some critical self-awareness. Yoga teachers and purveyors of self-help manuals offer the counter-mantra, 'be mindful in the present'. I am suggesting that a more qualitative approach to temporality that looks closely at the thought and behavioural patterns that get lumped under presentism would be more productive than hand-wringing about the 'tyranny of the present'. The current dominant temporal paradigm of post-industrial, cosmopolitan society might better be described as 'Anticipatory Bit-Time'. This phrase captures two tendencies: (1) we are an archiving society that chops time into small, moveable bits, and (2) that we have a strong tendency to live in a state framed by the near-future. But even this dominant paradigm may be changing (an assertion I will expand upon in the very near future!).

So, what about archaeology? Archaeology, as many have noted, is the antiquarian practice par excellence. Archaeologists produce antiquity. We have helped define modernity by showing what it is not. *If* the history of grand narratives is dying, as Foucault wanted and Hartog seems to fear, then surely old school archaeology must be dying too? Some branches may be but the subfield of historical archaeology has striven to respond to Foucault's critique of teleology. The field has also struggled to define itself in temporal terms. The prevailing definition is synonymous with the archaeology *of* modernity (circa 1450 forward). Until recently, it would be rare to read about components that dated later than about the First World War. Once we arrived in a period with living narrators who can provide a memory of events, archaeology seemed to stop. But now even that has changed. Starting in the 1990s, archaeologists began to pay more attention to the 'recent past', although where the divide between the 'present' and the 'recent past' lies is usually left unspecified (Buchli and Lucas 2001; Graves-Brown, Harrison and Piccini 2013; see also the *Journal of Contemporary Archaeology*). Archaeologists, perhaps better than historians, have long known that such periodization is more a matter of heuristics than reality. The cut-off between the past and the present is, if not arbitrary, culturally relative (Problem Number Five for the anti-presentists, who never define the boundary). As the subfield has gained momentum, more practitioners now call what they do an 'archaeology of the contemporary'.

Old school scholars ask: how can this be archaeology at all? Isn't it by definition a study of past societies? Clearly, archaeologists of the contemporary are in the process of redefining what archaeology is (I now explain to students that it is simply the study of human–material relations). I have to wonder whether Eriksen et al. would take this archaeological movement as a symptom of 'the tyranny of the present'. I accept the implication of the alarmists (as unreflective as it may be) that the interpenetration of popular and scholarly temporalities has significant effects. But perhaps this seepage is productive, not dangerous. In the next section, I will show how I am letting everyday temporalities inform my own work as an archaeologist of the contemporary. Doing so allows me to see that popular conceptions of collective time are on the verge of a tectonic shift. This shift goes so deep it involves how we (those living in post-industrial, cosmopolitan and increasingly secular spaces) think about the most fundamental timeline of all: our own lives, and deaths.

An archaeology of contemporary death

Frederic Jameson takes the anxious critique of presentism to a startlingly personal level when he diagnoses one possible cause for what he thinks of as our delusional entrapment in an eternal present. He says, 'perhaps our own attitudes on the subject [of destiny and fate] are conditioned by the modern American concealment and sanitization of death' (Jameson 2003: 709). Jameson does little more with this intriguing suggestion. However, Philippe Ariès (1974, 1981), in his opus on Western death, connected the way death was imagined and treated as a symptom of the gestalt of each period. Although not explicitly one of Ariès's themes, I will trace here how ideas about the afterlife and the ways they reverberated upon individual trajectories necessarily involves a paradigm of temporality. Ariès's scheme identified four (later, five) basic phases of Christian European death. 'The Tame Death' of the early medieval period is one in which death was considered natural, reflecting 'the conviction that the life of a man is not an individual destiny but a link in an unbroken chain, the biological continuation of a family or a line that begins with Adam and includes the whole human race' (Ariès 1981: 603). The second phase, the 'Death of the Self', marks the beginnings of a more pronounced individualism in the late medieval period continuing through the Renaissance and the Enlightenment (ending with the 'Remote and Imminent Death' of atheism). Life became unpredictable and death was a violent rupture. From the Romantic period into the Victorian era, some amelioration of this crisis in death appeared in the form of a focus on enduring love and the development of a death cult: 'The next world becomes the scene of the reunion of those whom death has separated' (Ariès 1981: 573). Aspects of this death culture and its memorialization practices (monuments, mourning jewellery, obituaries, death photography, etc.) never entirely went away. These phases should not be seen as entirely replacing one another, but as overlapping and evolving cultural formations. As one reviewer says, Ariès's approach was, 'a mélange of the synchronic and the diachronic' (Porter 1999: 83; for other critiques, see Stone 1978; Whaley 1981). For my purposes, what is important is not whether Ariès's periodization is solid, but that in each case a more general temporal gestalt is embedded in attitudes towards death.

This brings us to the contemporary moment and Ariès's 'Invisible Death', which could also be titled the sanitized or medicalized death of the twentieth century. This cultural period marks the colonization of death by science and industry. Death represents a failure of the body; it becomes dirty and embarrassing. Outside the professional sanctuaries of funeral homes, communal rituals started to break down. To cover the shame, embalming and restoration aimed to create a lifelike 'memory picture', which suggested the deceased were only sleeping. These practices led, according to Ariès, to a society that behaved, 'as if death did not exist' (Ariès 1981: 613). This denial of death, developed in its most extreme form in the United States, was made easier by the sequestering of the corpse in morgues, funeral homes and suburban cemeteries. Or by eliminating it altogether through the even more sanitary practice of cremation. In a world in which one's own death is denied and that of others rarely spoken about, the present, indeed, expands exponentially because there is no clear endpoint, no imagined future.

This brings us back to Jameson, who could just as well be citing Ariès on 'the modern American concealment and sanitization of death' (Jameson 2003: 709). What I want to emphasize is that this comment made in passing by Jameson indexes his intuition that our attitudes towards death are bound up with our dominant temporal paradigm in everyday life. I would argue that it is impossible to say that one merely reflects the other; rather, they are co-constitutive. As accounted in my re-interpretation of Ariès' phases of Western death, the phenomenological temporality of life tends to cohere with conceptions of death. A sequestered denial of death, with funeral practices broken into little bits of standardized professionalism and non-linear 'memory pictures' reproduced at a funeral service fitted with the inadmissible long future and modular character of 'Anticipatory Bit-Time'.

However, Jameson and Ariès only bring us up to about the end of the twentieth century. It is starting to look like we will need to label a new period. The denial of death, Ariès' 'Invisible Death', is breaking down and being replaced by a new gestalt. I will illustrate what I mean with some snapshots from my own research on contemporary death practices in the United States. However, the movements that I will describe have parallels in the UK, Australia and Western Europe. Nonetheless, it is safe to say that an extreme form of sanitized death was practised in the United States in the twentieth century. I am also comfortable saying, as a result of research by myself and others, that American death is now going through a kind of post-industrial revolution. In the conclusion, I will return to what all this seems to portend: if death practices are changing, then the dominant temporal paradigm may be as well. While this transformation is still emergent and uncertain, I believe we are witnessing the beginning of the end of what has been called presentism.

To date, the most significant work on modern American death practices remains journalist Jessica Mitford's classic exposé, *The American Way of Death* (1963, revised 1998), which documented the ways that the American funeral industry standardized this important life ritual and professionalized what used to be a form of family care. Viewing of the embalmed body became a standard practice of a proper funeral among Christian and secular Americans. Despite Mitford's critique, for decades little changed in American funeral practices. But between 2000 and 2015, the cremation rate doubled and now one-half of all Americans choose this disposition of the body with rates projected to reach 70 per cent by 2030. Northern California, where cremation rates are already at 80 per cent, is also the epicentre of two newer movements – green burial and at-home (or DIY) funerals. In this chapter, I will focus on these last two because they are newer trends and adherents are particularly articulate about the values that drive their choices.

Since the fall of 2015, with my collaborator, filmmaker Daniel Zox, I have been travelling the United States, from the Midwest to New Orleans to California, conducting interviews. The simple question at the heart of the project is: What does the changing face of death tell us about American life? We follow key innovators who are transforming the treatment of human remains and forms of memorialization. We also speak to everyday Americans and ask them two key questions: *what do you want done with your body after you die?* and *what do you think happens to us after we die?* Although our focus is contemporary society, we are engaged in a classic archaeological operation: how do the ways in which a society treats its dead reflect its cosmology, its values, its organization? In what follows, I zero in on those moments when temporality was invoked.

In addition to innovators, we spoke to over twenty conventional funeral directors and staff members to get their perspective on how funeral practices are changing. While they have been criticized by Mitford and others for being the main agents of the depersonalization of death in the United States, these professionals often express a deeply compassionate orientation – and a pronounced worry that most Americans seeking their services are in too much of a hurry.

Jason is an independent funeral director located in rural Louisiana.[1] He says that funerals are becoming smaller – and shorter. He says that this is because 'as a culture, we have less time'. He cites a fact referenced by many other conventional funeral directors I spoke to: that the traditional American funeral used to take several days (in the range of three to five): a three-day wake and vigil, followed by a funeral ritual and then a separate graveside ritual. Now, most funerals last half a day, at most. Some services take as little as twenty minutes. The wake has been replaced by an optional hour or two before the service for viewing (of the body) and visitation (with the family), or been eliminated altogether. If a burial is the chosen disposition, often only a few family members are present to witness the internment, if anyone is there at all. Cremation, unless the family members are Hindu or Buddhist, connotes no expected rituals at all and is often handled via email and postal delivery of the remains.

The reasons for this speed-up in the conventional funeral is both attitudinal and structural. Jason says that people just don't think they are important anymore, but also that families are so scattered, over hundreds or thousands of miles, that the travel involved takes significant time. Even if their employer offers bereavement leave (not a protected right or standard benefit in the United States, see Cann 2014: 3–10), it is rarely more than three days, two of which are eaten up by travel. Those living on precarious hourly wages often have no paid leave at all and can't afford to go many days without pay.

This compression of time has meant a transformation of funeral space. Jason selected the ranch-style house converted into a funeral home because the chapel area was small. This means that with the dwindling attendance at conventional funerals, the room might still feel full and not so sad. These businesses were once *homes*, as another one of my interviewees said. Sometimes the funeral director's family lived upstairs, but these capacious buildings also provided sleeping rooms, kitchens and eating areas for family members who were coming from out of town. Funeral homes were in part hospitality businesses for an extended ritual that intentionally suspended the rhythm of labour and life.

The majority of the professional funeral directors I spoke with expressed a variation of the concern that most of their clients are moving too fast. They worry that grieving itself is being short-circuited by the speed of life. The end-stage of Ariès's 'Invisible Death' stage needs an additional qualification: the death ritual has sped up and barely interrupts the flow of life. Here one does get the sense that the temporal paradigm is one of speed, in which we barrel towards a near-future (while denying the long-future of death) and rarely pause to appreciate the present. But, as most all of my interlocutors *also* asserted, these conditions and the overall depersonalization of death may be coming to an end. There are two growing movements in American death practice that reflect this with particular clarity: one revolves around the preparation of the corpse and rituals in the immediate period after death, and the other embraces the long durée of human matter and energy.

DIY death

One of the fallouts of the industrialization of death in twentieth-century America is a confusion between standard practice and legality. As a result, many Americans operate under the misconception that only a licensed funeral director can prepare the body for burial or cremation, or that the corpse must, as soon as possible after the heart stops, be transferred to a morgue (if an autopsy is required) or a funeral home. Juridically, freedom of religion has always allowed family care of the body (washing, dressing, visitation) in a home, and religious minorities such as the Amish and Orthodox Jews were never forced to adopt professionalized death care. Another popular misconception is that the corpse is a source of dangerous contamination, but there are very few diseases that survive the host's death (even the perception that cholera originates from dead bodies is incorrect (World Health Organization 2018)).

A similar misunderstanding ruled throughout much of the twentieth century that the only place to legitimately *begin* life was in a hospital. But the home birth movement of the 1970s attempted to change that perception and led to the rise of a generation of lay midwives and doulas who worked to demedicalize the natural process of birth. Some of these same women, or those influenced by them, have begun to switch their attention to the demedicalization of the other end of the life-cycle.[2] Throughout the United States, but especially along the West Coast (Washington, Oregon and California), a grassroots movement advocating for at-home body preparation and funerals is growing. In this movement, not only is the professional funeral home bypassed as a locale for services, but embalming is rejected. The values emphasize family-centred care and chemical-free processes. The primary rationale for a home funeral is that direct contact with the loved one's body aids in the grieving process by overcoming the denial of death.

Grace runs a small consultancy based in Northern California, but she travels all over the country training individuals to become 'death doulas', or to prepare for a death in their own family for which an at-home funeral is planned. In the course of her 20-year career, she has worked with over 400 families. Her description of the process is suffused with temporality. For one thing, the clock is slowed way down – back, in fact, to the timeline of the pre-industrial era. Although theoretically an at-home funeral could take place very quickly – within twenty-four hours as practised by Orthodox Jews and traditional Muslims – absent these religious traditions, Grace's training programme presumes a three to four day timeline during which the body is washed by family members, dressed and perfumed with essential oils, and placed on dry ice. Family and friends are then welcomed to visit with the deceased over a period of days. Or, those outside the immediate family are invited for a particular ritual or phase of the wake and funeral. There is a strong focus on *re*-personalizing the experience – decorative objects, dress, food served, music played, scents, etc. – should reflect the likes and personality of the deceased. Rituals are often ad hoc and improvised according to the lifestyle and values of close family and friends.

Grace says that people around the world keep the corpse at home for three days, and there is a reason for this beyond the need to allow adequate time for visiting and rituals, or even to verify (prior to modern medicine) that the individual was not just in a deep coma. That is, in those three days, the non-embalmed body undergoes a series of transformations. Death, she says, 'is not an event, it's a process'. It takes a while for the body's systems to shut down. Immediately after death, the body takes a while to cool. Rigor mortis peaks around thirteen hours after death but it usually lasts no more than two days, after which the tissues relax again, often resulting in a peaceful expression coming over the deceased's face. This transformation is something Grace believes to be a vital passage for loved ones to witness. By the third or fourth day, the skin starts to fade and shrink and the body 'looks like a shell'. The death process is coming to an end. Importantly for Grace, at that point death cannot be denied – there is no one home in that shell. The body becomes unfamiliar and uncanny. Loved ones can then accept that the spirit has moved on. The body no longer *is* the loved one, but a collection of mere bones and tissues, cells and molecules.

In addition to training other death doulas, Grace oversees at-home funerals for clients in her community. But education remains her main task – to educate family members about options, about what to expect, and what steps to take. She often gets a call in the middle of the night from panicked family members once someone has passed away at home, wondering what they should do. The first thing she tells them is: 'There's no rush. Go get some rest.' As Alexa Hargerty notes in her own study of the home funeral movement: 'One of the expressions frequently heard in the movement is "death is not an emergency"' (Hagerty 2014: 436). This message is both a surprise and a relief to Americans accustomed to speeding through life. It also contradicts their conditioning to think of death as a sudden failure of the body followed by a dangerous liminal state. Naturalizing death for Grace means slowing it down.

This deceleration extends to the period after the funeral. Opportunities for memorialization and ritual observance do not have to be restricted to those three to four days. In the case of a close friend whose death and directions for an at-home funeral served as Grace's calling to this work, it was not until over a year later, when she was on a white water rafting trip, that she scattered her share of the ashes. At that moment, she felt not closure but 'completion with the deepest of the grief'. Another way in which at-home funerals work against the denial of death is by keeping the relationship between the dead and the living open. For those like Grace working to naturalize the death process, the dead are never entirely gone. Their spirit gets broken up and redistributed into memory snapshots and momentary flashbacks. But it also, along with the body's constituent molecules, gets absorbed into the environment and eventually transformed into animals, plants and minerals. Grace expresses a belief in a general form of reincarnation. Although the long future of death is vague, it is definitely not final. Death marks not the end of life, but its transformation into another form. It is a form of recycling. Grace says that for her own arrangements, she is intrigued by a proposed project to compost human bodies. Her death beliefs are consistent with an emerging temporality of life itself that is not fast and linear, but slow, distributed and cyclical. It is reflected in everything from the 'slow food' movement to recycling habits, to the self-help command to 'be present'.

Green burial

Readers may be more familiar with the green burial movement (also called natural burial in the UK or forest burial in Germany (Hockey et al. 2012)). As with DIY funerals, one of the main tenets involves moving away from embalming and the sanitation of death that in the cemetery is extended through the use of concrete vaults and metal caskets. These material practices express important aspects of Ariès's

'Invisible Death': the desire to delay or deny decomposition, and the belief that the corpse poses a contaminating danger to the living. But what the decaying corpse may have presented most dangerously is a confrontation with the end of one's own story. In the linear, heavily narrativized temporality of late modernity, every story and every movie have an ending. But a different time gestalt is reflected in the growing popularity of green burial. As reflected in the culture of DIY funerals, death is not an ending but a transformation.

Lucas is an entrepreneur in California who several years ago purchased a small town cemetery north of San Francisco and began developing sections of it for traditional Jewish and green burials. He saw a market for this choice in death among the generally wealthy, educated and environmentally conscious local population. Although a businessman, he can reflect on what he has learned about life by falling into this business through a sideline as a website developer for funeral directors. He notes that the American denial of death is still very much alive: 'I laugh when someone says, "if I die" because it's "*when* I die". Although Lucas himself is trying to bring change to a conservative industry, he notes that things are changing anyway because the Baby Boomer generation demands personalization in all of their consumer choices. But there are larger values and trends coming into play as well. He believes that climate change is starting to instil a greater sense of responsibility and a realization that denying our own deaths is causing harm to the planet – both in terms of the disposition of the body (the chemicals used in embalming and the fact that cremation pumps most of our personal carbon into the atmosphere) and in terms of the speed with which we consume in our disposable lifestyle. He links the way Americans have lived to how they die and notes that the mid-twentieth century was all about conspicuous consumption – from the cars we drove when living to the fancy casket we rode into oblivion. And now people are starting to question both the greed and speed of life – which translates into a lower profile death. He says that because people's memories can be sustained in a digital afterlife via platforms like Facebook, stalling decomposition is no longer as important. He thinks we are coming back to a 'dust to dust' approach to the body.

In addition to body treatment being chemical-free, the green section of Lucas's cemetery has guidelines for the other material components of death. The body must be in a natural fibre shroud (and ideally any clothes should also be natural fibre) or a coffin made of unpainted wood and fastened with dowels rather than metal. Markers can be natural stone (uncut), preferably locally sourced. They can have a name and date cut into them, but otherwise should not be ostentatious. Some families opt for no markers at all. Further, landscaping is restricted to native plants – the aim is to 're-wild' cemetery space. In fact, the cemetery has a designation as a National Wildlife Federation Certified Habitat. After the burial and on anniversaries, family members may leave votive artefacts of remembrance, but these too should be of natural materials. Plastic is especially discouraged. On our visits to the cemetery, we saw peacock feathers, sea shells, paper notes and pebbles left on the graves. In one case, a loved one had gone the extra distance to carve a replica of a cell phone out of organic wood to leave on the grave. Perhaps no other artefact expresses the conflicting temporal values struggling for dominance in American life today: a tension between the addictive speed of technological life and the soothingly slow process of organic decay. When I asked Lucas about what he thinks happens to us after we die, he says 'we return to a vastness'. The theme of return, like Grace's version of reincarnation, suggests a deep break with the linear times of Christian eschatology and Enlightenment progress.

The popularity of green burial may also index a growing temporal consciousness of a deep future – a mirror image of the deep history that climate change awakens (Chakrabarty 2009). Those who embrace green burial not only refuse to deny death, they welcome gradual decomposition and are no longer attracted to the clock-stopping magic of embalming. For them, death is imagined as a definitive but slow process of disintegration and return. And it is not just a choice for the elite green consumer. Two women we met – one a nurse and another a manicurist – said they were 'excited' about green burial and the fact that a new cemetery had just been permitted for their rural county. In response to a question about what she wanted for her own burial, the nurse said: 'I know it sounds a little morbid, but just kind of let the natural decomposition process happen the way it is naturally supposed to happen.' And she wants her body to feed a tree, to give back to the planet in some small way.

Conclusion

In this chapter, I have made two central arguments. The first is that the anxieties about presentism expressed by historians are muddled by a number of analytical confusions, the most critical being a simplistic reliance on an unqualified division of the past–present–future and a tendency to confuse lived temporality with historical narrativity. My second argument, made with the assistance of Philippe Ariès, is that death practices are a powerful index of broader temporal gestalts that more pervasively define the tempo and phrasing of life itself.

My sense is that we are witnessing not only a new kind of death, but a new temporal paradigm for a post-industrial, post-petroleum world. Given the ways in which practitioners and adherents articulate how these new (or returned) death practices relate to other cultural currents, such as movements to simplify and live with fewer commodities, and an ethic centred on caring for the long-term health of the planet, I predict that the tension between industrial and green death will continue to build until there is a shift in the temporal paradigm. The problems these emerging values respond to are unlikely to disappear.

It is important to point out that these efforts to slow down the process of death and allow decay to do its work go hand-in-hand with a different type of affective language permeating funeral practice in the United States. We are moving from mourning rituals to 'celebrations of life'. This important change is sweeping across the landscape of death care, affecting funerals with more conventional material practices as well as the alternative practices I've described here. Celebrations represent a broad-based shift away from narrating a linear plotline (a life) that came to an (always tragic) end, to a form of memorialization that makes use of the bit-time of the present. At celebrations of life, it has become standard practice to project a montage of images from the individual's life that focus on the happy times and funny moments in the deceased's life, even if it was an untimely death. The focus has shifted away from the end of the story to its constituent and recombinant parts. Obituaries are a form of fiction that force a linear narrative upon the chaos of lived life. And while they are still used, particularly for the older generation, photo collages and 'memory pages', where snapshots of the past can be endlessly re-arranged, experienced and re-posted in virtual space, have taken a much more central place in American memorialization. More and more, it appears we may live and die as small recycling bits of matter and spirit that defy linearity. Historians' histrionics aside, the death-denying 'tyranny of the present' is on its way out and the future is expanding into a long, natural cycle of regeneration. As for the future of narrativity, if the close relationship between temporal experience and the historiographic imagination holds, then archaeology – as the discipline that excels in recombining small fragments into new patterns – may not be dying at all, but coming into its own as a postmodern practice.

Acknowledgements

I would like to extend my sincere gratitude to Marek Tamm, Laurent Olivier and Bjørnar Olsen for an invitation to participate in the seminar in Oslo, and to the participants there for the lively discussions that continue to stimulate my thinking. I also thank my wildly talented collaborator, Daniel Zox. Financial support for the research reported here was provided by the John D. and Catherine T. MacArthur Foundation and the Lichtstern Fund of the Department of Anthropology, University of Chicago. Any errors or overreaching remain my own.

Notes

1 The identities of interviewees have been anonymized to protect confidentiality. Direct quotes are verbatim from filmed interviews archived by the author. Research was conducted under University of Chicago IRB protocol IRB15-1236 (exempt).
2 There are a small number of men who seek training for at-home funerals (though more than there are male midwives). The gender contrast between professional and at-home funeral personnel is stark and worthy of study.

References

Ariès, P. (1974), *Western Attitudes Towards Death from the Middle Ages to the Present*, Baltimore, MD: Johns Hopkins University Press.
Ariès, P. (1981), *The Hour of Our Death: The Classic History of Western Attitudes Toward Death over the Last One Thousand Years*, transl. H. Weaver, New York: Alfred A. Knopf.
Augé, M. (1992), *Non-lieux: Introduction à une anthropologie de la surmodernité*, Paris: Seuil.
Buchli, V. and Lucas, G., eds (2001), *Archaeologies of the Contemporary Past*, London: Routledge.

Cann, C. (2014), *Virtual Afterlives: Grieving the Dead in the Twenty-First Century*, Lexington, KY: University Press of Kentucky.

Chakrabarty, D. (2009), 'The Climate of History: Four Theses', *Critical Inquiry*, 35 (2): 197–222.

Derrida, J. (1994), *Specters of Marx: State of the Debt, the Work of Mourning and the New International*, transl. P. Kamuf, New York: Routledge.

Eriksen, T. H. (2001), *Tyranny of the Moment: Fast and Slow Time in the Information Age*, London: Pluto Press.

Foucault, M. (1982), *The Archaeology of Knowledge and the Discourse on Language*, transl. A. M. Sheridan Smith, New York: Pantheon.

Fukuyama, F. (1992), *The End of History and the Last Man*, New York: Free Press.

González-Ruibal, A. (2008), 'Time to Destroy: An Archaeology of Supermodernity', *Current Anthropology*, 49 (2): 247–79.

Graves-Brown, P., Harrison, R. and Piccini, A., eds (2013), *The Oxford Handbook of the Archaeology of the Contemporary World*, Oxford: Oxford University Press.

Hagerty, A. (2014), 'Speak Softly to the Dead: The Uses of Enchantment in American Home Funerals', *Social Anthropology/Anthropologie Sociale*, 22 (4): 428–42.

Hartog, F. (2015), *Regimes of Historicity: Presentism and Experiences of Time*, transl. S. Brown, New York: Columbia University Press.

Hockey, J., Green, T., Clayden, A. and Powell, M. (2012), 'Landscapes of the Dead? Natural Burial and the Materialization of Absence', *Journal of Material Culture*, 17 (2): 115–32.

Jameson, F. (2003). 'The End of Temporality', *Critical Inquiry*, 29 (4): 695–718.

Mitford, J. ([1963]1998), *The American Way of Death Revisited*, rev. edn, New York: Vintage.

Porter, R. (1999), 'The Hour of Philippe Ariès', *Mortality*, 4 (1): 83–90.

Stone, L. (1978), 'Death and Its History', *New York Review of Books*, 12 October, 22–3.

Trouillot, M.-R. (1995), *Silencing the Past: Power and the Production of History*, New York: Beacon.

Virilio, P. (1997), *Open Sky*, transl. J. Rose, New York: Verso.

Virilio, P. (2004), *The Paul Virilio Reader*, ed. S. Redhead, New York: Columbia University Press.

Whaley, J. (1981), 'Introduction', in J. Whaley (ed.), *Mirrors of Mortality: Studies in the Social History of Death*, 1–14, London: Europa.

World Health Organization (2018), 'Cholera Fact Sheet'. Available online: http://www.who.int/mediacentre/factsheets/fs107/en/ (accessed 27 February 2018).

12

Rewilding Time in the Vale do Côa

Caitlin DeSilvey

Opening

For much of the twentieth century, both history and ecology were understood to be entities with a certain structure and orientation – gradually progressing along more or less linear paths towards states of increasing stability, set within a shared interpretive framework of succession and serialization. Now, the storyline has shifted. We live in an era in which concepts of stability have been superseded by an insistence on contingency; singular linear pathways have been replaced with multiple, interleaving possibilities; coherence has given way to complexity. This general shift is evident in both ecological thinking and in contemporary discourses around time and history, and has the effect of troubling foundational precepts and overturning previous assumptions about the way the world works. Some have diagnosed this temporal and ecological upheaval as a signature feature of the Anthropocene, in which the deep past and the deep future are subject to unpredictable processes of interpenetration and cross-contamination, which converge in a volatile present (Dibley 2012). In this chapter, I aim to examine temporality and ecology in relation with each other, through the concept of rewilding. In rewilding, I argue, emerging, alternative frameworks of ecology and history are fused, as the desire for restoration (to an imagined ecological baseline) is replaced by an embrace of radical ecological uncertainty (which draws on latent pasts to animate possible futures). I explore these ideas through reference to a specific landscape – the Vale do Côa in north east Portugal.

Temporalities of rewilding

The concept of rewilding can refer to multiple different contexts and practices, and its definition is frequently contested and debated (Lorimer et al. 2015; Helmer et al. 2015; Jepson 2016; Navarro and Pereira 2012; Monbiot 2014). Many rewilding initiatives share, however, a focus on supporting processes of naturalistic grazing and predation (Lorimer and Driessen 2014; Robbins and Moore 2013), often attempted through the reintroduction of keystone species to formerly intensively managed landscapes. Rewilding has emerged into academic and ecological discourse alongside a broader re-evaluation of core ecological concepts, in which assumptions about ecological succession towards stable climax states are being replaced with new paradigms that explore the significance of ongoing disturbance and dynamic change in the formation of non-equilibrium ecologies and novel ecosystems. The implications for the practice of ecological restoration have been profound, as summarized by Stephen T. Jackson and Richard J. Hobbs: '[P]erhaps the most natural feature of the world in which we find ourselves is continual flux [. . .]. If natural states are elusive, if the environment is always changing and ecosystems are always coming and going, and if multiple realisations are normal, then the premises underlying ecological restoration to a historic standard come into question' (Jackson and Hobbs 2009: 567–8).

Within critical academic discourse, opinion is divided on whether rewilding should be classified as a conservative and reactionary attempt to return ecological systems to a pre-human past or a radical experimentation with possible ecological futures. Questions of history and temporality – the nature of time and the time of nature – are central to this debate.

The term 'rewilding' contains within it an implicit temporal orientation, which suggests both that there existed a prior state of 'wildness' and that it is possible, or desirable, to restore elements of its structure and function – claims which have been thoroughly critiqued by contemporary scholars (Castree 2013; Cronon 1996; Jackson and Hobbs 2009). Dolly Jørgensen has argued that rewilding's focus on the reintroduction of animals which have been 'extirpated by humans' implies a baseline 'before human habitation' (2015: 486). She catalogues the different historic reference points that guide goal-setting in rewilding initiatives, and concludes: 'Rewilding as currently practiced disavows human history and finds value only in historical ecologies prior to human habitation. The rewilding concept has been deployed in a myriad of ways to exclude humans in time and space from nature' (Jørgensen 2015: 487). This critique suggests that any attempt to 'return' to a pre-human past is inherently suspect, and relies implicitly on a conceptualization of time as linear and irreversible.

Others have argued, however, that the temporalities of rewilding are not so neatly organized along a clear demarcation between the past and the present, and that representing rewilding as a desire to 'restore' a past state misses the point. The release and reintroduction of selected animal species has become a core strategy in rewilding efforts, but the ecological outcome of these interventions is often unknown, and the emphasis usually lies on creating the conditions of possibility for the (re)establishment of autonomous natural processes, rather than restoration as such (DeSilvey and Bartolini 2019). In a recent policy brief, Frans Schepers (managing director of Rewilding Europe) and Paul Jepson explain:

> [T]he baseline for conservation policy in many European nations has been preindustrial agriculture, which requires the protection and maintenance of wildlife-rich patches of cultural landscapes through active scientific management. This conservation approach, which has been compared to restoring a painting that then needs curating, is at odds with the process-oriented ethos of rewilding and the uncertain ecological and conservation dynamics this entails.
>
> Schepers and Jepson 2016: 25

They go on to describe rewilding as: 'Taking inspiration from the past but not replicating it, by developing new natural heritage and values that evoke the past but shape the future – with the point of reference in the future, not in the past' (Schepers and Jepson 2016: 26). The relationship between the past and the present in this statement is considerably more slippery (if not sloppy) than suggested by the critique summarized above.

Jamie Lorimer and Clemens Driessen, in their research on Heck cattle, have explored the way that rewilding engages with 'dynamic future pasts' (2016: 647), a term that seems more sympathetic to the temporal complexity which characterizes many rewilding initiatives. In these initiatives, the past emerges into the present as an active and constitutive force; latent materialities (and biologies) emerge to shape unpredictable futures. The past provides 'inspiration' but not necessarily evidence; efforts are directed towards production of a 'new natural heritage', with a future-orientation that evokes past patterns. Some scholars have proposed that 'neo-wilding' would be a more appropriate term to describe what is happening in these contexts (Bridgewater 2015).

These ideas have a clear resonance with the work of scholars who are exploring alternatives to the chronological, historicist 'time regime' (Hartog 2015; Tanaka 2015), and their proposals for the study of 'mnemohistory' (Assmann 1997; Tamm 2013, 2015), 'relational time' (Harvey 1996; Fitzpatrick 2004) and 'heterogeneous time' (Serres and Latour 1995; Schwanen 2007). Consider Laurent Olivier's musings on the implications of the re-evaluation of historical time, read in relation to the Jackson and Hobbs quote above:

> [I]f historical time is no longer a time which links, little by little, events which strictly follow on from each other – in a word, if time is now released – it can then create a correlation between events which are very distant from each other. If the past remains embedded in the present, it can therefore reawake[n] and reactivate in the present processes which were thought to be over for good, because they belonged to a past which was over and done with.
>
> Olivier 2004: 209

Olivier writes of composite, heterogeneous time, characterized by the persistence of elements of the material past in present physical environments – ideas also explored in depth by geographers in relation to specific places and landscapes (Pred 2004; Crang and Travlou 2001; Bartolini 2013; Bastian 2014; Massey 2006). Bruce Braun has recently argued that the Anthropocene calls for an understanding of time that acknowledges both how the 'past haunts the present' (Braun 2015: 240) and how time flows 'toward us, from the future to the present' (Braun 2015: 239). This chapter picks up on these ideas to imagine what it might look like to 'rewild' time, exploring rewilding as a conceptual metaphor which opens out alternative temporalities of release and recurrence.

A river in time

The Côa River cuts a northward course from its source in the mountains near Sabugal, Portugal, winding 135 kilometres to meet the Douro River below the town of Vila Nova de Foz Côa, in the far northeast of the country, close to the Spanish border (Figure 12.1). In this remote and rugged location, ancient people left their trace in an open air art gallery along the banks of the river. Most of the rock art was created during the Upper Paleolithic, roughly 20,000 years ago, and depicts the animals that shared the prehistoric landscape, including horses, ibex, aurochs and deer. More than a thousand rock art carvings and paintings have been found at seventy different sites, and more continue to be discovered. New carvings appear to have been created sporadically into the modern period, and images of trains, boats and aeroplanes sometimes appear adjacent to the depictions of extinct fauna.

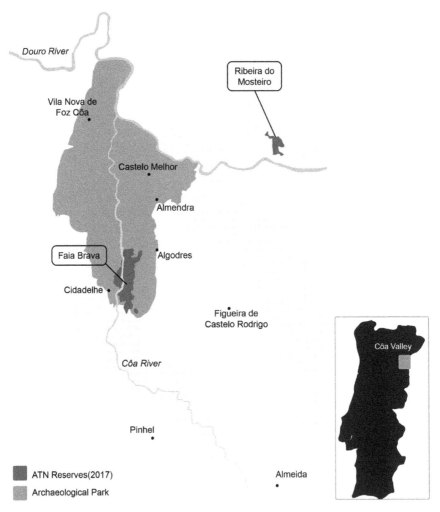

Figure 12.1 Map showing the confluence of the Douro and Côa Rivers, in relation to the Côa Valley Archaeological Park and ATN reserves. Produced by the University of Exeter Design Studio.

Although there is some evidence of continuity in the rock art tradition, by the second half of the twentieth century the presence of the carvings and paintings had been all but forgotten (Luís and García Díez 2008). Many of the villagers who formerly tended their fields and grazed animals in the steep fields and pastures along the river had passed on or moved away, and those who remained kept the knowledge of the rock art to themselves, with no reason to share it with outsiders. The depopulation of rural Portugal – an effect of mass emigration, falling birth rates and changing rural economies – meant that an already remote area became even more isolated during the course of the twentieth century. When a dam was proposed for the Côa in the 1990s, the concentration of carvings was (re)discovered by surveyors and archaeologists and brought to public attention (Lawson 2012). UNESCO classified the lower stretches of the Côa River valley as a World Heritage Site in 1998; the area was protected in an archaeological park and interpreted in a new museum. The Upper Paleolithic engravings in the Côa have been described as 'an exceptional illustration of the sudden development of creative genius during the dawn of human's cultural development' (Gomes and Lima 2009: 4). Recent research suggests that the engravings were associated with seasonal hunting camps, where dispersed tribal groups would come together to 'fulfill their economic, social and cultural needs' (Aubry, Luís and Dimuccio 2012: 543; Gomes and Lima 2009: 2); the collective, artistic depiction of their animal prey likely served a symbolic or ritual purpose which remains unknown, and unknowable.

The global recognition of the rock art and the creation of the archaeological park occurred against a backdrop of continued depopulation and land abandonment. Between 2001 and 2011 the region's population declined by 2 per cent every year ('Wo Europa wächst und wo es schrumpft' 2015). In the scattered villages above the valley, mostly elderly residents remained, living in homes alongside the ruins of former dwellings. As villages emptied out, the once-cultivated fields and grazing meadows became overgrown with broom and scrub. One group of people saw an opportunity in the disused agricultural lands. In 2000, a group of biologists established the Faia Brava reserve, on parcels of land just upstream of the main concentration of rock art. Their organization, Associação Transumância e Natureza (ATN), initially focused on improving the habitat for raptors, but they soon began to experiment with the reintroduction of horses and cattle, in the hope that their grazing activity would improve habitats and reduce fire risk, by gradually edging out the scrub vegetation and creating space for a mosaic of open meadows and revegetated woodland (a landscape type known in Portugal as 'montado').

Since 2012, ATN has been working with Rewilding Europe to run a rewilding pilot project in the Faia Brava reserve. In 2016 they released a new population of horses into an extension of the reserve (bringing the total reserve area to over 1,000 hectares), and they are supporting the animals as they gradually adapt to the rugged conditions and transition to a 'de-domesticated' semi-wild state (Lorimer and Driessen 2016). The organization is also participating in the Tauros back-breeding programme (which involves selective breeding to produce a contemporary breed that resembles the extinct auroch) and have submitted proposals to reintroduce the Pyrenean ibex. By minimizing active management and returning 'iconic European nature species' to the landscape, they hope to create 'a true wilderness area ... where natural processes work on their own' (ATN 2015).[1]

For the purposes of this chapter, I will focus on one aspect of the Faia Brava rewilding initiative: the proposed ibex introduction. The ibex (also known as the *bucardo*) was once common in Iberia, and profile images of their goat-like bodies and distinctive sweeping horns appear in many of the carvings along the river (Figure 12.2). As agriculture came to dominate the landscape and hunting pressures took their toll, ibex were gradually cornered into remote parts of the region, and several distinct sub-species arose in isolated populations. The Portuguese ibex subspecies (*Capra pyrenaica lusitanica*) became extinct in 1892, but the related Pyrenean ibex (*Capra pyrenaica pyrenaica*) was declared extinct only in 2000 (Folch et al. 2009). When ATN proposed the ibex for reintroduction in the Côa as part of their rewilding initiative, they intended to introduce animals from the Geres Mountains in the north, where they had spread from a reintroduced Spanish population. The reintroduced ibex would have taken their place alongside Faia Brava's 'semi-wild' horses and cattle.

However, the Portuguese national nature conservation body, ICNF, twice rejected the application for ibex reintroduction, claiming that there was no 'physical evidence' of their former presence in the landscape, despite the extensive depiction of ancient ibex in the carvings (personal communication, 25 November 2016). Presumably, archaeological documentation of bone fragments and other tangible remains would have made ICNF more inclined to consider the reintroduction plan; the carvings were deemed to be inadmissible as ecological evidence. The decision, also, however, contains within it the assumption that ecological restoration to a historic baseline, when informed by appropriate evidence, is possible. The idea that the reintroduced ibex

Figure 12.2 Upper Paleolithic ibex carving at Penascosa (Rocha 5B 1). Reproduced with permission of the photographer, João Romba.

would take their place in a novel ecosystem, characterized by emergence and uncertainty, is not entertained. In this sense, the rejection of the ibex reintroduction can be read, in part, as the residue of a conception of linear, singular time. Reintroduction is explicitly framed as a 'return' to a point along a prior temporal trajectory, rather than an expression of the past in the present, with unpredictable future effects.

The interpretation of the ibex images in the Museu do Côa, the main interpretive site for the archaeological park, also falls into line with this temporal conservatism. Inside, in a series of darkened rooms, the visitor can view backlit panels with reproductions of many of the most significant carvings discovered to date. The museum organizes the carvings into thematic groupings ('horses', 'aurochs', 'ibex') and describes each theme as a sign: 'Each rock art theme must be understood as a sign that, in combination with other themes, produces *discourses*. The communitarian meaning of a given *place* is behind the specific *discourse* of that same place.' The museum sorts the respective themes along projected timelines, with distinct periods marked out to indicate when the carvings were created, and when their creation ceased. The interpretive panel devoted to the ibex discourse shows that ibex appear in the rock art up to 10,000 BC. With the dawn of the Mesolithic, the ibex disappear from the representational timeline; the timeline itself ends in 1995. In the museum space, periodization operates as a tool for controlling time, breaking it into sequences and organizing it into a linear progression (Tanaka 2015). The ibex carvings belong to the past, 'the beyond'. The museum interpretation – in line with the ICNF rejection – seems to close off the potential for the images to signify otherwise, or to reach into the future.

In a curious parallel development, the extinct ibex has also become entangled with another experiment that radically unsettles assumptions about ecological and historical time. Shortly before the death of the last surviving Pyrenean ibex in 2000, scientists preserved skin samples (ear scrapings) from the individual in liquid nitrogen. Using DNA taken from these skin samples, in 2009 the scientists were able to clone a female Pyrenean ibex (whom they named 'Celia'). The experiment was celebrated as a successful attempt at 'de-extinction' (Folch et al. 2009). The newborn ibex kid died shortly after birth due to physical defects in its lungs. In this reorganization of time and ecology, extinction is no longer 'forever', and latent genetic potential is drawn on to invent previously unthinkable future-natures (Ogden 2014). The cautionary tale presented by the instance of the cloned ibex exists in an uneasy relation to the softer experiments with reintroduction and rewilding, which are more focused on restoring certain ecological interactions and functions than on bringing back particular life forms or species (Adams 2017: 4).

Aesthetic–causal alliances

One particular carving, etched into an upright slab at Quinta da Barca (Figure 12.3), provides a glimpse of another way of thinking about the ibex in relation to landscape and temporality. It shows an ibex with two heads: one head is looking forward and the other appears to be looking back. The two heads are linked in an arc made by their touching horns. Archaeologists have interpreted this image as marking a major innovation in the representation of movement, which came over 14,000 years ago (Baptista 2015: 203). By showing the heads in two positions, the artist implies that the ibex has just turned, and the static form is broken with the impression of animation. The way the carving is oriented along the river, the ibex head that turns over the back of the animal looks downstream, towards the part of the valley where most of the ancient carvings have been found; the forward-facing ibex head looks upstream, towards Faia Brava, and the future vision represented by the rewilding pilot project.[2]

Until their rediscovery in the 1990s, the Côa carvings, and the ancient ibex, remained a latent presence in the landscape – a reservoir of dormant potential. In conceptions of chronological time, causality is assumed to emerge from flow in a

Figure 12.3 Two-headed ibex carving at Quinta da Barca (Rocha 3). Reproduced with permission of the photographer, António Martinho Baptista.

unilinear direction (Tanaka 2015: 162). Timothy Morton, in contrast, asks what difference it would make to understand time not as a passive medium but as an effect that emerges from our encounters with objects and images (Morton 2013: 34–5). Causality, in his opinion, is fundamentally an aesthetic process. He explains this concept in his discussion of his encounter with a painting by Australian Aboriginal artist Yukultji Napangati:

> The image is not a mute object waiting to have its meaning supplied by a subject, nor is it a blank screen; nor is it something objectively present 'in' space. Rather the painting emits something like electromagnetic waves, in whose force field I find myself. The painting powerfully demonstrates what is already the case: space and time are emergent properties of objects. . . . The aesthetic form of an object is where the causal properties of the object reside.
>
> Morton 2013: 35

If we are willing to accept (even provisionally) that time and causality are emergent properties of objects, then we can understand the ibex images in the rock art as aesthetic forms that cast effects both 'backwards' into the past and 'forwards' into the future, bending and twisting along the way to interrupt expectations of the 'has been' with expressions of what might yet be (Olsen 2010: 128). Such a perspective collapses temporal distance to allow the images to exist not 'in time' but as objects that 'time' in their own right, with the perception of temporality activated by encounter (Morton 2011: 153). Following on from ideas explored by Bernard Stiegler (1998), we can perhaps understand the ibex images as a form of 'tertiary memory', stretching across generations: the carved images function as a prosthetic memory support, reactivated by our gaze, and our touch (Figure 12.4).

Here we begin to see how linear, chronological time might be rewilded to (re)introduce other temporal frameworks. The 'process-oriented ethos' that defines ecological approaches to rewilding (Schepers and Jepson 2016) could be adopted to enliven our understanding of how the world 'times', with a renewed focus on experimental epistemologies and emergent relationships. Rewilded time might encourage recognition of the way time flows and eddies, speeds up and slows down, iterates and irritates, pleats and plaits (Serres and Latour 1995). Bronislaw Szerszynski elaborates on what it might look like to 'release' time in this way:

> [T]ime in the non-human world as much as the human world can be seen as displaying multiple, overlaid temporalities, and qualitative characteristics, such as those of intention and adaptation. Such accounts render problematic any simple distinction [. . .] between the wild and the domestic. Making the environment temporally meaningful [. . .] could even perhaps be seen as restoring rather than imposing a qualitative dimension to time, and thus at one and the same time taming time – making it socially meaningful – and setting it free – releasing it from the strictures of quantitative clock time that have been imposed on it by the discourses of modern science.
>
> Szerszynski 2002: 189

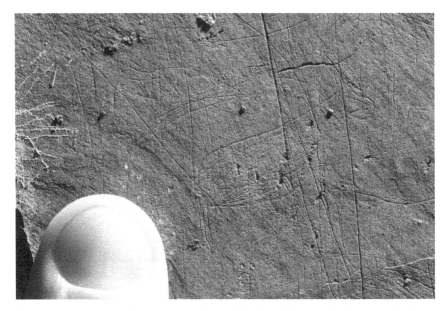

Figure 12.4 A very small carving of an ibex at Vale de João Esquerdo. Reproduced with permission of the photographer, Mário Reis.

The rewilding experiment on the Côa can be understood as a kind of temporal ecological activism. The conservationists responsible for managing the Faia Brava reserve take care, however, to explain that the Paleolithic carvings do not provide a literal reference for their reintroduction plans. They see the carvings instead as a 'portrait of what people saw and valued' in the ancient landscape, and also a record of the way that humans and animals have coexisted in the Côa for thousands of years. Their interest is not in the rock art in isolation, but in the 'landscape behind the engravings' (personal communication, 26 January 2015). For them, the rewilding initiative is not about reaching some arbitrary baseline of prehistoric wildness, but about the process of 'becoming wild' again, in the context of the present, and appreciating how the past can animate the future.

Kathryn Yusoff writes about rock art as a 'gesture of time given to the future' (2015: 391) and, as such, she suggests its aesthetic charge lies in its power to actualize different temporalities: 'The image holds the survival of its coming into being, and its survival through geologic time,' she writes; it also 'fore-sees the future, in its creative power to survive as a possibility' (Yusoff 2015: 400). In the Côa river valley, the rock art opens up a 'space of communication' (Yusoff 2015: 399) in which we recognize that we share a 'corporeal heritage' with bodies that are not our own (Yusoff 2015: 396). This space of communication connects us, through our encounters with the rock art, with the people who lived in the Côa valley thousands of years ago; but it also, critically, connects us to the animals who lived in that landscape as well, and who impelled the human inhabitants to idealize them in their rock art imagery, for unknowable symbolic or ritual reasons. In Morton's terms, the images operate as 'aesthetic–causal alliances with nonhumans', performing time in our encounter with them (Morton 2011: 154).

Stefan Tanaka has argued that only a 'history without chronology' allows us to recognize discontinuous patterns of co-evolutionary change, born out of extended interaction between animals and people over time (Tanaka 2015: 179; LeCain 2016). One might argue that what we are witnessing now can be understood as co-*devolutionary* change, which unstitches the agricultural advances of the Neolithic to weave a future that integrates elements of older, more unpredictable and autonomous, human–animal relations. If, as Tanaka claims, linear, chronological time forces us into a 'default progressivism' and an attendant politics of growth and accumulation, then rewilded time opens up the possibility of intentional decline and creative deceleration, and the formation of new Anthropocene storylines, which allow us to reimagine human/nonhuman relations in a more reciprocal and receptive mode (Tanaka 2015; see also Kallis and March 2015). Lesley Head has suggested that we should cultivate an appreciation of spatial and temporal variability in our understanding of past relationships between humans and nonhumans, in order to prepare ourselves for the conceptual labour that is required to think ourselves into the Anthropocene creatively, open to contingency and chance (Head 2014). The work of these scholars suggests that it may be an opportune moment to rewild our conceptualizations of time, opening ourselves to the possibility of release, multiplicity and convergence. The future assembled through the practice of rewilding (in the Côa, if not elsewhere) is not about restoration, but about understanding conservation as a 'series of wild experiments – speculative practices uncertain of future outcomes' (Lorimer 2015: 9).

Acknowledgements

A first draft of this chapter was completed while the author was resident at the Centre for Advanced Study in Oslo, Norway, as a fellow on the research project 'After Discourse: Things, Archaeology and Heritage in the 21st Century'; the chapter benefited from comments from the research group and from participants in the CAS 'Past Presences' workshop in December 2016. Field research was supported by 'Heritage Futures', an Arts and Humanities Research Council (AHRC) 'Care for the Future: Thinking Forward through the Past' Theme Large Grant (AH/M004376/1), awarded to researchers at University College London, University of Exeter, University of York and Linnaeus University (Sweden). I am grateful to Nadia Bartolini, Heritage Futures Transformation theme Research Associate, and Antony Lyons, Senior Creative Fellow on the Heritage Futures project, who shared the fieldwork experience in Portugal and informed this work through our ongoing intellectual and creative collaborations. Additional thanks to ATN (Associação Transumância e Natureza) and ACÔA (Friends of the Côa Museum and Archaeological Park), Bárbara Carvalho, Pedro Prata and the other individuals who participated in our research in the Côa Valley and generously offered their insights and expertise.

Notes

1   The rewilding pilot project in the Côa Valley features in several films produced by Heritage Futures Senior Creative Fellow Antony Lyons, including Gifts to the

Future – Episode 2 (https://vimeo.com/246869108) and Côa Valley – Voices 1 (https://vimeo.com/245361962).
2   Thank you to Bárbara Carvalho for drawing the significance of the orientation to my attention.

References

Adams, B. (2017), 'Geographies of Conservation 1: De-extinction and Precision Conservation', *Progress in Human Geography*, 41 (4): 534–45.

Assmann, J. (1997), *Moses the Egyptian. The Memory of Egypt in Western Monotheism*, Cambridge, MA and London: Harvard University Press.

ATN 2015 = Nature Conservation Strategic Plan Figueira de Castelo Rodrigo, Portugal.

Aubry, T., Luís, L. and Dimuccio, L. A. (2012), 'Nature vs. Culture: Present-Day Spatial Distribution and Preservation of Open-Air Rock Art in the Côa and Douro River Valleys (Portugal)', *Journal of Archaeological Science*, 39: 848–66.

Baptista, A. M. (2015), 'Parque Arqueólogico do Vale do Côa – Portefólio I', *Côa Visão: Economia, Ciência e Cultura*, 17: 187–244.

Bartolini, N. (2013), 'Rome's Pasts and the Creation of New Urban Spaces: Brecciation, Matter, and the Play of Surfaces and Depths', *Environment and Planning D: Society and Space*, 31: 1041–61.

Bastian, M. (2014), 'Time and Community: A Scoping Study', *Time and Society*, 23: 137–66.

Braun, B. (2015), 'Futures: Imagining Socioecological Transformation – An Introduction', *Annals of the American Association of Geographers*, 105: 239–43.

Bridgewater, P. (2015), 'Rewilding the World for the Future: Using Novel Ecosystems as a Key Conservation Tool', unpublished paper presented at 'Wild Thing? Managing Landscape Change and Future Ecologies', 9th to 11th September 2015, Sheffield Hallam University.

Castree, N. (2013), *Making Sense of Nature*, London: Routledge.

Crang, M. and Travlou, P. S. (2001), 'The City and Topologies of Memory', *Environment and Planning D: Society and Space*, 19: 161–77.

Cronon, W. (1996), 'The Trouble with Wilderness: Or, Getting Back to the Wrong Nature', in W. Cronon (ed.), *Uncommon Ground: Rethinking the Human Place in Nature*, 69–90, New York: Norton.

DeSilvey, C. and Bartolini, N., (2019), 'Where Horses Run Free? Autonomy, Temporality and Rewilding in the Côa Valley, Portugal', *Transactions of the Institute of British Geographers*, 44(1): 94–109, https://doi.org/10.1111/tran.12251.

Dibley, B. (2012), '"The Shape of Things to Come": Seven Theses on the Anthropocene and Attachment', *Australian Humanities Review*, Available online: http://australianhumanitiesreview.org/category/issue/issue-52-may-2012/ (accessed 12 June 2018).

Fitzpatrick, T. (2004), 'Social Policy and Time', *Time & Society*, 13: 197–219.

Folch, J., Cocerob, M. J., Chesnéc, P., Alabart, J. L., Domínguez, V., Cognié, Y., Roche, A., Fernández-Árias, A., Martí, J. I., Sánchez, P., Echegoyen, E., Beckers, J. F., Sánchez Bonastre, A. and Vignon, X. (2009), 'First Birth of an Animal From an Extinct Subspecies (Capra pyrenaica pyrenaica) by Cloning', *Theriogenology*, 71 (6): 1026–34.

Gomes, P. D. and Lima, A. C. (2009), *Vale do Côa, a Landscape of Freedom, Between Prehistory and Medieval Villages: A Tour Around the Archaeological Park and a Trip from Malcata to Planalto Mirandês*, Vila Nova de Foz Côa: Parque Arqueológico do Vale do Côa.

Hartog, F. (2015), *Regimes of Historicity: Presentism and Experiences of Time*, transl. S. Brown, New York: Columbia University Press.

Harvey, D. (1996), *Justice, Nature and the Geography of Difference*, Oxford: Blackwell.

Head, L. (2014), 'Contingencies of the Anthropocene: Lessons from the "Neolithic"', *The Anthropocene Review*, 1: 113–25.

Helmer, W., Saavedra, D., Sylvén, M. and Schepers, F. (2015), 'Rewilding Europe: A New Strategy for an Old Continent', in H. M. Pereira and L. M. Navarro (eds), *Rewilding European Landscapes*, 171–90, New York: Springer.

Jackson, S. T. and Hobbs, R. J. (2009), 'Ecological Restoration in Light of Ecological History', *Science*, 325: 567–68.

Jepson, P. (2016), 'A Rewilding Agenda for Europe: Creating a Network of Experimental Reserves', *Ecography*, 39 (2): 117–24.

Jørgensen, D. (2015), 'Rethinking Rewilding', *Geoforum*, 65: 482–88.

Kallis, G. and March, H. (2015), 'Imaginaries of Hope: The Utopianism of Degrowth', *Annals of the Association of American Geographers*, 105: 360–68.

Lawson, A. J. (2012), *Painted Caves: Palaeolithic Rock Art in Western Europe*, Oxford: Oxford University Press.

LeCain, T. J. (2016), 'How Did Cows Construct the American Cowboy?', in M. W. Ertsen, C. Mauch and E. Russell (eds), *Molding the Planet: Human Niche Construction at Work, RCC Perspectives: Transformations in Environment and Society*, 5: 17–24.

Lorimer, J. (2015), *Wildlife in the Anthropocene: Conservation After Nature*, Minneapolis: University of Minnesota Press.

Lorimer, J. and Driessen, C. (2016), 'From "Nazi Cows" to Cosmopolitan "Ecological Engineers": Specifying Rewilding through a History of Heck Cattle', *Annals of the American Association of Geographers*, 106: 631–52.

Lorimer, J., Sandom, C., Jepson, P., Doughty, C., Barua, M. and Kirby, K. J. (2015), 'Rewilding: Science, Practice, and Politics', *Annual Review of Environment and Resources*, 40: 39–62.

Luís, L. and García Díez, M. (2008), 'Same Tradition, Different Views: The Côa Valley Rock Art and Social Identity', in I. Domingo Sanz, D. Fiore and S. K. May (eds), *Archaeologies of Art: Time, Place, and Identity*, 151–70, Walnut Creek, CA: Left Coast Press.

Massey, D. (2006), 'Landscape as a Provocation: Reflections on Moving Mountains', *Journal of Material Culture*, 11: 33–48.

Monbiot, G. (2014), *Feral: Rewilding the Land, Sea and Human Life*, London: Penguin.

Morton, T. (2011), 'Objects as Temporary Autonomous Zones', *Continent*, 1: 149–55.

Morton, T. (2013), *Realist Magic: Objects, Ontology, Causality*, Ann Arbor: Open Humanities Press.

Navarro, L. M. and Pereira, H. M. (2012), 'Rewilding Abandoned Landscapes in Europe', *Ecosystems*, 15: 900–12.

Ogden, L. (2014), 'Extinction is Forever . . . Or is It?', *BioScience*, 64 (6): 469–75.

Olivier, L. (2004), 'The Past of the Present: Archaeological Memory and Time', *Archaeological Dialogues*, 10 (2): 204–13.

Olsen, B. (2010), *In Defense of Things: Archaeology and the Ontology of Objects*, Lanham: AltaMira Press.

Pred, A. (2004), *The Past Is Not Dead: Facts, Fictions and Enduring Racial Stereotypes*, Minneapolis: University of Minnesota Press.

Robbins, P. and Moore, S. A. (2013), 'Ecological Anxiety Disorder: Diagnosing the Politics of the Anthropocene', *Cultural Geographies*, 20: 3–19.

Schepers, F. and Jepson, P. (2016), 'Rewilding in a European Context', *International Journal of Wilderness*, 22: 25–30.

Schwanen, T. (2007), 'Matter(s) of Interest: Artefacts, Spacing and Timing', *Geografiska Annaler: Series B Human Geography*, 89: 9–22.

Serres, M. and Latour, B. (1995), *Conversations on Science, Culture, and Time*, Ann Arbor, MI: University of Michigan Press.

Stiegler, B. (1998), *Technics and Time: 1. The Fault of Epimetheus*, transl. R. Beardsworth and G. Collins, Stanford: Stanford University Press.

Szerszynski, B. (2002), 'Wild Times and Domesticated Times: The Temporalities of Environmental Lifestyles and Politics', *Landscape and Urban Planning*, 61: 181–91.

Tamm, M. (2013), 'Beyond History and Memory: New Perspectives in Memory Studies', *History Compass*, 11 (6): 458–73.

Tamm, M., ed. (2015), *Afterlife of Events: Perspectives on Mnemohistory*, Basingstoke: Palgrave.

Tanaka, S. (2015), 'History Without Chronology', *Public Culture*, 28: 161–86.

'Wo Europa wächst und wo es schrumpft' (2015), Available online: http://www.bbsr.bund.de/BBSR/DE/Home/Topthemen/bevoelkerung_europa.html (accessed 28 March 2018).

Yusoff, K. (2015), 'Geologic Subjects: Nonhuman Origins, Geomorphic Aesthetics and the Art of Becoming Inhuman', *Cultural Geographies*, 22: 383–407.

Conclusion

A Creed That Has Lost its Believers? Reconfiguring the Concepts of Time and History

Aleida Assmann

The term 'conclusion' is a hint that this book is about to reach its closure. What is expected at this point is a pragmatic summary of central ideas of the foregoing chapters. In complying with this expectation, I hope to do the opposite of closure, however, which is to encourage the reader to think beyond the cover and to take away from the book some ongoing issues, inspirations and irritations.

The crisis of the modern time regime

Irritation is indeed a key word that resonates through all the essays of the volume. It has to do with the discovery that 'our' moorings in time – which have been taken for granted and considered as self-evident, universal and unchangeable – suddenly turned out to be contingent, debatable and unreliable. In other, more objective words: what is referred to today as the 'modern time regime' and functioned as the backbone of Western culture of modernization, has been revealed during the last two or three decades as a construction that privileges Western politics and arts while devaluing and eliding other cultural options. Together with the notion of time the modern concept of history attracted critical attention and was itself historicized.

What exactly happened in this process? The implicit nexus that had held together the three temporal dimensions of past, present and future suddenly eroded. First of all, the *past* was no longer considered neatly cut off from the present, existing at a safe distance from which professional historians could deal with it in a purely objective manner. Instead, it proved to weigh heavily on the present and, after longer periods of silence, it returned with full force, for instance in the voices of traumatized victims who made claims on the present. In this light, cutting the past off from the present appeared to be a strategy supported by those who wished to let bygones be bygones and used their power to decide when to end a period and to stop certain claims and issues issuing from the past. In this view, history was no longer a clearly detached subfield of culture, but proved to be entangled with issues of law and memory.

Second, the *present* is no longer what it used to be. Within the conceptual frame of the modern time regime, it was not even a temporal modality but only the point of transition, the tipping point when the future tilts into the past. Why, we may ask, was the present, the only temporal zone that humans can shape and inhabit with their memories (retention) and expectations (protention), conceived as a moment without extension? The answer is that modern time was conceptualized as rapid motion, symbolized by an arrow moving from the past into the future.

This explains, third, why the *future* used to be the centre of gravity in the modern time regime. In this temporal system, everything was geared to the future. The future was for the temporal compass what the North Pole is for the spatial compass: a steady and reliable source of orientation-in-movement. The future was a continuous promise, harbouring utopian energy and serving as the 'telos' of a narrative of progress and liberation. 'Leave the past behind and move forward towards a better future!' This was, in a nutshell, the amazingly convincing and popular message inscribed into the time regime of modernity. It collapsed, however, when the past became sticky and resisted being shed and left behind like the skin of a snake, and the future morphed with ecological knowledge from an eternal utopia of promises into the gloomy prospect of ongoing extinction in the Anthropocene with a new mandate for joining forces to save the planet for future generations. We are living today, to quote Zoltán Boldizsár Simon (Chapter 4), with a 'simultaneity of highly optimistic and extremely pessimistic perceptions' of the future, so how can we salvage the positive energy that is so vital for human existence?

The past, the present and the future have not only dramatically changed their valence and meaning, but also the ways in which they have been connected. The first chapter in this book, by Chris Lorenz, is a detailed analysis of François Hartog's contribution to this topic. Hartog has described the formerly self-evident model of coherence that had prevailed in the time regime of modernity in the following way:

> The future illuminating the past and giving it meaning constituted a *telos*, called, by turns, 'the Nation', 'the People', 'the Republic', 'Society', or 'the Proletariat', each time dressed in the garb of science. If history dispensed a lesson, it came from the future, not the past. It resided in a future that was to be realized as a rupture with the past, or at least as a differentiation from it.
>
> Hartog 2015: 102, cited by Lorenz in this volume p. 25

Hartog did not only register the waning of the modern time regime, he was himself hit by it with the force of a seismic shock. He observed and described in great detail the emergence of a new vocabulary of key terms (*maître-mots*, *grands mots d'époque*) such as 'victim', 'witness', 'testimony' and 'trauma', which he identified as elements of a new paradigm of memory, commemoration, heritage and identity. According to Hartog, this new paradigm abolishes the ontological border between the past and the present and is exclusively focused on an enlarged present that is weighed down by the past and saturated with it, growing into monstrous proportions. Hartog's term for this new form of temporality is 'presentism', a mode of temporality that he also defines as 'a black hole in time', the 'tyranny of the instant' or 'the treadmill of the unending now'. Presentism refers to a present that has absorbed the future and the past.

The devaluing and pathological language in which Hartog describes this consequential change reflects the fact that he experienced it as a power struggle, fearing the immediate loss of the institutional authority and public influence of the historian. This vantage point made it impossible for him to welcome the new paradigm as a possible extension of the history paradigm; instead, he pitted one against the other as deadly enemies, denouncing 'memory' as the ultimate other, doom and end of 'history'. No wonder that he writes in such a gloomy tone about a threat and crisis, a pathology and catastrophe, leading inevitably to the demise of modern History, the end of the autonomy of professional historiography and possibly also to the decline of Western culture. After Fukuyama had pronounced the end of history in 1990, Hartog pronounced the end of modern historiography in 2013. His book is titled: *Croire en l'histoire* (Hartog 2013); history as we knew it, he seems to suggest, has become a creed that has lost its believers.

The authors of the essays in this volume start from the same observation that time is out of joint, but they do not necessarily follow Hartog's dismal assessment of the situation. They start from the point where Hartog ends. Indeed, the past, the present and the future are no longer what they used to be, they have acquired other meanings and valance and are no longer automatically connected and interrelated by the syntax of a modern temporality that had enforced linearity and causality – all these topics are taken up in the book and discussed as open-ended.

It is a trivial observation that the natural element of the historians has always been the past. Less trivial, however, is the question: 'when does the past begin?' In the last century? Fifty years ago? Ten years ago? Last year? An hour ago? The break between the past and the present is an all-important one, as it defines and demarcates different disciplines. But how can we track down and identify that 'ever-mobile fault line of the past' (James Simpson)? There are currently clear signs that the past is moving closer and closer towards the present. Two chapters deal with this tendency. Jean-Pierre Legendre and Laurence Ollivier (Chapter 10) provide a striking example relating to the change of attitude towards family heirlooms and antiquities in France over the last two decades. As the boom in flea markets and the decline of the antiques business show, the willingness to transmit objects and values across generations has dramatically decreased, while vintage objects from the 1950s to 1970s are rapidly gaining in value, moving the past closer and closer to the present. The authors attribute this to 'the ever-increasing demands of a consumer society that favours the ephemeral' and is unable to view itself in the longterm. Shannon Lee Dawdy (Chapter 11), writing about an archaeology of the contemporary, argues 'that popular conceptions of collective time are on the verge of a tectonic shift. This shift goes so deep it involves how we (those living in post-industrial, cosmopolitan and increasingly secular spaces) think about the most fundamental timeline of all: our own lives, and deaths'.

Now that the three time zones have fallen apart, new basic questions need to be asked: Do the past, present and future form alternative alliances and enter into new configurations? Who is affected by the fundamental change of the temporal order? What new issues can be addressed that had hitherto been rendered invisible? In other words: the crisis of the time regime can also be a stimulus for scholarly attention, reflection, investigation and debate. Historicizing and reconfiguring past–present–and–future presents a great challenge and chance for interdisciplinary investigation and cooperation. My discussion of the themes and essays of this volume will focus on five topics: reconfiguring concepts of history and historiography, alterity of the past or continuity, scales of time, the experience of historical time in the arts and the multiplicity of temporalities.

Reconfiguring concepts of history and historiography

Time is not a new topic for the theory of history and historiography. The first half of the twentieth century was exploding with new philosophies of time. Another engaged meta-discourse on time emerged after the 1960s and 1970s, inspired by writers like Fernand Braudel, who introduced the notion of different scales of time, Claude Lévi-Strauss, who distinguished between 'hot' (or modern) cultures, predicated on change, and 'cold' (or pre-modern) cultures predicated on continuity and homoeostasis, and Reinhart Koselleck, who introduced the divide between the realm of experience (the past) and the realm of expectation (the future). In addition, questions of time such as dating, chronology and periodization were always controversial and an integral part of historical methodology. What has changed, however, is the fact that some of the solid implicit assumptions about time that had been backed up by these theorists and had been taken for granted in the discourse have been eroded, shaking the very foundations of the professional field.

One of the 'holy cows' of modern histor(iograph)y, for instance, has been the imperative to break with the past. The future, as Hartog (2015: 105) put it, 'was to be realized as a rupture with the past, or at least as a differentiation from it'. Koselleck (1979) spelled out the urgency of this first law of disconnecting the past from the present. As long as historical witnesses are talking, he argued, the past is still in the grip of the present. Only when these partial voices with their vested interests have ceased to interfere can the historian take over and present an objective account of the past. As already underlined, drawing a clear borderline between the past and the present is never easy, but it was considered absolutely mandatory to establish history as a professional discipline. The emphasis on this ontological borderline is constitutive of the discipline, and, at the same time, it was also one of the most popular and effective tools of ordering time within historiography. Historians have vigorously emphasized the notion of 'breaking up time' (Lorenz and Bevernage 2013), pointing to violent ruptures and discontinuities, but they had never considered the possibility that this very emphasis on rupture might be a pattern that is firmly inscribed into their own cultural frame of normative modernism.

Ruptures and breaks are the medium and tools of modernization. Every social, cultural, political and artistic project that presents and understands itself as modern, draws its legitimation from acts of breaking with tradition and the past. We call modern whatever distances itself consciously, radically and often also violently from previous conditions and behaviour. The word modern stands for the decision to think in new directions and to do things differently from how they were done previously, to embark on a new path and to free oneself from traditions and the burden of the past. The term 'to break' carries associations of violence, destruction, liberation and renewal in such a way that the positive resonances of liberation and renewal outweigh and justify violence and destruction as legitimate ends to these means.

Here are two examples showing that the concept of rupture and breaking is losing some of its normative force. Charles Maier, member of the international scientific advisory board of a 'House of Austrian History' in the making was asked to comment on a mission statement of the project in 2015. This was his advice: 'Do watch the jargon and fashionable terms. [...] Avoid overusing such concepts as "Brueche" as if they're self-evident. By and large they mean periods when residents of Austria are willing to put each other in jail or resort to violence. Let's not gloss over the realities.'[1] He warns against overemphasizing this pattern and advises his colleagues to recognize 'historical breaks, contradictions and controversies in balance with bridges and continuities' that link the past to the present.[2]

To create a certain balance between rupture and balance, Jürgen Osterhammel elaborated a historical theory that suspends canonized breaks and ruptures, focusing on longer continuities. His key question is: 'How much past do we need to understand the present?' (Osterhammel 2017: 186). He introduced the term 'temporal horizon' for the stretch of time that is needed to explain an event in the past 'historically'. Osterhammel comments: 'A horizon is the far and moving border of the visible. I use the term here in a specific way. My question is not: How far can we see? but: How far do we want and do we need to look' (Osterhammel 2017: 192) – in order to understand an event in terms of its becoming, emanating out of a concatenation of events? By privileging longer continuities over iconic ruptures, as, for instance, the year of the Iranian revolution in 1979 over 9/11, he also alerts us to media effects and cultural patterns that we no longer question because they have been deeply internalized.

Alterity of the past or continuity?

Medievalist and professor of English, James Simpson, has recently reignited the discussion of the old problem of periodization with new arguments and fervour. He argued that a normative break in historiography has separated early modern culture from its religious medieval roots and origins, dividing not only historical periods but also professional fields and their scholarly focus, perception and traditions of interpretation (Simpson 2018: 6). Simpson criticized the artificial 'religions' vs 'secular'-dichotomy that supports this conventional break and legitimizes the end of an old world and the beginning of a new one. Instead, he emphasized that religion is 'a profound mover' and that 'without understanding religious cultures (regardless of whether or not we are believers), and especially the religious cultures of early modernity, we have no compass into the cultural history of what follows'. Simpson criticizes what he calls a 'synchronistic historicism' according to which historical periods are 'hermetically sealed, or, to change the metaphor, divided by epistemic crevasses, [...] denying the intelligibility of one period to another' (Simpson 2018: 10). Instead, he practises a 'diachronic historicism' that constructs 'narratives of the longue durée', using seismic concepts such as 'pre-tremor, aftershock, absence, reverberation, and resonance'. His research is focused on '"different", "queer" temporalities as operating simultaneously but with differing durations, thereby potentially opening the present up to different pasts at any moment' (Simpson 2018: 17). He is confident that once we overcome the habit of seeing the Middle Ages as wholly 'other', 'we will come to understand ourselves as children of our whole history, whether we like parts of that story or not. We are immanent to that history, part of history's problem and therefore part of its solution' (Simpson 2018: 18).

It is all but easy to organize, to regulate and to evaluate temporal distance. Modern historiography started with the mission of separating the present from the past, thereby creating conditions of objectivity and autonomy of the past independent from the grip of the present. This practice was described as 'breaking'; and such a breaking that ensured the alterity of the past was seen as the central obligation and responsibility of the historian. While modern history was premised on breaking in order to guarantee the alterity of the past, memory was considered to be a tool for constructing sameness of and continuity with the past. History, Lynn Hunt (2002) claimed, 'should not just be the study of sameness, based on the search for our individual or collective roots of identity. It should also be about difference'. Victoria Fareld (Chapter 3) describes a case that challenges this clear opposition between historical pastism and memorial presentism. She points to a project of students at various universities protesting against the memorial culture of their universities, which they denounced as colonialist and racist. In 2015, they focused their protest on statues of Cecil Rhodes, the apex of the British colonial project in public institutions in Cape Town and Great Britain, pointing to the colonial and racist message that these statues retain, prolong and project into the present. In doing so, the students drew attention to a blind spot in British Imperialism. They were, however, immediately criticized for their identity politics and for 'kidnapping the past for present concerns'. Historians stigmatized the intervention of these student activists time and again as 'presentism', but this presentism is obviously not 'a symptom of a denial of otherness'. They do not insist on sameness but, quite on the contrary, on *breaking* with this particular colonial past that these monuments celebrate and uncritically continue into the present. They respond to the fact that the monuments today have become problematic because they are experienced as a bitter provocation by former colonial subjects. Far from enforcing the presence of the past as misguided advocates of presentism, therefore, these students insisted on *difference* and demanded a *break* with current memorial practices.

Cases like these can be easily multiplied. In Germany, for instance, there is a growing issue about how to deal with the many monuments of the First World War that glorify war and were reframed in the Nazi period for ideological purposes. We have become historically distanced and morally estranged from many of the political claims and messages that monuments in our build environment continue to represent and express. They can be metaphorically referred to as 'ghosts' of the past 'haunting' the present, but in a more precise language they are remnants of a different historical period with a message that jars with the present. How do we deal with the aftermath of history, with these untimely, non-contemporary historical relics that continue to deliver their messages to a changed present? The examples show how hopeless it is to frame such issues in the blunt terms of 'pastism' versus 'presentism'.

The new modes of temporality have become much more complicated as we are no longer dealing only with history writing, but also with history preserving across the ruptures of historical periods. We are living at a time in which we are experiencing the ruptures and estrangements from historical periods in the present; in various societies people are estranged from their colonial or communist past and have become sensitive to the normative text and subtext of preserving such monuments and commemoration practices. Instead of blaming the students' project on blind iconoclasm, putting them in the same class as the Taliban or IS-troops destroying world heritage, it might be more constructive to think about new ways that help to historicize and contextualize history in the public space. Fareld's chapter suggests that there is indeed a third possibility besides the alternative of either fetishizing or eliminating a monument, and that is its preservation as a historical *document*. The general description of a 'present' that is saturated with the past and is experienced as an unlimited realm of simultaneities cannot take us very far. Undeniably, 'memory' in the shape of monuments has become a vital part of a 'history' that is still felt and contested in the present. After the normative syntax of the temporal nexus has eroded, we have to look for new, more complex, and possibly even contradictory framings that can help us to think of such problematic monuments in terms of 'anachronisms'. Such a framing could include more voices and emphasize the past in the present and the present in the past by preserving more than one perspective and interpretation.

Scales of time

Fernand Braudel has introduced the notion of scale into historiography, distinguishing between three basic modes of temporality: 1) very long and extended periods (*longue durée*), 2) middle-range trends and developments (*conjoncture*) and 3) short, fast and sudden reversals (*événement*).[3] His grammar of historical temporalities establishes an interesting correlation between duration and change: the longer the duration, the smaller the change; the shorter the duration, the greater the change.

The first half of the twentieth century saw a boom of new constructions of temporality. It grew out of a deep discontent with the historicist paradigm and the urge to break with the dominant Western narrative asserting linearity, coherence and progress. Particularly in times of revolutionary crisis like the 1920s and 1930s, the temporality of the moment (*Augenblick*, *Kairos*) moved into the focus of philosophers who celebrated the quality of sudden and radical reversals, explosive events and violent force. Hans Ruin (Chapter 5) presents the interwar years of the 1920s and 1930s as a period saturated with revolutionary conceptualizations of time, enforcing on the right and left political spectrum new existential modes of temporality. In combining historicism and existentialism, Martin Heidegger's temporality of the moment emphasized the 'inescapable historical situatedness of subjectivity, thinking and truth, indeed of life'. In the short interval between the First and the Second World War, new theories emerged in which 'being in time' suddenly became the solution to the historical predicament, urging the radical decision to embrace a new world (like that of Nazi ideology) at the expense and willing destruction of the old world. Ruin presents Walter Benjamin's contemporary vision of a time of abrupt suddenness, emphasizing its messianic and epiphanic power as Heidegger's mirror image at the opposite end of the political spectrum. Liisi Keedus (Chapter 6) offers another interesting constellation of post-Hegelian responses to historical moments, confronting Franz Rosenzweig's option for religion and the Jewish spirit that 'breaks through the shackles of time' after the First World War with Mircea Eliade's rediscovery of the myth of the eternal return after the Second World War.

Seen from hindsight in the aftermath of the Second World War and its cataclysmic violence, the term 'event' changed its meaning. It lost most of its utopian and messianic overtones and became associated with the language of trauma. The new formula of 'unprecedented change' (Zoltán Boldizsár Simon in Chapter 4) signalled a clear distance from the revolutionary potential of the Now. In one of her books, Anne Fuchs describes the negative aura of the 'impact event' by changing the perspective from that of the actors to that of the victims. She refers to such events as 'seismic historical occurrences' breaking into the habitual life-world with extreme forms of violence 'that are perceived to spectacularly shatter the material and symbolic worlds that we inhabit' (Fuchs 2011: 11–12).

Rupture is an abrupt form of change; change is a minimal condition of rupture. There is no concept of history that can discard change. Zoltán Boldizsár Simon emphasizes in his chapter that the topic of history is and has always been 'change over time in human affairs', and an important task of a philosophy of history is 'to conceptualize, understand, account for and enable change in human affairs'. The question is, however, whether this is a specific problem for *Western* societies, or, given the changed contexts of an entangled global world and the Anthropocene, this project could also be conceived of in more connected and trans-cultural terms.

Moving from small to large scale, we arrive at a new form of *longue durée* that is today dubbed 'big history'. This concept of history vastly transcends the 4,000 years of documented written history and includes the much longer cosmic time of nature and geology. It merges the time of humans with the time of nature, collapsing the time of human action with the time of the natural world. The time frame and scale of 'big history' connects all the life sciences, integrating the different time regimes of natural evolution and human history, making them permeable to each other. In this new form of world history, natural sciences and human historical sciences have merged: 'paleontology, evolution biology and astrophysics are rightly acknowledged as historical sciences, as they are also dealing with temporal transformations' (Osterhammel 2017: 189).

This form of history also registers change and has its breaks, ruptures and periodizations. A new historical period, as Helge Jordheim (Chapter 2) informs us, was marked in 2017 when a group of scientists issued the worldwide warning of the 'sixth mass extinction event'. After five other causes for mass extinction, including asteroids and the eruption of volcanos, it is now the human species itself that has stepped on the stage of cosmic history as a collective actor, propelling and precipitating climate change and the extinction of many biological species. Human and natural history are interacting here in a new way, posing a new problem to historians who are moving beyond their traditional historical time frame of 6,000 years and are opening it up to 540 million years. Jordheim resorts to chronology to cope with this huge change in temporal scale. For him chronology means 'to return to a historiographical practice that is able to think about timescales and periodizations in the plural, to try out different durations, periodic structures and rhythms, compare them and map out their similarities and their differences, or, if you like, their synchronicities and their non-synchronicities'.

History, in other words, has arrived in the Anthropocene. From a larger ecological perspective, which includes environmental history and climate change, human action is no longer interpreted in terms of the human will of dominating and shaping the world, but rather in terms of the enormously destructive effects and reversible or irreversible changes of this will. The concept of 'ecological sustainability' has introduced a new time regime that makes humans accountable for processes that had hitherto lain outside the range of human responsibility. In the lens of sustainability, a holistic approach to time and change is required in order to bring a derailing world back into a state of balance. This involves a new understanding of human action and responsibility that challenges under apocalyptic auspices the notion of the irreversibility of historical time and is now introducing the hope for a reversibility of ecological time. Caitlin DeSilvey's essay (Chapter 12) on the concept of 'rewilding' deals with the possibility of such a reintroduction or 'return' of animals to a place where they have grown extinct. This practice challenges a linear history of ecological successions, replacing it with a temporality of ongoing disturbance and dynamic change in the formation of new ecosystems.

Historical experience and aesthetic representations

Roland Barthes has used the distinction between 'studium' and 'punctum' to characterize different modalities of time in the act of perception: one that takes time, effort and patience, and one that hits the consciousness or moves the emotions in a direct touch and encounter. This distinction between a slow and a fast mode of cognition has been associated with other basic distinctions regarding the experience of time in the arts such as long and short, mediated and unmediated, representation and presentation, signs and signals, mostly with normative implications privileging the direct over the indirect mode. Heidegger had already made ample use of the term 'authenticity', praising the force and intensity of the existential moment at the expense of more deviant and slower modes of representation and cognition. In the current media discourse, as Johannes Grave shows in this volume (Chapter 7), the power of images is also being invoked as a privileged medium to capture and release the emotional force of historical experience and to offer an immediate sensual and perceptual access to the past. In these contexts, the temporal dimension of the experience of history and the suddenness of an impact still play an important role, but the conceptual framing has changed. In the phrase 'presence of an absence' a new twist is introduced that guards against the danger of falling back into the tracks of too easy dichotomies.

Anne Fuchs (Chapter 8) continues this topic by exploring aesthetic strategies of contemporary photographers whose work undermines the persuasiveness of iconic images of historical moments and experiments with different technical devices to foreground the dimension of time. Pointing, for instance, to 'the temporal multi-layeredness of the photographic image by distinguishing between the "time in a photograph" and the "time of a photograph"' she convincingly shows that a photo does not necessarily freeze a moment but can itself incorporate forms of duration and historical temporality.

In his analysis of architectural reconstruction, a cultural practice that has became popular in Eastern and Western Europe since the 1990s, Torgeir Rinke Bangstad (Chapter 9) also questions a flat notion of presentism. He uses the notions of 'timeliness' and 'untimeliness' to point to the multitemporal properties of objects and thus the different historical layers involved in heritage practice. 'Material remains store memories of past events' and these memories 'occasionally find their way back into the present in unsolicited ways'. For this reason it is impossible, he argues, to determine 'unequivocally whether heritage is *of* the past or the present'.

The multiplicity of temporalities

The modern idea of history was built on a consensus that the culture of modernity was founded on the discovery of an abstract, homogeneous and non-sensuous concept of time. Reinhart Koselleck dated this origin of modern history to around 1770 in the period of Enlightenment and connected it with a linguistic change happening at the same time: the replacement of multiple histories existing only in the plural by a general and inclusive concept of History existing in the singular. Together with this discovery, as Lucian Hölscher has pointed out, an equally abstract concept of a general 'future' emerged that replaced the notion of specific futurities. These huge abstractions made it possible to order events in a long-term perspective and to generate the confidence of scientific control. Time became an amazingly inclusive 'dispositive' for a construction of world history; it offered the possibility to map all events within a new single frame. The historian, placed at the tipping point of the present, surveyed the extension of the past and the future stretching into vast and endless temporal spaces and embraced the vision that it was now possible to scientifically explore both dimensions. According to Hölscher, this concept of History is 'not an anthropological given, it is not a presupposition of human existence in general, but a specifically historical way of thinking'. In 1999, at the threshold of the millennial future, he added: 'We do not know how long this form of thinking will continue to exist, but we are able to reconstruct how and when it came into being' (Hölscher 1999: 10).

Since Koselleck has discovered the consequential transformation from 'histories' to 'History' at the origin of modernity and *as* the origin of modernity, we are now witnessing the reverse process from 'History' to 'histories'. This cannot mean, however, that we are moving backwards in time, but that we are ceasing to ontologize the modern time regime, acknowledging its constructive character. By restricting its value and scope, we are leaving space for other possibilities. Seen from this new perspective, the modern time regime is not the last word nor is it a dead end. It is still indispensable and functioning in many contexts, but it is no longer the exclusive option and has become more self-conscious and self-critical concerning its own history and universal claims.

'It might be useless to look for unity,' writes Hartog (2015: 184), 'if a certain dispersion or simply a multiplicity of different regimes of temporality happened to characterize (and distinguish) our present.' What Hartog articulated as a speculative hypothesis,

Chris Lorenz has transformed in Chapter 1 into a positive statement that sums up a consensus of this book and binds all of the chapters together: 'This fundamental multiplicity of times [...] implies that the past can no longer be conceived as the ontological object that modernist historians reconstruct from a fixed observer position because past–present–future distinctions are made differently in different "timescapes". The task of this volume is to rethink historical time, promising 'New Approaches to Presentism'. Embracing the idea of multiple temporalities it takes the tension out of the topic with which Hartog had invested it. Together with this de-dramatization the melancholy tone has disappeared. The change of tone is connected to a change of perspective: we have left Hartog's strictly national/European/Western perspective and joined a 'postmodernist', 'transnational' or 'postcolonial' perspective. Terms like 'multi-' or 'polychronic' signal a turning away from the hegemony of the modern time regime that had covered up, devalued and dismissed other past–present–future configurations. When Dipesh Chakrabarty (2000: 108) claimed that 'the writing of history must implicitly assume a plurality of times existing together', he was arguing from a non-Western point of view against the dominant, repressive and exclusionary force of the modern time regime. In his book *Time and the Other*, ethnologist Johannes Fabian had started this discourse in 1983 with a formula that became influential. He spoke of a 'denial of coevalness', coining even a new English term to point to the irreconcilable non-synchronicity between the two cultural time zones inhabited by the ethnographer and his or her informant (Fabian 1983). This clash between temporal cultures, he argued, is built into the hegemonic character of the time regime of modernism and colonialism that classifies other regions of the world and their cultural time regimes as 'backward', 'cyclical' or 'static'. By creating a temporal abyss that categorically disconnects different ontological, historical and cultural time zones, these countries had not only been cut off from the path of progress and a glaring future, they were also excluded from political partnership and the possibility of meaningful interaction, starting in the dialogue between ethnographer and informant. Almost two decades later, Dipesh Chakrabarty (2000: 108) argued that 'the writing of history must implicitly assume a plurality of times existing together, a disjuncture of the present with itself', and Berber Bevernage (2015: 351) even went so far as to encourage philosophers of history to 'break with the idea of the fully contemporaneous present and instead embrace that of radical noncontemporaneity or noncoevalness' (see the Introduction for these quotes).

Mikhail Bakhtin was among the first to theorize cultural constructions of time. He introduced the term 'chronotope' in 1975 and recommended looking for a multiplicity of temporal ontologies in literary genres and narratives, historical epochs and different societies (see Bakhtin 2008). Bakhtin criticized the assumption that we are living in only one homogeneous and universal time regime that was created in the Enlightenment. Instead, he explored a multiplicity of cultural temporalities that allow for different modes of being in time. As these always exclude other possibilities, it is vital to understand better the cultural modalities, choices and constraints in our relation to time. Coming to terms with the multiplicity of cultural temporalities does not necessarily imply a postmodern relativism, nor a state of total confusion; instead, it rather implies coming to terms and living together with multiple time regimes in a global culture.

Notes

1   Charles Maier, email to Oliver Rathkolb from 2 September 2015, Re: 3. Beiratssitzung HGÖ, 2.
2   Charles Maier, email to Oliver Rathkolb, commenting on the mission statement of a 'House of Austrian History', 2 September 2015.
3   'The longue durée, cyclical phases (*conjoncture*), and events fit together easily, for they are all measurements on the same scale. Hence, to enter into one of these temporalities is to be part of all of them' (Braudel 2009: 198).

References

Bakhtin, M. M. (2008), *Chronotopos*, transl. M. Dewey, afterword M. C. Frank and K. Mahlke, Frankfurt am Main: Suhrkamp.
Bevernage, B. (2015), 'The Past Is Evil/Evil Is Past: On Retrospective Politics, Philosophy of History, and Temporal Manichaeism', *History and Theory*, 54 (3): 333–52.
Braudel, F. (2009), 'History and the Social Sciences: The Longue Durée', transl. I. Wallerstein, *Review*, 32 (2): 171–203.
Chakrabarty, D. (2000), *Provincializing Europe: Postcolonial Thought and Historical Difference*, Princeton, NJ: Princeton University Press.
Fabian, J. (1983), *Time and the Other: How Anthropology makes its Object*, New York: Columbia University Press.
Fuchs, A. (2011), *After the Dresden Bombing: Pathways of Memory 1945 to the Present*, Basingstoke: Palgrave Macmillan.
Hartog, F. (2013), *Croire en l'histoire*, Paris: Flammarion.
Hartog, F. (2015), *Regimes of Historicity: Presentism and the Experiences of Time*, transl. S. Brown, New York: Columbia University Press.
Hölscher, L. (1999), *Die Entdeckung der Zukunft*, Frankfurt am Main: Fisher.
Hunt, L. (2002), 'Against Presentism', *Perspectives on History*. Available online: https://www.historians.org/publications-and-directories/perspectives-on-history/may-2002/against-presentism (accessed 16 October 2018).
Koselleck, R. (1979), *Vergangene Zukunft. Zur Semantik geschichtlicher Zeiten*, Frankfurt am Main: Suhrkamp.
Lorenz, C. and Bevernage, B. (eds) (2013), *Breaking up Time. Negotiating the Borders between Present, Past and Future*, Göttingen: Vandenhoeck and Ruprecht.
Osterhammel, J. (2017), *Die Flughöhe der Adler. Historische Essays zur globalen Gegenwart*, Munich: C. H. Beck.
Simpson, J. (2018), 'Trans-Reformation English Literary History', unpublished manuscript.

Index